OMIGOSH --- IT'S HIM AGAIN!
TAXI
WALT DISNEY
Distributed by King Features Syndicate, Inc.

I0822208

WALT DISNEY'S

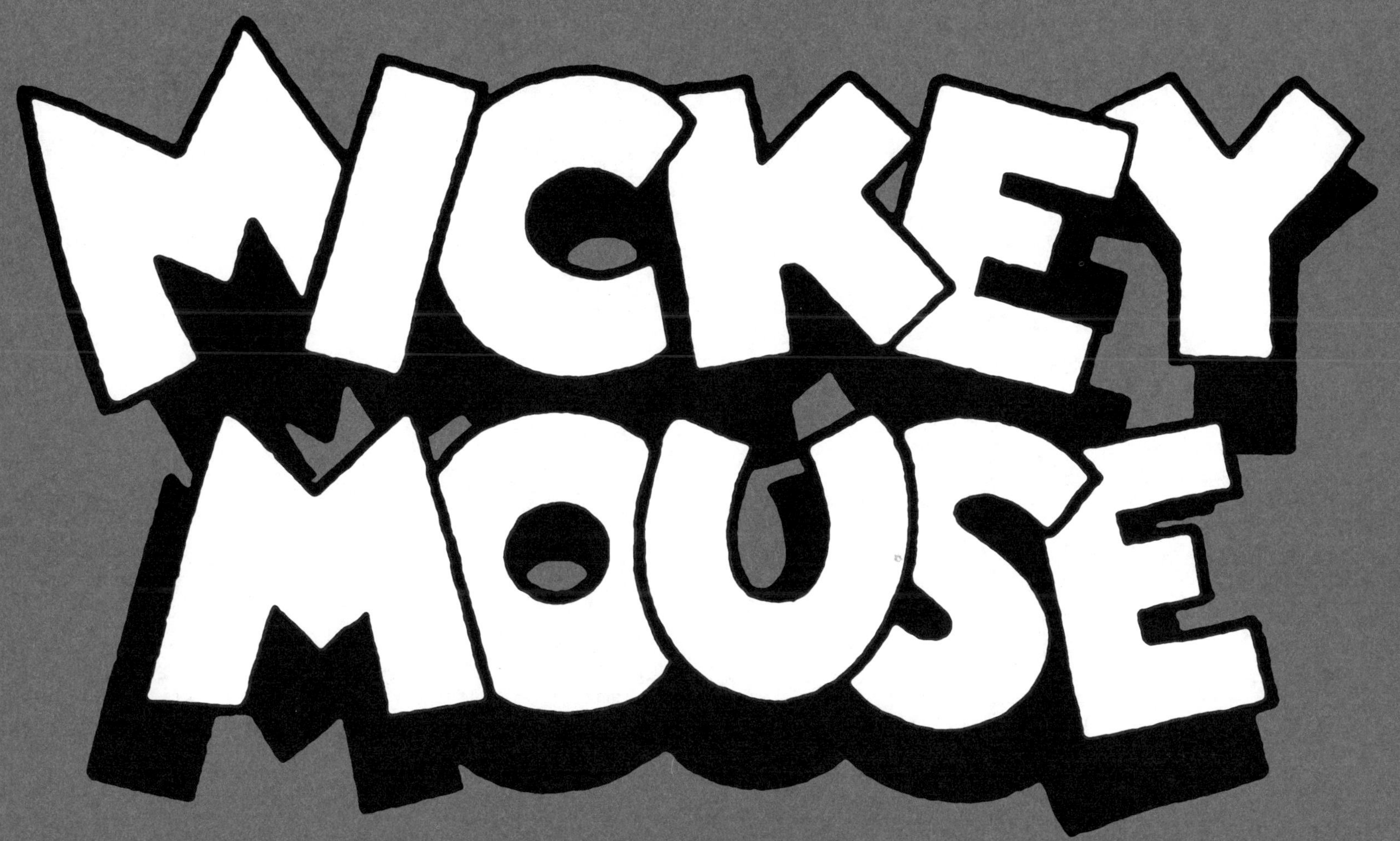

BY FLOYD GOTTFREDSON

WALT DISNEY'S

"OUTWITS THE PHANTOM BLOT"

BY FLOYD GOTTFREDSON

Series Editors: David Gerstein and Gary Groth

FANTAGRAPHICS BOOKS

Right: An early 1940s Phantom Blot reappearance came on this World War II insignia for the US Navy's Composite Squadron 8. Art by Hank Porter; image courtesy Dennis Books; information courtesy David Lesjak.

© WALT DISNEY

The Floyd Gottfredson Library

Series Editors: DAVID GERSTEIN and GARY GROTH
Series Designer: JACOB COVEY
Designer: TONY ONG
Production: PAUL BARESH
Associate Publisher: ERIC REYNOLDS
Publishers: GARY GROTH and KIM THOMPSON

Walt Disney's Mickey Mouse "Outwits the Phantom Blot" is copyright © 2014 Disney Enterprises, Inc. Text of "Of Mouse and Man: Gags and Gravitas" by Thomas Andrae is copyright © 2014 Thomas Andrae. Text of "The Heirs of Gottfredson: Osamu Tezuka" by Ryan Holmberg is copyright © 2014 Ryan Holmberg. All contents copyright © 2014 Disney Enterprises, Inc. unless otherwise noted. All rights reserved. Permission to quote or reproduce material for reviews must be obtained from the publisher. Fantagraphics Books, Inc. 7563 Lake City Way, Seattle, WA 98115.

Special thanks to:

Randall Bethune
Big Planet Comics
Black Hook Press, Japan
Nick Capetillo
Kevin Czapiewski
John DiBello
Juan Manuel Domínguez
Mathieu Doublet
Dan Evans III
Thomas Eykemans
Scott Fritsch-Hammes
Coco and Eddie Gorodetsky
Karen Green
Ted Haycraft
Eduardo Takeo "Lizarkeo" Igarashi
Nevdon Jamgochian
Andy Koopmans
Philip Nel
Vanessa Palacios
Kurt Sayenga
Anne Lise Rostgaard Schmidt
Christian Schremser
Secret Headquarters
Paul van Dijken
Mungo van Krimpen-Hall
Jason Aaron Wong
Thomas Zimmermann

To receive a free catalogue of graphic novels, newspaper strip reprints, prose novels, art books, cultural criticism and essays, and more, call 1-800-657-1100 or visit our website at www.fantagraphics.com.

Distributed in the U.S. by W.W. Norton and Company, Inc. (800-233-4830)
Distributed in Canada by Canadian Manda Group (800-452-6642 x862)
Distributed in the U.K. by Turnaround Distribution (44 (0)20 8829-3002)
Distributed to comic stores by Diamond Comics Distributors (800-452-6642 x215)

ISBN 978-1-60699-736-9

Printed in Singapore

MICKEY MOUSE'S MENTORS include Chief O'Hara, Captain Doberman, and Captain Churchmouse: seasoned adventurers and detectives whom—as an eager amateur—Mickey yearns to emulate. As a teenage Disney comics fan, *I* wanted to emulate Disney comics historian Joe Torcivia, my guiding light on many a convention floor. Or is "light" the wrong word? For to this day, no Disney character grabs Joe quite like the dark, spooky Phantom Blot! And it is to my longtime friend Joe that this blotty volume is dedicated. Who else?

Of course, our Blot wouldn't even be an inkdrop without many other friends and helpers. First come Ken Shue, Disney Publishing Worldwide's Vice President of Global Art and Design Development, and his Secretary Iliana Lopez, who enabled us to remaster the Gottfredson strips in this volume.

Numerous other scholars contributed artwork, essays, knowledge, and archival items. We're grateful to Director Rebecca Cline and Contractor Kevin Kern at the Walt Disney Archives. I'd also like to thank Thomas Andrae, Gary Apgar, Alberto Becattini, Geoffrey Blum, John Clark, Byron Erickson, Leonardo Gori, Jonathan Gray, Carl Guderian, Ryan Holmberg, Thomas Jensen, Roy Kooijman, Thad Komorowski, Susan Lindstrom, Larry Lowery, Craig McCracken, Anne Marie Mersing, Frank Stajano, Malcolm Willits, and Francois Willot.

Others, too, have provided crucial support and encouragement. First and foremost come my parents, Susan and Larry Gerstein, and my brother Ben. Then come friends including Céline and Stefan Allirol-Molin, Christopher and Nicky Barat, Jerry Beck, the late Diane Disney Miller, César Ferioli, Fabio Gadducci, Didier Ghez, Colleen Gottfredson Toomay, Jan Gottfredson, Joakim Gunnarsson, the Hake's Americana staff (including Alex Winter, Terence Kean, and Deak Stagemeyer), Andy Hershberger, Nelson Hughes, Lars Jensen, Mark and Cole Johnson, Vincent Joseph, J. B. Kaufman, Mark Kausler, Jim Korkis, Raquel Lopez, Mike Matei, Geoffrey Moses, Floyd Norman, Martin Olsen, KaJuan Osborne, Jesse Post, Stefano Priarone, Tarkan Rosenberg, Travis Seitler, Warren Spector, Tom Stathes, Kwongmei To, Ted Toomay, Esther Torcivia, Francois Willot, Germund Von Wowern, and Wilbert Watts.

Why, that's almost as many people as the Blot has disguises! Indeed, Disney scholars learn about new Blot crimes all the time. Most recently, Joe Torcivia—Joe again!—observed how an episode of the TV classic *The Adventures of Superman*, "The Mystery of the Broken Statues" (1952), finds a gang of crooks smashing cheap plaster statues in order to find hidden items stowed in a few of them. Hmm... in Gottfredson, the Blot smashed cheap *cameras* to find a chemical formula hidden in *one* of them! The "Blot" story had just been reprinted in 1949; did Superman copy it? Was Super *Goof* involved? Joe and I may ponder this one forever.

No—wait... *he'll* have to stop and read this book sometime.

—David Gerstein,
November 2013

TABLE of CONTENTS

Setting the Stage

The Adventures: Floyd Gottfredson's Mickey Mouse Stories With Introductory Notes

The Gottfredson Archives: Essays and Special Features

TABLE of CONTENTS

PREVIOUS PAGE: These 1938 model sheets by Fred Moore helped defined Mickey's modern eye treatment. Images courtesy Walt Disney Photo Library.

ABOVE: This 1945 studio model sheet captures the childish naïvete of Gottfredson's Morty and Ferdie, who make their daily strip debut in this volume. Art by Les Elton; image courtesy Walt Disney Photo Library.

OF MOUSE & MAN

FLOYD GOTTFREDSON AND THE MICKEY MOUSE CONTINUITIES

1938-1940: GAGS AND GRAVITAS

» *Foreword by Thomas Andrae*

The comics in this book represent a fascinating transition within Mickey's adventures. After a string of exceptionally thrilling story arcs in 1935-1937, we now see a reversion to the more comedic, gagged-up serials of the early years.

The shift can be explained by a number of factors. In 1938 Gottfredson and his team started soliciting gag ideas from Disney staffers; inserting the results into continuity naturally made the strip funnier. But the change was also prompted by the political upheavals of the era. With Hitler invading and annexing countries in Europe at a rapid pace, Mickey's adventures abroad became increasingly problematic. Gottfredson may have desired to give his readers some relief from frightening world events.

In practice, however, the new gag stories were not quite an escape from the outside world. Whereas earlier *Mickey* comedies had often been driven by simple slapstick, Gottfredson's gags now invoked a darker, more eccentric and cynical tone—in response both to troubled times overseas, and to the continued frustrations of a Depression that seemed unending. "Mickey Mouse Meets Robinson Crusoe" (1938) was loosely inspired by the 1935 cartoon *Mickey's Man Friday*. But "Crusoe" vastly differs from earlier film-to-strip adaptations—beginning with the opening, as Gottfredson directly states that the story to follow is just a film! This framing device breaks the strip's usual illusion of reality—the idea that we are reading Mickey's "real" life—and logically implies that preceding Mickey adventures may *also* have been only Hollywood fiction.

ABOVE: Gottfredson's "Robinson Crusoe" blurred the bounds between cartoon and comics "reality." Goofy's gripe about a grasshopper in the December 15, 1938 daily references *Goofy and Wilbur* (1939). Publicity drawing by Hank Porter; image courtesy Walt Disney Photo Library.

This subversion of narrative "realism," while treated casually in the strip, reflects a credibility crisis that gripped America as a new war approached. Many people believed that World War I was manufactured by munitions companies to promote the sales of arms; that American propaganda had artificially drummed up war fever in 1917, and was now poised to do so again. Consequently, the country became strongly isolationist: loath to engage in another foreign fight.

At the same time, however, Americans also believed in the myth of American exceptionalism. This was the idea that the country's democratic institutions—and the abundance of cheap land on the frontier—freed America from the class divisions, religious intolerance, and feudal institutions of the Old World.[1] The myth of this unique history, many felt, destined America to spread freedom around the globe—and in 1938, this meant that only America could save Europe from its authoritarian excesses.

Once again, Gottfredson reflected the zeitgeist. In *Mickey's Man Friday*, Mickey himself played a Robinson Crusoe figure; in Gottfredson's story, Mickey is shipwrecked *along* with Crusoe, allowing Gottfredson to contrast the two. In Daniel Defoe's original novel, Crusoe was an archetype of rugged individualism and European superiority, embodied in his ability to survive on a desert island almost unaided. In Gottfredson's version, the European is clueless and almost helpless without an American—Mickey—to protect him.

Similarly, at tale's end, we learn that two balmy British scientists observed our friends in peril from cannibals; but didn't rescue them, for fear of contaminating their scientific study. They wanted to learn whether Mickey and Crusoe could survive unaided! The scientists' behavior invokes a stereotype of the British as hidebound and obsessed with rules, implying that Europe is unprepared to defend itself—and that American intervention might be risky.

Apart from world politics, Gottfredson's "Crusoe" reflects changes in Mickey himself. In past volumes we have seen how, as Mickey became a more adult character, he took more of a straight man role. Comedy stemmed less from Mickey than from the bizarre, eccentric characters he encountered. Here, Crusoe is one such eccentric; so are Friday and his fellow island natives. Invoking the era's insensitive African-American stereotypes, Gottfredson turns Defoe's original Caribs into Blacks who speak in fractured Southern dialect. Friday in particular—a loyal and resourceful servant in both Defoe and *Mickey's Man Friday*—is now almost as clueless as Crusoe: a lazy adolescent who perpetually asks for food. The mix of anachronism, geographical displacement, and stereotype makes the tale feel almost like a surreal dream. All the better to paint Mickey as the lone voice of reason.

Mickey's role is reinforced by a transformation in his looks. In 1938, when the Disney studio held a party to celebrate the completion of *Snow White and the Seven Dwarfs* (1937), animator Ward Kimball put pupils in Mickey's eyes on the cover for the party program. The alteration, carried over to cartoons and comics, not only made Mickey more anthropomorphic—it corresponded to his becoming more straitlaced; even parental, as when facing a very childish Crusoe.

"The Plumber's Helper" (1938)—seemingly a simple on-the-job comedy—continues the more cynical tone of the late 1930s *Mickey* strips, and once again ties into the politics of the time. New Deal legislation had recently codified workers' rights to unionize, to bargain collectively, and to be protected from employers' unfair labor practices. However, these protections ran into conflicts with New Deal opponents and business leaders. Gottfredson's story embodies these conflicts.

Mickey's plumber boss Joe Piper at first seems to be a stereotypically incompetent and indolent workman, protected against fair competition by a bigwig contractor and a crooked government regulator. As part of a scheme to rob Piper's clients, Piper is funneled all the fat contracts in town—no matter how low other honest plumbers might bid! The scenario is an implicit swipe at the "closed shop" system—which required employers to hire union employees—and the New Deal regulations that enforced it. In

RIGHT: Gottfredson used plot synopses to solicit gag ideas for stories. This one, for "Mickey Mouse Meets Robinson Crusoe" (1938), dates from late in the story's production; it summarized the plotline thus far, then requested gimmicks for the climactic sequence. Image courtesy Hans Perk.

OUTLINE OF CURRENT MICKEY MOUSE DAILY COMIC STRIP

"ROBINSON CRUSOE"

This is essentially an adventure and personality story, relying for gags largely on the personality and character of Crusoe and Friday, with Mickey carrying the principal action and adventure stuff.

CHARACTERS: Mickey Mouse, one of two lone survivors from a shipwreck, who is cast away on a desert island with--

Robinson Crusoe, a timid soul, whose characteristics are exactly the opposite from the resourceful adventurer of the story book. He is dismayed and fearful of the jungle and its inhabitants and looks to Mickey to lead the way in everything. His comments about his wife show that he has been a henpecked husband.

Friday, a goofy little native character that Mickey and Crusoe adopt as their servant. His principal traits are laziness, a constant hunger and a great aptitude for lying. He never tells the same version of a story twice.

Minor Characters are the cannibals, who constitue the chief menace, and a balmy scientist, who shows up on a ship which Mickey and Crusoe escape in at the close of the story.

LOCALE: A mythical tropic island, inhabited by cannibals who speak English with a colored accent. The island can also contain any kind of animal without regard to normal geographical limits.

SYNOPSIS

Following a shipwreck, Mickey and Crusoe, with a raft and a few necessary supplies, are cast up on a desert island. Crusoe is overcome with fear of the unknown dangers on the island and tries two or three silly attempts to escape. Mickey recognizes that they may be marooned for some time and insists upon building a strong stockade as protection against wild beasts and savages. They construct a crude hut within the stockade and prepare to settle down.

They are alarmed at once, when a section of the fence caves in and an elephant walks through, followed by a lion and tiger. After a big scare and some gag business with the animals, Mickey and Crusoe are amazed to find them as tame as house cats. They have a tough time trying to drive them off and only succeed when Crusoe makes bogey-man faces which frighten the animals away.

Rid of the animals and their stockade repaired, Mickey and Crusoe set out to explore the island. Some distance away they discover a human footprint and terrified at the thought of savages being near, they run back to the safety of their stockade, only to discover a lone native already making himself at home there. This, of course, turns out to be Friday. Follows various gags on Friday wanting to eat all the time, the various tall stories of who he is and how he got there. Finally he is accepted as a servant and shows great ingenuity in training a parrot and a turtle to do his work for him.

conservative philosophy, unions were considered restrictive, destroying initiative, and the New Deal was cynically seen as rigged in unions' favor.

Adding to the cynicism, Gottfredson ultimately reveals that Piper and his gang are in fact out-of-work actors—performing menial labor only as a means to an end. Through Piper's scheming, the story effectively blames city corruption on the *lumpen* unemployed, victimizing honest workers and the well-to-do alike. Pretty dark for a hometown comedy.

ABOVE: Fantômas was a murderous master thief in French fiction. In the film *Fantômas* (1913), René Navarre plays the bandit in a costume that anticipates the Blot.

Darkness and cynicism also pervade the single major *non*-comedic tale Gottfredson produced at this time. 1939's "The Phantom Blot" is arguably Gottfredson's finest story; certainly it contains his most memorable villain. The serial appeared only months before World War II erupted in Europe. Hitler had taken over Austria and was poised to annex Poland, which would bring U.S. allies Britain and France into the war. Gottfredson's story is suffused with paranoia, revealing how close to home Americans felt the threat had come; Nazis might someday invade America! No longer could a foreign menace be dealt with only in foreign lands. The Blot, a sinister agent for a foreign syndicate, operates among us and threatens both our security and the world's.

To make his villain look particularly malevolent, Gottfredson clothed the Blot in a body-length black cloak with only vertical holes for eyes, giving no clue as to who or what lurked beneath. As one of his victims described him, he looked like a "black ghost." "I had been visualizing a character who looked like that," Gottfredson observed, "who we could do a mystery with. So [Merrill De Maris] suggested a story involving stolen cameras and a waterfront locale."[2]

The Blot's name and costume were inspired by two Black boys called "the Blots" in one of the artist's favorite comic strips, Walter Hoban's *Jerry on the Job*. "They were like Siamese twins," Gottfredson recalled, "who moved and talked in unison and were coal black except for their white eyes and lips." Other period racial imagery also influenced the Blot: according to Gottfredson, "the Blot was slightly based on... the phrase 'the [*n-word*] in the woodpile.'" The now-disused, derogatory expression refers to an undisclosed, highly suspicious fact or entity—much like the Blot. In Western culture, darkness is often associated with evil, and African-Americans have unfairly been blighted by the connection. Of course, the Blot himself is Caucasian under his cloak.

Gottfredson originally called his character just "the Blot"; while he is also called a "phantom" in the story, the words are never linked. But in 1941, a comic book reprint titled the story "Mickey Mouse Outwits the Phantom Blot," and the name stuck. Fans—and even Gottfredson—tended to refer to the villain as the *Phantom* Blot after that; for like a phantom, the Blot is a ghostly presence, watching and hearing everything. We first see him stealthily trailing Mickey, then sitting unobserved in the back of Mickey's cab as the Mouse rides to the police station. Gottfredson even adopted the Hoban Blots' habit of walking in unison for one panel that shows the Blot creeping in step behind Mickey.[3]

Though the artist drew immediate inspiration from Hoban, the Blot's inky form had been percolating in his mind for years. The Fox, created by Walt Disney for the first strip adventure, was also a black-clad figure, as were the villainous Bat Bandit and the cloaked scientist in *The Mad Doctor* (1933), the film cartoon that inspired Gottfredson's "Blaggard Castle" (1932).[4] Villains dressed all in black had been common film fare since Louis Feuillade's movies about the French terrorist Fantômas, and Gottfredson was fascinated by these shadowy figures.

Gottfredson's period cynicism enters the story when the lines between Blot and Mickey blur—for even the straight-arrow Mickey must dirty his hands in order to defeat the Blot. Soon Mickey, too, is wearing a black robe and stealing cameras, even

ABOVE: Walter Hoban's "Blots"—from the comic strip *Jerry on the Job*—were insensitive ethnic stereotypes, but a major inspiration for Gottfredson's most memorable villain.

grasping one from the hands of a defenseless little girl! To defeat such an insidious foe, Mickey must become his mirror image. On the eve of war, the Blot symbolized the fear that battle might lower us—voluntarily or not—to the level of our enemies.

The fact that the "kindhearted" Blot can never kill in person, instead devising elaborate traps to murder Mickey in his absence, makes him particularly diabolical. In effect, his devices are self-destruction machines, designed to make the Mouse murder himself. Bound and drugged, with a noose around his neck, Mickey is placed on a high rafter, so that when he falls off, he will hang himself; or his foot is tied to the trigger of a gun, so that when he is forced to move, the weapon will discharge. These devices have roots in the suicide gags in Gottfredson's "Mr. Slicker and the Egg Robbers" (1930)[5] and Pete and Sylvester Shyster's rigged shotgun in "The Great Orphanage Robbery" (1932), but nobody other than the Blot was so consistently ingenious in meting out deathtraps.

For the Blot, these murder-in-absentia weapons fill an important psychological need: by a kind of twisted reasoning, they absolve him from responsibility, since he is never present when the traps are sprung. For Gottfredson, they solved an editorial problem: "This was done because we couldn't do any killing in the strip. We had to show violence in a tongue-in-cheek way, so we could only go so far." In creating a reason for murderous devices that would threaten but never quite kill Mickey, Gottfredson gave the Blot a twisted mind like that of no other villain in the strip, making him into a truly frightening adversary.

In the thrilling boat-and-aquaplane chase that concludes the story, Mickey is again the underdog who barely manages to beat a more powerful villain; he triumphs only through tenacity. The final scene imposes a bit of wartime propaganda. Like earlier stories, the tale of the Blot revolves around a great mystery: seemingly worthless cameras are being stolen for no apparent reason. It turns out that the formula concealed in the Blot's camera was stolen from an American firm that intended giving it to hospitals at cost, for the betterment of mankind; but a foreign syndicate wants to adapt it to make war material "more powerful than any ever known." The United States and her enemies were thus drawn in simple, black-and-white terms as America girded itself for war.

The decade's end saw decreased interest in programs of social reform and a retreat from the radicalism of the early 1930s. Some now perceived the New Deal as a failure, and grew cynical about the mushrooming powers of the Roosevelt administration's federal government. The threat of war and Fascism dampened interest in social experimentation as foreign affairs—rather than domestic issues—became paramount in Americans' eyes.

Indications of these shifts are evident in "The Miracle Master" (1939), a story about Mickey's discovery of a magic lamp that houses a wondrous genie. Atypically for Gottfredson, the story doesn't explain away its supernatural events—other than to leave the reader wondering if it was all a dream! While this story returns to the period's more typical gag-dominated style, its darker, misanthropic reflections on humanity keep Gottfredson's cynicism front and center. Although "Miracle Master" Mickey is well intentioned and performs magnificently good deeds, they all backfire. Thus Gottfredson considers a possibility never entertained before: that even a hero's actions may have unpredictable consequences—perhaps, ironically, mocking their creator's intentions.

The art and initial premise of "The Miracle Master" were based on the 1940 cartoon *Pluto's Dream House*, in which Mickey digs up a magic lamp.

However, there is no genie in the film; the character was dropped during production, surviving only in Disney's monthly *Good Housekeeping* feature—and in Gottfredson's strip. As he had done throughout the 1930s, Gottfredson looked beyond the finished cartoon for ideas.

Indeed, "The Miracle Master" took special inspiration from a recent H. G. Wells film, *The Man Who Could Work Miracles* (1936). The film follows George McWhirter Fotheringay, a small, timid haberdasher's assistant who is given unlimited power by a Roman-style god. Unequipped to deal with his new abilities, George at first creates goodies for himself and his friends, then follows advice from his vicar. But George becomes arrogant, and when he stops the Earth from revolving on its axis, his magic threatens to destroy the world. In "The Miracle Master" Mickey, too, is unable to harness his powers at first—but the focus of the story is on people's reactions *to* his magic, *not* on his lack of control over it.

Gottfredson effectively used the magic theme to satirize liberal programs of social reform. When Mickey decides to help the poor with his magic, he reflects 1930s liberal/humanitarian beliefs—the theory that people's living conditions caused their problems, and that the poor were not responsible for their plight. Films like *Dead End* (1937) blamed slums for juvenile delinquency and crime. "Those people are all right!" Mickey proclaims to the genie. "It's just the way they've had to live!" Mickey transforms the city dump into beautiful, park-laden housing, which he offers rent-free to the slum dwellers. But the result is a liberal reformer's nightmare. The poor are so cynical that they think Mickey is a swindler, and they refuse to move into his magically built dwellings.

Mickey's attempt to aid the disadvantaged is equally thwarted by local officials. A large bureaucracy had grown up as a result of Roosevelt's creation of a welfare state; Gottfredson felt this bureaucracy had rendered officials blind to humanitarian impulses. Instead of congratulating Mickey for his

good deed, the police put him in jail for building without a permit. And the mayor and his cronies are grafters, using city regulations to steal Mickey's housing project. In the process, as in "The Plumber's Helper," labor unions come in for a drubbing. The mayor condemns Mickey for not using local labor; even the genie is unionized, refusing to perform miracles after his four-hour shift!

The genie's needs also figure in the story's climax, when Mickey travels to Genieland and makes all of its citizens rich. Alas, the poor genies are peevish cranks who complain about whatever they get. En masse, they chase Mickey out of town and threaten to boil him in oil; now that they have everything, they believe they have nothing left to live for!

Gottfredson suggests that even if poverty were eliminated, the poor would still be miserable. Whether or not one agrees, the story is still a brilliant

LEFT: "From a mouse to a miracle man!" H. G. Wells' *The Man Who Could Work Miracles* (1937) helped spawn Gottfredson's "Miracle Master" serial. Image courtesy Heritage Auctions.

ABOVE: "Mickey's Magic Lamp"—changed to *Pluto's Dream House* (1940)—was adapted for Disney's monthly *Good Housekeeping* page. The feature turned current cartoons into painted picture stories told in verse. Art by Tom Wood; image courtesy Walt Disney Archives.

satire of the paradoxes involved in building a utopian society. We might do well to compare "The Miracle Master" with the earlier "Great Orphanage Robbery" (1932), in which Mickey is not only successful in helping the poor, but becomes a symbol of hope for all those in need. We see how far Gottfredson and his America had traveled since the early 1930s.

Mickey's inability to aid others is also the theme of the last story in this collection, "An Education for Thursday" (1940). Friday, of "Robinson Crusoe" fame, sends his brother Thursday to live with Mickey for an extended visit to America. In a continuity break from "Crusoe"—was it a movie story, or did it really happen?—Friday now utilizes pidgin English rather than Southern dialect, and Thursday can't speak English at all. The comedy hinges on his inability to understand what Mickey wants, as well as his unfamiliarity with civilization.

If Gottfredson's late 1930s cynicism previously colored his views of workers, economics, and domestic government, now we see it applied to foreign spheres. Thursday exemplifies the "child/savage" stereotype of Black Africans in older American culture. Though an adolescent, he acts like an ungovernable child. At times he is friendly and obedient; unlike the "Robinson Crusoe" cannibals, Thursday is never intentionally dangerous. He worships Goofy like a god—but he creates chaos wherever he goes.

To some extent, the story was inspired by earlier Mickey adventures dealing with mischievous children—such as "Mickey's Nephews" (1932)—and wayward animals, like "Oscar the Ostrich" (1936). In the latter, animals function as surrogate children and Mickey as frustrated father figure. With Thursday, the relationship is similar, as Mickey tries to assimilate the "child" into grownup American culture. The gags are based on 1930s misperceptions of Africa as a primitive, uncivilized society—regardless of its actual states, culture, and history. Mickey's effort to employ Thursday with a Cab Calloway-type Black jazz band is especially telling. According to popular prejudice, Blacks possessed an innate wildness because of their "primitive" African ancestry; jazz bands could sublimate the wildness into socially acceptable venues.[6]

For Gottfredson, however, the African-American bandleader "Cal Cabway" can be incorporated into middle-class society; the foreigner Thursday cannot, and so he must go home at the story's conclusion. By implication, "An Education for Thursday" registers isolationist fears of America becoming involved with, and intervening on behalf of foreign nations. Like Mickey's attempt to educate Thursday, the effort was seen as potentially dangerous, costly, and burdensome.

With the beginning of World War II, of course, this became a moot point. Hitler and the Axis powers challenged the freedom of *all* democratic nations, and America had to join the fight in order to help shift the tide. We'll see how Mickey moved toward joining the fight in our next book. •

1 Godfrey Hodgson, *The Myth of American Exceptionalism* (New Haven: Yale University Press, 2009), pp. 9-29.

2 This and later quotes: Floyd Gottfredson, interviews with the author, 1970s-80s.

3 Gottfredson liked the creeping-in-step gimmick and used it again in 1940 in the western *Mickey* adventure, "The Bar-None Ranch." It is likely Hoban and Gottfredson had seen this done in vaudeville routines and early movies.

4 Thomas Andrae, "Of Mouse and Man: Adapting Mickey," in *Walt Disney's Mickey Mouse: Trapped on Treasure Island* (Vol. 2 of this series), p. 9. The comic appeared several months before the film's release, but was inspired by it in development.

5 The gags feature a lovelorn Mickey failing to end it all. For the inspiration behind this sequence, see David Gerstein, "Sheiks and Lovers," in *Walt Disney's Mickey Mouse: Race to Death Valley* (Vol. 1 of this series), p. 72.

6 Burton W. Peretti, *The Creation of Jazz: Music, Race and Culture in Urban America* (Chicago: University of Illinois Press, 1994), p. 54.

LEFT: Gottfredson's cynical 1939 view of poverty marked a sharp contrast with earlier days. This 1931 Christmas ad features two poor orphan kittens who would feature in "The Great Orphanage Robbery" (1932) strip serial. Art by Floyd Gottfredson and Al Taliaferro; image courtesy Garry Apgar.

Reading Pictures:

THE VISUAL LANGUAGE OF FLOYD GOTTFREDSON

» *Appreciation by Craig McCracken*

I'VE MADE MY CAREER as a cartoonist working in animation with cartoons like *The Powerpuff Girls*, *Foster's Home For Imaginary Friends*, and currently Disney's *Wander Over Yonder*. In that work, I've always tried to put an emphasis on bold designs in which characters, ideas, or feelings can be broken down into clean, simple iconic symbols. Much of the inspiration for this, though, was not found on TV or on the movie screen—but in the comic section of the newspaper in the work of Floyd Gottfredson, who to me was one of Disney's best cartoon directors.

I have been drawn to cartoon images since I can first remember; and like most kids, I was especially transfixed by Mickey Mouse. My mom tells a story of finding a two-year-old me in a trancelike state, hypnotically staring at that classic smiling, arms-behind-back, foot-out pose of Mickey that then appeared on a lot of T-shirts. I just *loved* that image. Still do.

There's something about Mickey that just makes me happy. Which is just as obvious as saying "the Beatles made great music," "Hawaii is an amazing place to vacation," or "food tastes good."

Mickey. Mouse. Makes. People. Happy.

And as a kid, I loved staring at that beaming symbol of joy and innocence. He was my friendly, happy-go-lucky pal. Nothin' got his goat, and everything was swell!

Then something happened when I got a little bit older. I discovered—in the pages of *The Smithsonian Collection of Newspaper Comics* (1977)—a Mickey I hadn't seen before.[1] This Mickey wasn't just standing there, mouth agape and arm outstretched as if he were a hand model for an unspecified future product yet to come. No. This Mickey was worried. This Mickey was scared. This Mickey was determined. And, most surprising of all, this Mickey was mad!

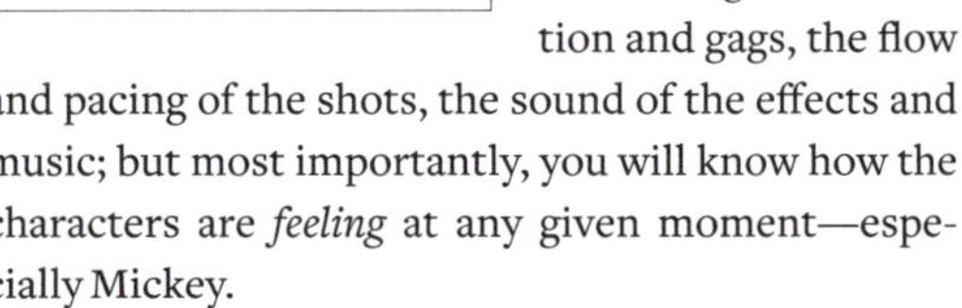

Yep. Brows furrowed, teeth gritted, shoulders up, hands tensed into claws. This was not the same happy-go-lucky pal I had on my shirts, sheets, shoes, and shelves. This guy made plans, he solved mysteries, he got out of scrapes, he outwitted the thugs—and he saved the day! He expressed a wide range of emotions that transformed this two-dimensional image of joy into a deep, multifaceted character who seemed to feel the way I felt; and thus he became alive to me. This was the best Mickey I had ever *seen*, and it was all because of Floyd Gottfredson.

Now, I say *seen* and not *read*, because herein lies Gottfredson's genius. His ability to *distill a feeling, action, or emotion down into a graphic symbol that reads instantaneously* made it almost unnecessary to read the words to understand what was going on. Don't get me wrong—these strips are filled with great stories that are totally worth reading, but those narratives are made even stronger because...

The pictures *told* the story.

Floyd got his start at Disney in the Animation Department, and you can tell: his strips really move. The characters flow through the panels like key poses in an animated scene. Looking at these strips in sequence is like watching a really great adventure cartoon. Try it out. Take any of the strips contained in these volumes and just quickly skim the panels. Though you may not know the specific details of the plot, you will find that you begin not only to fill in the timing of the action and gags, the flow and pacing of the shots, the sound of the effects and music; but most importantly, you will know how the characters are *feeling* at any given moment—especially Mickey.

You can track the emotional beats of any Gottfredson story just by looking at the expression on Mickey's face.

1 The *Smithsonian Collection* reprinted the Mickey Mouse serial "Race for Riches" (1935) in its entirety. "Race" also appears in Vol. 3 of this series.

Usually a plotline will start out with the we all know and love. Then something happens that makes Mickey and head out on an adventure!

As the story continues, Mickey will have a fair share of along the way, but most of the time it's a lot of

You always know how deep you are in a Gottfredson story when all you see are days and days of

Despite Mickey's small victories, the villains always end up getting the jump on him, making Mickey

Now this is when our little hero digs deep and decides to for what is right, thus saving the day! Then Mickey returns home to But we know that this is short-lived, for soon something troubling will make Mickey ...and once again, our heroic mouse will be off on another adventure!

Just you watch—and I mean *watch*. For Floyd Gottfredson directed some of Disney's best Mickey Mouse animated cartoons never filmed! (Note: the headshots above were all pulled, in approximate chronological sequence, from "The Mighty Whale Hunter" adventure found in *this* volume!) •

FACING LEFT: This iconic "arms-behind-back" Mickey pose—a favorite of both Craig McCracken and Andy Warhol—was based on an image drawn by animator Fred Moore for the cartoon *Puppy Love* (1933).

FACING RIGHT: The comics Mickey in archetypal happy and angry moods. From Gottfredson's 1931 marketing model sheet; images courtesy Disney Publishing Worldwide.

RIGHT: Gottfredson's original art for part of a "Mighty Whale Hunter" strip (see page 30 for the end product). From the Craig McCracken collection.

MIGHTY WHALE HUNTER

FEBRUARY 7, 1938
–
JULY 6, 1938

CRAFT(TINT)ING A WHALE OF A TALE

It's safe to say that "Mickey Mouse, Mighty Whale Hunter" is an underappreciated gem. At least in the United States, that is, where the story has only been reprinted once in modern years.

That lack of reprinting should be surprising, since the story lives up to the same high standard as most of Gottfredson's *Mickey* serials in the later half of the 1930s. It's an exciting adventure set in a fully realized setting (a whaling ship), populated with lifelike secondary characters, told with humor and suspense—and just the right touch of both pathos and sympathy.

It's tempting to think the reason "Mighty Whale Hunter" has been allowed to fade into obscurity is that whale hunting itself is mightily politically incorrect. But then again, the story is actually *anti*-whaling: Mickey *saves* not one but two whales from the villainous Pegleg Pete.

So perhaps the story owes its obscurity to the equally politically incorrect stereotypes of the Chinese cook Hi See—complete with queue and pidgin English dialogue—and Pedro, a seeming Italian who talks a little like Chico Marx. But Hi See, if portrayed with 1930s insensitivity, is still Mickey's smart confidante. And Pedro is actually *Portuguese*: an admiring spoof of Spencer Tracy as Manuel Fidello in *Captains Courageous* (1937).

But no, neither concerns about whaling nor ethnic imagery would have prevented "Mighty Whale Hunter" from being reprinted during thirty or forty years of "less concerned" times. I submit that the real reason it got buried is because of Gottfredson's use of craftint, which he debuted to masterful effect in "Mighty Whale Hunter." Just look at the sunrise in the February 22 strip (took my breath away the first time I saw it in all its full-size six-column glory!), or the painterly effects on the sea and waves throughout.

Gottfredson was able to achieve these "painterly" effects because craftint is a shading technique in which the artist draws on special illustration board that has crosshatch lines chemically embedded into it. The lines are brought out by (you guessed it) *painting* on the board with either of two chemicals—or both. The disadvantages to the artist are that the paper is expensive, and that you can't really make whiteout corrections without ruining the chemical patterns.

The use of craftint also presents many disadvantages to the would-be reprinter. At highly reduced sizes, the crosshatch patterns muddy up even worse than the more standard zip-a-tone shading. Throwing color on top of it gives really weird tones (check out the earlier reprint, 1980's *Goofy: Best Comics*). And worst of all, you can't separate the strips' panels to remount them to the comic book format. Or rather, you *can*—and you can certainly trim off art to make the panels fit the width of a comic book, but you can't easily *add on* art at the edges to justify the pages (as Western Publishing frequently—and very poorly—did with their Gottfredson reprints).

But lucky you! For this Fantagraphics edition, you get the strips in almost full-size horizontal glory. You finally get a chance not only to enjoy a sadly obscure classic from the golden age of the *Mickey Mouse* comic strip, but to marvel at how good a comic artist Floyd Gottfredson really was.

— Byron Erickson

BACK FROM THEIR ADVENTURES ACROSS THE SEA, MICKEY AND MINNIE SETTLE DOWN AGAIN IN THE OLD HOME TOWN.

R-7

AFTER SOME TIME AT HOME, A SPIRIT OF RESTLESSNESS BEGINS TO GROW ON MICKEY. MINNIE IS THE FIRST TO RECOGNIZE THE SYMPTOMS.

R-9

MINNIE IS STILL TRYING TO PERSUADE MICKEY TO STAY AT HOME AND GIVE UP ADVENTURING.

YOU MAKE ME SO MAD! A NICE HOME AND EVERYTHING, AND NOW YOU WANT TO GO WHALE-FISHING! WHAT NEXT?
WHAT NEXT? I HAVEN'T THOUGHT THAT FAR!

WELL, LET ME TELL YOU ONE THING, MICKEY MOUSE! I'LL NOT HAVE YOU ROAMING THE FOUR CORNERS OF THE EARTH ALL THE TIME!
BUT I—!

EITHER YOU GIVE UP YOUR WILD IDEAS OR GIVE UP ME!
?

!
---AND I KNOW YOUR DECISION! VERY WELL! GOOD-BYE!!
R-10
WALT DISNEY

WOMEN ARE FUNNY, PLUTO! HERE'S MINNIE SORE AT ME FOR GOIN' ON A WHALIN' VOYAGE I HAVEN'T EVEN PLANNED ON!

BUT IT WOULD BE FUN TO--- OH, H'LO, GOOFY!
WHUT WUD BE FUN?

CATCHIN' WHALES! THE THRILL O' THE CHASE! THE TANG OF SALT SPRAY, AS THE HARPOONED MONSTER TEARS THROUGH THE WAVES, LIKE NOTHIN' AT ALL! FINALLY--HE TIRES--YOU'VE GOT HIM---!

HUH? WHAT'D Y' SAY?
I SED, GOSH-DARN YUH, YUH'VE MADE ME DISSATI'FIED WITH THUH FINEST MESS O' FISH I EVER CAUGHT!
R-11
WALT DISNEY

I SURE WISH I COULD GET ON A WHALIN' VOYAGE!
NOT ME! AFTER DE-LIBERATIN', I FINDS IT'S TOO DANG'ROUS--- AND A LOTTA WORK!

WELL, I GUESS THERE'S NO EXPEDITION WE COULD JOIN, ANYWAY!
NO? OH--- THEN I'LL GO WITH YUH!

MEN WANTED
DESTRUCTIVE WHALE!! LIBERAL BOUNTY
LADY DAFFODIL"
NO WEAKLINGS NEED APPLY!
HEY! WHAT'S THIS?
?
R-12

MEN WANTED!
FOR VOYAGE TO NORTHERN WATERS
FOR PURPOSE OF CAPTURE OF
DESTRUCTIVE WHALE!!
LIBERAL BOUNTY WILL BE PAID!!
APPLY TO CAPTAIN OF BOAT "LADY DAFFODIL"
FOOT OF MAIN ST. WHARF
NO WEAKLINGS NEED APPLY!
WALT DISNEY

OH, BOY! THAT'S OUR CHANCE!
MEN WANTED FOR VOYAGE TO NORTHERN WATERS!! FOR PURPOSE OF CAPTURE OF DESTRUCTIVE WHALE!! LIBERAL BOUNTY WILL BE PAID!! APPLY TO CAPTAIN OF BOAT "LADY DAFFODIL" FOOT OF MAIN ST. WHARF NO WEAKLINGS NEED APPLY!!
NOT ME! I AIN'T HANKERIN' TO MESS WITH NO DEE-STRUCTIVE CRITTER!

AW--C'MON! IT'LL BE THE THRILL OF A LIFETIME! AND BESIDES---!
B'SIDES WHUT?

---THE SIGN SAID "NO WEAKLINGS NEED APPLY" SO IF YOU DON'T APPLY, WHAT'LL PEOPLE THINK?
GAWRSH! THEY'LL THINK I AIN'T MAN ENUFF! WHY--THUH LOW-DOWN GOSSIPIN' POLE-CATS---I'LL SHOW 'EM!
R-14

AIN'T NOBODY GONTER CALL ME A WEAKLIN', B'GAWRSH! BRING ON YER DURN WHALE!
FISHING SUPPLIES
WALT DISNEY

THE IDEAR! PEOPLE CALLIN' ME A WEAKLIN'! NUTHIN'S GONTER STOP ME FRUM WHALE-HUNTIN' NOW!
EXCEPT, MAYBE, WE WON'T GET TH' JOB! THEY MIGHT HAVE ALL THE MEN THEY NEED!

THEY AIN'T HAD ANYBUDDY 'TIL THEY SEE ME! WHERE'S THIS "LADY DAFFY-DIL"?
I GUESS THAT'S HER AT THE END O' THE WHARF!

WE WANTA SEE THE CAPTAIN, PLEASE!
AN' WE AIN'T FOOLIN', NUTHER! WE'RE GONTER KETCH THAT WHALE!

JOE---TAKE THESE GENTS TO THE OLD MAN! HE'S BEEN LAYIN' AWAKE NIGHTS, WAITIN' FOR 'EM!
FER TWO CENTS, I'D---!
CAREFUL, GOOFY! THIS CREW LOOKS KINDA TOUGH!
WALT DISNEY
R-15

CAPTAIN
WALK RIGHT IN, SIRS! THE CAPTAIN AWAITS YORE PRESENCE!

WELL?
CAN Y' USE TWO GOOD MEN?
---A COUPLA FEAR-LESS WHALE KETCH-ERS?

AYE--THAT I CAN! YE'VE COME TO THE RIGHT SHIP, ME HEART-IES!
GAWRSH--THANKS!
UH--THANK YE, SIR!

WELL? DON'T STAND THERE LIKE BELAYIN'-PINS! IF YE'VE GOT TWO GOOD MEN--BRING 'EM IN!
R-16

WHAT? Y' EXPECT ME TO HIRE YOU?
I NEED MEN -- NOT SWABS O' YOUR SIZE!
!

I'LL DO ANY KIND O' WORK Y' WANT, SIR! JUST GIVE ME A CHANCE!
LISSEN, CAP! DON'T LET MICKEY'S SIZE FOOL YUH! HE KIN LICK ANY WHALE IN TH' OCEAN, I BETCHER!
FIDDLESTICKS!

BUT I'M MIGHTY BAD IN NEED O' HANDS, SO I'LL TAKE YOU, ANYWAY!
NO YUH WON'T, CAP! YUH TAKES MICKEY OR YUH LOSES ME--!
R-17

---AND IN THET CASE, YUH PROB'RLY LOSES YER WHALE! THINK IT OVER, CAP!
WALT DISNEY

BETTER DECIDE, CAP! WE JERNS YER CREW TOGETHER--OR WE DON'T JERN!

IF I WASN'T SO DANGED SHORT-HANDED, I'D--! ALL RIGHT--BUT YOU'RE TOO SMALL FOR ANY JOB BUT CABIN-BOY!
OKAY! I'LL TAKE IT, SIR!
R-18

GET YOUR DUNNAGE AND REPORT ON BOARD IN THE MORNIN'! WE SAIL AT SUN-UP!
YES, SIR!
SEE YUH TOMORRER, CAP!

AND NOW THAT YOU'RE WORKIN' FOR ME, CALL ME, SIR!!
Y-- YES-- SIR!
WALT DISNEY

WELL, S'LONG, MICKEY! TOMORRER WE'LL BE SHIPMATES!
AND NOW, I GOTTA GO SAY G'BYE TO MINNIE! HOPE SHE'S NOT STILL SORE AT ME!

---SO I'M SAILIN' AT SUNRISE--AN' I THOUGHT---THERE'S NOT MUCH TIME---I'D BETTER---BETTER SEE Y' TONIGHT---!
INDEED? I'M FLATTERED!

---I--I GUESS I BETTER--GO NOW! Y' SEE, I'M SAILIN' AT SUNRISE AND---!
YES! YOU ALREADY SAID THAT!
R-19

BUT YOU'RE NOT SAILING WITHOUT THIS SWEATER! WHAT DO YOU THINK I'VE BEEN WORKING MY FINGERS OFF, FOR?
MINNIE! YOU OLD--- YOU---! OH, GOSH!

THE MOMENTOUS DAY IS HERE! MICKEY IS UP WITH THE FIRST FAINT LIGHT OF DAWN, READY TO JOIN THE CREW OF THE "LADY DAFFODIL", NORTHWARD BOUND ON A WHALE-HUNT.

SEVERAL DAYS OUT FROM PORT MICKEY AND GOOFY HAVE FOUND THEIR SEA LEGS AND ARE SETTLED TO THE ROUTINE OF THEIR JOBS. GOOFY TAKES HIS TURN WITH THE OTHER SAILORS, BUT MICKEY'S SMALL SIZE KEEPS HIM STILL A CABIN BOY.

S'MATTER, GOOFY-- DON'T Y' LIKE YOUR JOB?
THUH JOB'S ALL RIGHT! IT'S THUH GOL-DURNED WORK THET'S GITTIN' MUH DOWN!

I'M QUITTIN' RIGHT NOW! I'M THROUGH, I AM!
Y' CAN'T QUIT ON TH' HIGH SEAS! THAT'S MUTINY!
2-28

IT'S BETTER'N WORK! ANYWAY -- WHUT KIN THEY DO ABOUT IT?
NOT MUCH! THEY'LL JUST CHAIN Y' DOWN IN THE DARK HOLD WITH THE RATS FOR TH' REST O' TH' TRIP!

OH, A JOLLY SAILOR BOY AM I---YO HO--YO HO--YO HO-O--!
WALT DISNEY
Copr. by Walt Disney Enterprises 1938 / World rights reserved

PLENTY FAST DISH WASHEE! NICE WU'K!
THANKS, HI SEE!

Y' KNOW, YOU'RE THE ONLY GUY ON THIS BOAT THAT EVER SMILES! WHAT MAKES THE CREW SO CRABBY, ANYWAY?

MEBBE SO ON 'COUNT OF THIS BOAT ALLEE SAMEE HOODOO--VELLY BAD LUCK! SAILEH GUYS SUPASTISHEE!
HOW D'YA MEAN?
3-1

SAILEH GUYS NO CATCHEE 'NUFF FISH--BOSS-CAPTAIN, HE GO BROKEE--SAILEH GUYS NO CATCHEE WAGES ALL SEASON!
SO THAT'S IT!
WALT DISNEY

THE SHIP'S LOSIN' MONEY AT TH' FISHIN' TRADE---THE CAPTAIN'S TOO POOR TO PAY THE CREW---BUT HERE WE ARE---!
Copr. by Walt Disney Enterprises 1938 / World rights reserved

---GOIN' AFTER A RAMBUNCTIOUS WHALE THAT NO SHIP'S BEEN ABLE TO CATCH! HOW COME?
VELLY SIMPLE!

THIS SHIP CATCHEE WHALE, BOSS-CAPTAIN WIN BIG PLIZE MONEY--PAY OFF CLEW---EV'YBODY HAPPY! HOTSY-TOTS!
3-2

BUT THIS A BAD LUCK SHIP, SO WON'T CATCHEE WHALE!
WELL---GOOD GOSH--WE GOTTA CATCH IT!

GOOFY, HAVE Y' HEARD ANY O' THE MEN TALKIN' ABOUT THIS BEIN' A HOODOO BOAT?
YEAH! 'AT'S WHUT THEY ALL SAY!

AND THE CREW HASN'T BEEN PAID IN MONTHS?
YEP! THUH POOR, LOONEY SAPHEADS-- I TOLE 'EM WHUT IDJUTS THEY WERE!

UH-HAW! KIN Y' IMAGINE YOU OR ME, MICKEY, BEIN' DUMB ENUFF TO WORK ON A SHIP LIKE THET?
BUT WE ARE WORKIN' HERE, Y' DOPE!
3-3

HE'S RIGHT, B'GAWRSH! WE ARE!

WHAT D' YOU THINK, PEDRO?- WILL OUR BOAT BRING IN THE WHALE AN' WIN THE PRIZE?
BAH! THEES TUB, SHE BRING NO-THEENG BUT TRO'BLE! SHE'S NO LUCK NO TIME!

THEN OUR LUCK'S ABOUT DUE FOR A CHANGE!
YES--SHE'S CHANGE FROM BAD TO WARSE!
3-4

THEES WHALE WAN BEEG TOUGH GUY-- SWALLER US ALL IF SHE'S FEEL HONGRY! BUT WHO CARE? PTOOH!

BOY! IS THIS A JOLLY AND JOVIAL CREW? WOW!
WALT DISNEY

SEEMS LIKE EV'RYTHING DEPENDS ON CATCHIN' THAT WHALE!
HEAH! FOHGETEE 'BOUT WHALE AN' TAKEE DINNEH TO BOSS-CAPTAIN!

THIS WHALE, SIR--- WHY IS THERE A REWARD FOR IT?
AH, ME LAD-- THIS IS NO ORDINARY WHALE!

HE'S A STRANGE BEAST AND A BIG ONE! MANY A VESSEL'S COME T' GRIEF DISPUTIN' TH' RIGHT O' WAY WITH OL' BARNEY!

THEY CALL 'IM THAT 'CAUSE O' TH' BARNACLES ON HIM--- BRRHUMPH! WHAT ARE YE STANDIN' AROUND FOR? BE ABOUT YER BUSINESS!
AYE, AYE, SIR!
3-5
WALT DISNEY

GO AFT AND FETCH ME M' OILSKINS! LIVELY NOW!
AYE, AYE, SIR!

SO, THE OLE MAN WANTS HIS ILESKINS, EH? THAT MEANS A SPELL O' DIRTY WEATHER!
BUT, GOSH! TH' OCEAN'S LIKE A MILL POND!

SQUALLS COME UP MIGHTY SUDDINT IN THESE WATERS -- AND OLE BEAGLE-NOSE CAN SMELL 'EM WHILE THEY'RE STILL PUPS!
BOY! IF IT STORMS, I HOPE IT'LL BE A RIP-SNORTER!

DAD-BLAST YER SCUPPERS!! I SAID LIVELY!!
HO! HO! THERE'S ONE SQUALL FOR YE ALREADY, MATEY!
3-7
WALT DISNEY

WHAT'D I TELL YE! THE CAP'N KNOWS HIS WEATHER, DON'T HE?
Y' MEAN THIS IS GONNA BE A REAL STORM?

JIST THAT, SONNY! DAVY JONES HEZ ORDERED A SPESHUL BLOW TO SKEER LANDLUBBERS! SO, I'D ADVISE YE TO STAY BELOW AND ANCHOR YORE TEETH!

SO--- THINKS WE CAN'T TAKE IT, EH?
HUH! LAN' LUBBERS! IF I KNOWED WHUT IT MEANS, I'D SOCK 'IM DOWN.

ALL HANDS ON DECK! STAND BY AND MAKE FAST THE RIGGIN' FER A BLOW-W-W!!
3-8

STOW ALL LOOSE GEAR! BATTEN DOWN THE HATCHES!!

AVAST THERE! LEGGO THAT LINE AN' LET A MAN HAVE IT, YA LAN' LUBBER!

AYE, AYE, SAILOR!
WALT DISNEY
3-9

AT THE CRY OF "MAN OVERBOARD!" THE ENGINES OF THE "LADY DAFFODIL" ARE THROWN INTO REVERSE AND THE CREW RUSHES TO THE RESCUE!

MICKEY HAS WEATHERED HIS FIRST STORM ABOARD THE "LADY DAFFODIL" AND RAISED HIS STOCK WITH BOTH CAPTAIN AND CREW. HIS PRESENT PROBLEM, HOWEVER, IS A VERY SEASICK CHINESE COOK.

THERE SHE IS! THE CAPTAIN'S PET DISH, AND COOKED TO A "T"-IF I DO SAY SO!
3-17

THE COOK'S STILL SICK, SIR! I FIXED YOUR DINNER, MYSELF!
WELL, YE BEEN **LONG** ENOUGH ABOUT IT! I'M DANG NEAR STARVED!

WHAT IN BLUE TOPHET IS **THIS**? **FISH**?
Y-YES, SIR! BOILED COD!
Copr. 1938 by Walt Disney Enterprises World rights reserved

I THOUGHT--I HEARD YOU LIKED---!
WHAT? DON'T YE KNOW I HATE THE **SIGHT** OF A FISH? DO YE EXPECT ME TO **EAT** ONE? **GODFREY SCISSORS!**

I WOULDN'T EAT A DAD-BLASTED **FISH** IF I WAS STARVIN'! EV'RY MAN-JACK IN THE FO'CSLE KNOWS THAT!
SORRY, SIR--- I---!

3-18

TAKE THIS DAD-ROTTED MESS O' BILGE TRIPE--- AN' BRING ME SOME **FOOD**!
YES, SIR---!
WHAT TH---?

THANKS FOR YOUR **TIP**, OL' BOY! THE CAP'N ENJOYED THAT FISH SO MUCH, HE HAD TO SHARE IT WITH YOU!
WALT DISNEY

GOSH -- WOTTA LIFE! I SURE WISH HI SEE WOULD HURRY UP AN' GET WELL!

UH-HAW! LOOK WHUT I BRUNG YUH, MICKEY!
OH, **BOY**!
Copr. 1938 by Walt Disney Enterprises World rights reserved

I GOTTA BE GOIN', IN CASE TH' SKIPPER'S NEEDIN' ME!
ME ALL LIGHT!
SURE YOU'RE ALL RIGHT, HI SEE?
3-19

?
OW-W-W!
PLOP!
WALT DISNEY

HOW Y' FEELIN' TODAY, HI SEE?
OH, ME ALL LIGHT NOW-- EXCEPT STUMMICK FULL O' BUTTAFLIES!
3-21

I'VE BROUGHT YOUR LAUNDRY, SIR!
GOOD! ER-- JUST PUT IT ON THE BERTH!

WHAT IN TUNKET DO YE MEAN BY BARGING IN WITHOUT KNOCKIN'? GET OUT!
SWISH!

HMM-M! WHATEVER HE WAS FIGURIN' ON THAT PAPER, HE SURE DIDN'T WANT IT TO BE SEEN!
SLAM!
WALT DISNEY

HEY, WHUT'S TH' IDEAR O' SLEEP-WALKIN'?
HUH? OH -- I GUESS I WAS JUST THINKIN'!

ABOUT WHUT, F'R INSTANCE?
I GOT A HUNCH THIS VOYAGE IS A LOT MORE IMPORTANT THAN ANY OF US KNOW ABOUT!

SAY! WHERE'D Y' GET THAT PAPER?
THIS? OH, IT WUZ BLOWIN' ALONG THUH DECK AN' I SWEP' IT UP!
Copr by Walt Disney Enterprises 1938 World rights reserved

IT AIN'T NO GOOD! JEST A LOTTA BIG WORDS THET DON'T MEAN NUTHIN'!
3-22
WALT DISNEY

Y' FOUND THIS ON THE DECK? WHY, IT LOOKS LIKE AN IMPORTANT PAPER!
YEAH? WELL, SOMEBUDDY THROWED IT AWAY!

IT IS IMPORTANT! AND IT WASN'T THROWN AWAY, EITHER! IT PROB'LY BLEW OUT OF THE CAPTAIN'S CABIN!

BEG Y'R PARDON, SIR!
WELL? WHAT IS IT NOW?
Copr by Walt Disney Enterprises 1938 World rights reserved

THIS PAPER, SIR! IT---!
WHAT? WHERE'D YE GET THAT?
3-23

HOW'D YOU COME BY THIS PAPER? TELL ME THAT!
IT MUST'VE BLOWN AWAY, SIR! ONE O' THE MEN FOUND IT AND TURNED IT OVER TO ME!

HUMPH! AND YE READ IT, I CALC'LATE!
NO, SIR! ONLY ENOUGH TO SEE THAT IT'S YOUR PROPERTY!
3-24

HMM-M-M---VERY GOOD! WELL, THAT'S ALL!
AYE, AYE, SIR!
Copr. by Walt Disney Enterprises 1938 World rights reserved

NO, THAT AIN'T ALL! COME BACK HERE! AND CLOSE THE DOOR, CAN'T YE? GODFREY SCISSORS!
!
WALT DISNEY

Y' HAD SOMEP'N ELSE TO TELL ME, SIR?
YES! I'VE BEEN WATCHIN' YOUR WORK AND, UH--CONDUCT ON BOARD AND---!
TAPPETY! TAPPETY TAP
Copr. by Walt Disney Enterprises 1938 World rights reserved

SIT DOWN, WILL YE? AND DON'T BE SO DANGED NERVOUS!
?

AS I WAS SAYIN', ER--YE SEEM TO TAKE MORE INT'REST IN THIS VOYAGE THAN THE REST O' THE HANDS!
I GUESS MAYBE I DO!

SO--IT'S IN ME MIND TO TELL YE JUST WHAT THIS VOYAGE MEANS TO ME!
GOSH! THANK YA, SIR!
3-25

COME ON DECK A MINUTE, ME LAD!
YES, SIR!

WHAT D'YE THINK OF HER? THIS SHIP I MEAN!
SHE'S A BEAUTY, SIR! A SWELL BOAT!

SHE'S BEEN MY HOME FER OVER THIRTY YEAR! I KNOW EV'RY PLANK IN HER DECK--EV'RY NAIL, TOO! I'D SOONER LOSE ME ARM THAN THIS VESSEL!
?
3-26

BUT I DO LOSE HER IF WE DON'T CATCH THAT WHALE! CAN YE IMAGINE HOW I FEEL?
G-GOSH! I SURE CAN, SIR!
WALT DISNEY
Copr. by Walt Disney Enterprises 1938 World rights reserved

MICKEY LEARNS THAT NOT ONLY THE CREW'S WAGES DEPEND ON THE LONG-SOUGHT WHALE, BUT FAILURE ALSO MEANS THAT THE SKIPPER LOSES HIS SHIP, WHICH HE HAS MORTGAGED TO COVER EXPENSES OF THE VOYAGE.

3-28

THE "LADY DAFFODIL" REACHES HER GOAL AND MOVES IN AMONG THE OTHER FISHING BOATS, READY TO DROP HER ANCHOR.

3-29

HOW'RE THE FISH RUNNIN'?
THEY AIN'T! WHATEVER OL' BARNEY HASN'T ET, HE'S SKEERED AWAY!
3-31

IF SOMEBUDDY DON'T KETCH THAT WHALE, THE FISHIN' TRADE AIN'T WUTH A DIME!

WHALE OR NO WHALE, THIS IS A FISHIN'-BOAT! GET READY THE NETS AN' GO TO WORK!

HEY! WOT FOH YOU FOOL ALOUND ON DECK? YOU NOT FISHAMAN! PLENTY DISH WASHEE TO DO! MAKE SNAPPY!
!
WALT DISNEY

HERE I AM STUCK AT THIS JOB, WHILE THE SAILORS ARE OUT FISHIN'!
PHOOH! SAILEHS NO CATCHEE FISH, BUT YOU DO GOOD JOB WET WASHEE DISHES!
Copr. by Walt Disney Enterprises 1938 World rights reserved

BUT I WANT ADVENTURE -- ACTION! I WANTA HELP GET THAT WHALE!

!
THAR SHE BLOW-W-S!
OH, BOY!

OOM-PA-PAH!!
MAN THE GUNS--ER, TO THE BOATS--UH-- ALL HANDS ON DECK!
4-1
WALT DISNEY

OOM-PA-PAH!
GOSH! WHAT A WHOPPER!
4-2

YOU DON'T KNOW OLD BARNEY! WHEN HE SOUNDS, LOOK OUT!
BOY! THAT'S A BREAK--HE'S GOIN' DOWN!

O-MI-GOSH!
Copr. by Walt Disney Enterprises 1938 World rights reserved

VOOP! VOOP!

MICKEY GETS HIS FIRST SIGHT OF "OLD BARNEY," THE WHALE, WHEN THE MONSTER SUDDENLY POPS UP AT THE FISHING-GROUNDS AND PLAYFULLY TOSSES A DORY AND TWO MEN OUT OF THE WATER.

"OLD BARNEY'S" GREETING TO MICKEY AND HIS SHIPMATES IS TO PULL HIS FAVORITE TRICK OF DIVING BENEATH THE VESSEL AND BUMPING IT AS HE COMES UP.

AFTER THE SHORT BRUSH WITH THE WHALE, THE SKIPPER RETIRES TO HIS CABIN AND PEACE AND QUIET DECEND UPON THE SHIP.

SEVERAL DAYS LATER, THE WHALE HAS KEPT AWAY AND THE DAFFODIL'S MEN ARE SETTLED DOWN TO THE DULL MONOTONY OF FISHING.

4-9

Copr by Walt Disney Enterprises
1938 World rights reserved

IT'S NO USE! I CAN'T MAKE 'EM HEAR ME!
4-14

WHAT'S TH' IDEE? THE DAFFODIL'S H'ISTED HER ANCHOR --- SHE'S MOVIN'!
?

OOM-PAH OOOOM-PA-PAAAH!!
?
?
!
!

JUMPIN' JERUSHA-- WE'RE GONERS!
Copr. by Walt Disney Enterprises 1938 World rights reserved
WALT DISNEY

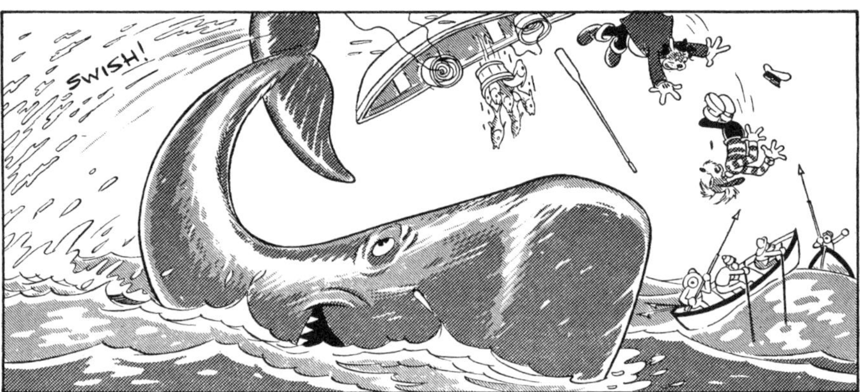
SWISH!

PICK UP THOSE TWO MEN! THEY'RE HURT!
I'LL GET 'EM, SIR!
4-15
WALT DISNEY

OOMP-PAH! PA-PA-PAH!!
WITH THE TWO INJURED MEN SAFELY ON BOARD THE DAFFODIL, THE OTHER BOAT CREWS ATTACK OLD BARNEY WITH HARPOONS.

F' GOSH SAKES! THOSE THINGS ARE ONLY TICKLIN' HIM!!
4-16
Copr. by Walt Disney Enterprises 1938 World rights reserved

I'LL TICKLE HIM! PULL CLEAR, YOU SWABS AN' GIVE ME A CHANCE FOR A SHOT!
WALT DISNEY

OLD BARNEY SEEMS ONLY AMUSED AT ATTEMPTS TO CAPTURE HIM WITH HAND HARPOONS. THE SKIPPER GETS READY TO TRY A SHOT FROM THE DAFFODIL'S GUN.

MICKEY IS IN THE SEVENTH HEAVEN OF DELIGHT. THE CAPTAIN FINALLY LETS HIM TAKE A BOAT AND GO OUT AS A FISHERMAN.

H'COME WE'RE GOIN' S' GOSH-DURN FUR OUT?
BETTER CHANCE FOR FISH! THE WHALE'S SCARED 'EM ALL AWAY F'M THE REG'LAR GROUNDS!

LOOKA HERE, MICKEY! YOU AIN'T PULLIN' A FAST ONE ON ME? WE'RE NOT WHALE-HUNTIN', YUH KNOW!
OH, SURE NOT! JUST FISHIN'!

THEN WHUT'S TH' IDEAR O BRINGIN' THESE ALONG?
WELL-L--IN CASE WE'RE ATTACKED, WE GOTTA DEFEND OURSELVES!

I SEE! WE TAKE A COUPLA TIN SPEARS AND ROW OUT INTA THUH MIDDLE O' NOWHERE--- TO DEFEND OURSELVES! HM-M-M!!
4-25

BOY-- IT SURE PAID TO COME 'WAY OUT HERE! WE'RE GETTIN' SOME REAL FISH!
YOU SED IT, B'GAWRSH! WE AIN'T BRINGIN' BACK NO SARDINES!

OOPS! I GOT ONE, NOW, THET I AIN'T GONTER KEEP!
WHAT'S THE MATTER WITH IT?

NUTHIN' MUCH! ONLY WE CAN'T BOTH OF US GIT IN TH' SAME BOAT!
?
4-26

---AND I AIN'T AIMIN' T'GIT OUT AN' WALK, B'GAWRSH!
WALT DISNEY

I'D LIKE TO S'PRISE THE CAPTAIN WITH A WHOPPIN' BIG BOATLOAD!
WE GOT MORE A'READY THAN TH' REST OF 'EM BRUNG IN!
THE FISH STOP BITING AND MICKEY AND GOOFY PADDLE THE DORY TO A NEW ANCHORAGE.

S'POSE WE TRY OUR LUCK HERE?
4-27

UH--DON'T LOOK NOW-- BUT I THINK WE'RE BEIN' FOLLERED!

WALT DISNEY

JUST AS MICKEY AND GOOFY ARE CONGRATULATING THEMSELVES ON THEIR FISHERMAN'S LUCK, OLD BARNEY POPS UP RIGHT BEHIND THEM!

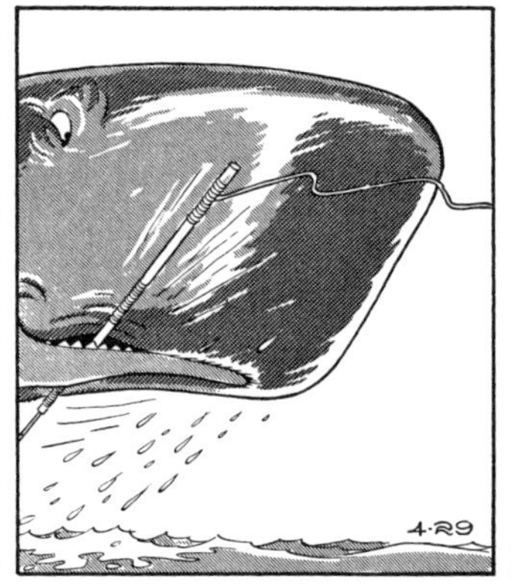

WITH THE HARPOON IN HIS TEETH, OLD BARNEY TOWS MICKEY'S BOAT ON A WILD RIDE. SUDDENLY, THE ROPE BREAKS----!!

4-30

VOO-O-O-OOP!
BOY--LOOK OUT! WHEN HE MAKES THAT FOG-HORN NOISE, HE'S UP TO SOMEP'N!

GAWRSH! HE'S DIVIN'!
THAT'S OUR CUE TO SCRAM!

BY GUM, WE'RE SURE STEPPIN' NOW!
YEH, BUT Y' MIGHT AS WELL PULL IN YOUR OARS!
5-2

WELL, KIN YUH BEAT THAT? WE'RE GOIN' FER A RIDE!
WALT DISNEY

THIS AIN'T BAD ATALL -- IT'S EASIER'N ROWIN'!
YEH-- BUT WHERE'RE WE GOIN'?

OOPS! RAININ', B'GAWRSH!
?
5-3

AH-H-H!

CLARABELLE WUZ RIGHT! SHE TOLE ME I'D NEED AN UMBRELLER ON THIS TRIP!
WALT DISNEY

OLD BARNEY, HAVING PLAGUED MICKEY AND GOOFY WITH HIS TRICKS AND EATEN THEIR FISH, FINALLY PICKS UP THE DORY AND HEADS BACK TOWARD THE "DAFFODIL."
WHADDYA KNOW? HE'S TAKIN' US TO THE SHIP!
GAWRSH! DURN OBLIGIN' O' THUH CRITTER!

ALL HANDS ON DECK! OL' BARNEY'S COMIN' OFF TH' STA'BOARD BOW!
5-4

GOOD GOSH! THE CAP'N'S GETTIN READY TO SHOOT!
HE DON'T EVEN SEE WE'RE HERE! HALP!!
WALT DISNEY

THE WHALE DIVES AND DISAPPEARS FROM SIGHT, LEAVING MICKEY AND GOOFY TO BE PICKED UP BY THEIR SHIPMATES.

5-6

WOTSA MATTEH? YOU ALLA TIME MOONIN' ALOUND! USTA BE SMAHT AN' SNAPPY!

I'M THINKIN' ABOUT OLD BARNEY! I WISH THERE WAS SOME WAY TO GET RID OF HIM WITHOUT KILLING HIM!
F'GOLLY SAKE! LITTLE TIME AGO YOU POSSESS GLATE ITCH TO BE WHALE-MAN!
Copr. by Walt Disney Enterprises 1938 World rights reserved

I KNOW -- BUT OLD BARNEY'S NOT THE "F'ROCIOUS MONSTER" THEY SAID HE WAS! HE SHOULDN'T OUGHTA BE KILLED!

THERE MUST BE SOME OTHER WAY! I'VE JUST GOTTA THINK OF IT!
HUMPH! ALLEE SAMEE GONE PLENTY KLAZY!
5-9

I'M GOIN' TO SEE THE CAPTAIN AND LET HIM KNOW JUST WHAT I THINK ABOUT OLD BARNEY!
YOU KLAZY! ALLEE TIME STICKEE OUT NECK!

THE NEXT TIME THAT WHALE HEAVES IN SIGHT, I'M GOIN' TO TAKE AFTER HIM! I'LL GET 'IM IF I HAVE TO CHASE HIM TO THE NORTH POLE!

I'M SICK O' LAYIN' AT ANCHOR WHILE TH' BRUTE GITS OFF! DO YE HEAR?
AYE, AYE, CAP'N!
!
5-10

GUESS I BETTER WAIT AWHILE --- HE'S KINDA BUSY!
WALT DISNEY

BOY! EARLY DAWN ON THE OCEAN! Y' CAN'T BEAT IT!

WELL, I'LL BE A --- F'GOSH SAKES!

CAPTAIN! THAT SHIP, SIR -- SHE WASN'T THERE LAST NIGHT!

SHE MUSTA SNEAKED IN WHILE IT WAS DARK! WHAT'S IT MEAN?
HMM-M! DANGED IF I KNOW- -- BUT I DON'T LIKE IT!
5-11

Sometime in the dead of night a strange boat has slipped in and dropped anchor near the fleet.

A MYSTERIOUS STRANGER HAS SNEAKED ABOARD THE "LADY DAFFODIL" AT NIGHT!

NO USE LAYIN' HERE JUST THINKIN'! MIGHT AS WELL TAKE A TURN IN THE FRESH AIR!

WHY CAN'T THERE BE SOME WAY TO MAKE OLD BARNEY LEAVE THIS SECTION FOR GOOD?
MAYBE THERE IS!

WHAT TH---? THAT'S NOT ONE OF OUR MEN!
5-16 WALT DISNEY

SOMEP'N WRONG HERE! THAT BIRD DON'T BELONG ON OUR BOAT!
5-17
Copr. 1938 by Walt Disney Enterprises World rights reserved

HEY, YOU!
!

PEG-LEG PETE!!

HAW-HAW-HAW! DIS IS A BETTER NIGHT'S WORK DAN I FIGGERED ON!

NOT ONLY DO I FIX T'INGS SO I'LL KETCH ME A WHALE, BUT I ALSO GITS ME A SARDINE DAT I BEEN WANTIN'! HAW-HAW-HAW!

CAME THE DAWN ABOARD THE "LADY DAFFODIL!"

WELL? WHAT'S GONE WRONG NOW?
5-18

PLENTY! SOME RAT'S CRIPPLED OUR ENGINES!
THIS SHIP CAN'T MOVE!

YE MEAN TO TELL ME OUR ENGINES HAVE BEEN TAMPERED WITH?
AYE, SIR! THEY'VE BEEN PUT ON TH' KIBOSH! IT'LL TAKE A WEEK OR MORE T' GET 'EM BACK IN SHAPE!
5-19

WHAT IN BLUE TOPHET DO YOU WANT?
VELLY SOLLY, PLEASE! --BUT LOTTA WUK IN GALLEY, AND NO CATCHEE MICKEY MOUSE!

BEG TO REPORT, SIR, THAT MICKEY MOUSE IS NOT ON BOARD!
!
?

Y' WON'T GET AWAY WITH THIS, Y' BIG TRAMP!
SO YUH DON'T 'PRECIATE ME HORSPITALITY? IS DAT NICE?
WALT DISNEY

OF ALL TH' GOSH-DARNED----! IT WOULD HAVE TO BE PEG-LEG PETE THAT TURNS UP AGAIN!

THAT'S WHAT MICKEY SAID TO ME, SIR! HE WISHED THE WHALE WOULD GET AWAY!
I KNOW! HE PRACTICALLY TOLD ME THE SAME THING!

YOU'RE SURE HE'S DESERTED?
AYE, SIR! WE'VE SEARCHED THE SHIP AND HE'S NOT ABOARD!
Copr 1938 by Walt Disney Enterprises World rights reserved
5-20

THE ONE MAN I THOUGHT I COULD TRUST! HE WRECKS THE ENGINES AND SKIPS OFF! IT'S HARD TO BELIEVE!
WALT DISNEY

SO YUH DON'T LIKE IT HERE ON D' "ORCA", HUH?
Copr 1938 by Walt Disney Enterprises World rights reserved

"DEAH ME, NO! I BELONG ON DE 'LADY DAFFODIL'! YES, INDEED --- DE 'LADY DAFFODIL'!"
5-21

GO AHEAD AN' CLOWN, Y' DUMB TRAMP! I STILL DON'T SEE WHAT Y' GAINED BY WRECKIN' OUR ENGINES!
DAT'S EASY! YOUR TUB WUZ D' ONLY ONE WID A CHANCE OF KETCHIN' DE WHALE!

NOW I KETCH HIM AND I WIN DE PRIZE MONEY, MYSELF---WID NO INNERFERENCE!
GIT IT, STUPID?
WALT DISNEY

ALL IS GLOOM ABOARD THE "DAFFODIL." HER ENGINES HAVE BEEN DISABLED AND THE ABSENT MICKEY IS BLAMED FOR THE CRIME.

WELL, PETE, OL' BOY-- --I'M LEAVIN'! BUT I GOT A LITTLE WORK TO DO, FIRST!
Copr. by Walt Disney Enterprises 1938 World rights reserved

LESSEE NOW-- DID I LOCK DE PADLOCK ON DE LI'L RAT'S DOOR? BLAZES! DO I HAFTER GIT UP AN' LOOK?

?
ORCA
PS-S-S-T!
5-26

ORCA
UH-HAW! IT'S ME!
OH, BOY! NOW I WON'T HAFTA SWIM IT!

MICKEY ESCAPES FROM PETE'S SHIP, AIDED BY GOOFY IN A DORY.
5-27

MIGHTY SWELL OF Y' TO COME AN' GET ME, GOOFY! HOW'D Y' KNOW WHERE I WAS?
I SEEN YUH FRUM THUH CROW'S-NEST!

LEMME THINK NOW! DID I LOCK DE RAT IN? YEAH--I REMEMBER --HE'S SAFE ENUFF!

F'GOSH SAKES! WHAT'S TH' IDEA OF ALL THE SECRECY?
UH-HAW-HAW! THUH CAP'N DON'T EVEN KNOW I SPOTTED YUH! I JEST SNEAKED OFF WITH THIS HERE BOAT!

YUH DON'T KNOW IT, BUT YOU'RE THUH GUY THEY ALL THINK BUSTED OUR ENGINES! THUH CAP'N WOULDN'T A-LET ME RESCUE YOU! NO, SIREE!

TH' CAPTAIN HAS SOME NERVE TO THINK I'D WRECK HIS ENGINES!
HE SORTA FIGGERED YUH WUZ TRYIN' TO PERTECT OL' BARNEY!

WELL, LET'S HURRY BACK TO THE SHIP AND GET THINGS STRAIGHTENED OUT!
YUH GOTTA ADMIT I DONE A PURTY NEAT RESCUE ACT, B'GAWRSH!
5-28

HOW FAR AWAY'S THE "DAFFODIL," ANYHOW? SEEMS T' ME WE'VE BEEN ROWIN' FOR MILES!
HUH?

UH--COME T' THINK OF IT, I KINDA FORGOT TO TAKE MUH BEARIN'S WHEN I LEFT THUH SHIP!
OF ALL THE---- GOSH KNOWS WHERE WE ARE, THEN!
WALT DISNEY

GOOFY, IN A ROWBOAT, HAS RESCUED MICKEY FROM PETE'S SHIP

HOWEVER HE HAS FORGOTTEN THE LOCATION OF THE "DAFFODIL AND THEY ARE LOST IN THE DARK NIGHT!

ON BOARD THE GOOD SHIP, "LADY DAFFODIL," THE ABSENCE OF GOOFY HAS JUST BEEN DISCOVERED

Copr 1938 by Walt Disney Enterprises / World rights reserved

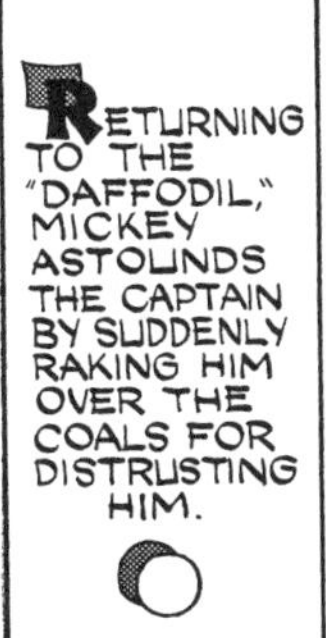
RETURNING TO THE "DAFFODIL," MICKEY ASTOUNDS THE CAPTAIN BY SUDDENLY RAKING HIM OVER THE COALS FOR DISTRUSTING HIM.

THINKIN' I DISABLED TH' ENGINES! OF ALL TH' GOSH-DARNED NERVE!
W-WHAT?

A GUY THAT CAN'T JUDGE HIS MEN BETTER'N THAT SHOULDN'T BE A CAPTAIN! HE'S GOT NO RIGHT TO BOSS A SHIP!
WHY-- WHY, YOU--!

HERE I WAS, KIDNAPED BY TH' BIRD THAT DID WRECK YOUR ENGINES! AND WHAT D' YOU DO? Y' BLAME ME!
BRRHMPH! NOW LOOK HERE-- S'POSE YE GO A BIT EASY WITH THET TONGUE!

I'VE EVEN FOUND A WAY TO GET RID O' THE WHALE FOR Y'-- BUT---!
YE HAVE? COME, COME, LAD-- OUT WITH IT!
6-6

YE'VE FOUND A WAY TO GET RID OF OL' BARNEY? WHAT IS IT?
IF I TOLD YOU, Y' WOULDN'T LET ME TRY IT! Y' DON'T TRUST ME!

ALL I'D NEED IS A BOAT AND A FEW SUPPLIES!
THAT'S ALL? AND I'M S'POSED TO LET YE HAVE 'EM WITHOUT KNOWIN' WHAT YE'RE UP TO!

ALL RIGHT-- LET OLD BARNEY KEEP ON RUININ' YOUR BUSINESS! I TRIED TO HELP Y'!

STOP! YOU WIN! BUT, BY THUNDER, YE BETTER MAKE GOOD YER WORD! I'LL TAKE NO ALIBIS!
6-7

IT BEATS ME! ONE MINUTE TH' OLD MAN'S GOIN' TO THROW YE IN IRONS --- NEXT HE TELLS ME TO GIVE YE WHAT-EVER YE WANT!
YEH! SOMEBODY MUST'VE CHANGED HIS MIND!
DANGER XXX

C'MON, GOOFY! WE'RE READY TO GO!
HUH?
WAZZAT?
I AIN'T GOIN' NOWHERES!

YES, Y' ARE! YOU'RE GOIN' TO HELP ME GET RID OF OLD BARNEY--- FOR GOOD!
?
!
6-8

NICE GUY YOU ARE! KEEP ME UP RESCUIN' YUH ALL NIGHT, AND NOW I CAN'T EVEN KETCH A NAP! ALL RIGHT, SIMON LEGREE!
WALT DISNEY

MICKEY AND GOOFY SET OUT IN A DORY EQUIPPED WITH AN OUTBOARD MOTOR.
MICKEY HAS A SECRET PLAN THAT HE EXPECTS WILL SETTLE THE WHALE PROBLEM FOR GOOD.

6-9

THE "DAFFODIL'S" DISGRUNTLED CREW PUZZLES OVER THE NEW SHIP THAT HAS JOINED THE FLEET.

SHE'S-A NO FEESHIN' BOAT!
AIN'T RIGGED FER WHALIN', NUTHER!
WOT BLASTED DIFF'RENCE DOES IT MAKE NOW?

WE GOT NUTHIN' MORE TO WORRY ABOUT! MICKEY MOUSE HAS ARRANGED TO SETTLE THE WHALE BIZZNESS FOR US! EV'RYTHING'S JUST DUCKY!

YES, IT IS!
6-13

!

ARMED WITH DYNAMITE, MICKEY AND GOOFY ARRIVE AT THE ICEBERG WHERE THEY HAVE SEEN THE FEMALE WHALE IMPRISONED.
6-14

YESSIR, THET SURE IS A SLICK IDEAR YUH GOT, MICKEY!
IF IT WORKS!
Copr 1938 by Walt Disney Enterprises World rights reserved

THAT CHUNK YOU'RE CUTTIN' OUGHTA PLUG TH' HOLE JUST RIGHT!

ALL SET! GET READY TO SCRAM!
DON'T WORRY--I AIN'T LOITERIN' IN THIS NEIGHBOR-HOOD!

THIS SUSPENSE IS ORFUL!
PUT-PUT PUT!
6-15

BA-ROOM!!!

YIPPEE! SHE'S LOOSE!
HOT DORG!
PRRRRRR-RR!!
Copr 1938 by Walt Disney Enterprises World rights reserved
WALT DISNEY

EV'RYTHING'S WORKED FINE--- SO FAR!
YEP! THE LITTLE GAL'S TAGGIN' RIGHT ALONG AFTER US!
Copr. by Walt Disney Enterprises 1938 World rights reserved

I ONLY HOPE WE'LL FIND OLD BARNEY AT THE FISHIN'-GROUNDS!
IT'S A CINCH! WE SAW 'IM HEADIN' FER IT!
6-16

TH' ONLY THING I CAN'T FIGGER IS HOW YUH KNEW THIS LADY WHALE'D FOLLER US!
THAT'S EASY! SHE'S BEEN LOCKED IN THAT ICEBERG A LONG TIME
AND SHE'S MIGHTY HUNGRY- ---

--- SHE WANTS TO EAT US!
WALT DISNEY

STEP ON IT! I DON'T WANTER BE ET!
CAN'T GO ANY FASTER! WE'RE DOIN' TH' LIMIT, NOW!
Copr. by Walt Disney Enterprises 1938 World rights reserved

I KIN SEE THUH FISHIN' BOATS 'WAY AHEAD!
THE HECK WITH THEM! WHERE'S OLD BARNEY?

THERE HE IS! ALMOST TO THUH BOATS!
OOMPAH-PAH!
GOOD GOSH! EV'RY SECOND COUNTS NOW!

UP ANCHOR! GIT MOVIN', YUH SCUM! DE TIME HAS CAME!
ORCA
6-17
WALT DISNEY

JUST MY DAD-BUSTED LUCK! HERE COMES OL' BARNEY AND --- JUMPIN' JERUSHA! WHAT'S THIS?
6-18
Copr. by Walt Disney Enterprises 1938 World rights reserved

OOM-PAH-- WUMPH?
WE MADE IT, MICKEY!
DAREN'T STOP! SHE'S RIGHT BEHIND US!

OO-O-O-O--OOOMP!
PA-PAH!
WALT DISNEY

MICKEY'S DARING PLAN SEEMS TO BE WORKING. HE HAS BROUGHT THE LADY WHALE TO OLD BARNEY'S.
ATTENTION AND IT LOOKS LIKE LOVE AT FIRST SIGHT!

TOODLE - OODLE - OOPS! PA-PAH?
OOMP! BA-BEE!
6-20
Copr. 1938 by Walt Disney Enterprises World rights reserved

UH-HAW! LOOKS LIKE WE'RE A SUCCESS!
SO FAR!

OH, MY GAWRSH! TH' "ORCA'S" COMIN'! PEG-LEG PETE'LL GIT BOTH OF 'EM!
WALT DISNEY

HAW-HAW! TWO WHALES, EH? WELL, DAT'S ALL RIGHT-- D' OLD TIME BOMB'LL TAKE KEER OF 'EM BOTH!
ORCA

BANG!!
ORCA

WELL, I'LL BE A BLINKIN' SO-AND-SO!
HEY! WHY'N'T YE LOOK WHERE YE'RE SHOOTIN'?
ORCA

BANG!
ORCA
6-21
WALT DISNEY

GAWRSH! OLE PETE'S GUN BLOWED UP! WHUT A BREAK FER THUH WHALES!

YEH, THE NIGHT I LEFT TH' "ORCA", I KINDA FIXED UP THAT GUN!
UH-HAW-HAW! MIGHTA KNOWED YUH HAD A HAND IN IT!
6-22

SAY! WHERE IS OLE BARNEY AND HIS GAL, ANYWAY?

THERE THEY GO! AND I GUESS THAT'S THE LAST WE'LL EVER SEE OF 'EM!
WALT DISNEY

OLD BARNEY AND HIS NEW-FOUND GIRL FRIEND HAVE CRUISED AWAY TO THE FROZEN NORTH, LEAVING MICKEY WELL-SATISFIED WITH THE SUCCESS OF HIS PLAN.

THE "DAFFODIL'S" JUBILANT CAPTAIN INSISTS ON MICKEY AND GOOFY CELEBRATING WITH HIM AT DINNER.

6-29

THE "DAFFODIL'S" CREW, GLUM AND SOUR FOR SO LONG, SNAP OUT OF IT WITH A WILD CELEBRATION
!
6-30

H'RAY!!
JIG IT, MATEY!
YO-HO!

UH-HAW! I'LL SHOW YUH SOME STEPS, B'GAWRSH!

WOT'S THAT --A HORNPIPE?
NOPE! IT'S THE SHAG!
HAW! HAW! HAW!

YOU ALL WRONG! MISTA GOOFY JOOSTA DANCE THE BAKED APPLE!
WALT DISNEY

OH, YOU CAN SEE--WE LOVE THE SEA--AS YOU CAN SEE--YO-HO!
7-1

!
!
AVAST, THERE! WHAT'S TH' MEANIN' O' THIS HIGH JINKS, WITHOUT ASKIN' ME?
?

WALT DISNEY

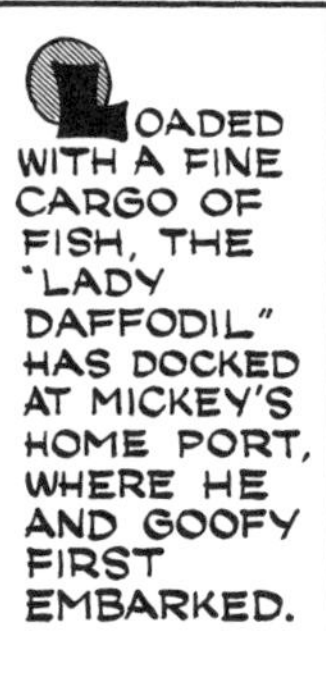
LOADED WITH A FINE CARGO OF FISH, THE "LADY DAFFODIL" HAS DOCKED AT MICKEY'S HOME PORT, WHERE HE AND GOOFY FIRST EMBARKED.
7-2

GOODBYE, ME LAD! I WISH YE'D ACCEPT A PART OF THE REWARD MONEY! YE SURELY EARNED IT!

NO, THANK Y', SIR! I ONLY SHIPPED FOR THE ADVENTURE! I'VE GOT ALL THE MONEY I NEED!

UXTRY! UXTRY! BIG STOCK CRASH! AMERICAN DRUM GOES BOOM!
GOOD GOSH!
HUH? WHUT'S IT TO YOU?
WALT DISNEY

BACK FROM A SUCCESSFUL WHALING VOYAGE MICKEY'S HIGH SPIRITS ARE JOLTED BY A HEADLINE IN THE LOCAL PAPER.

7-4

MICKEY DISCOVERS THAT WHILE HE WAS AWAY ON THE "LADY DAFFODIL," HE HAS LOST NEARLY ALL HIS MONEY IN A STOCK FAILURE. GOOFY IS ALSO A LOSER.

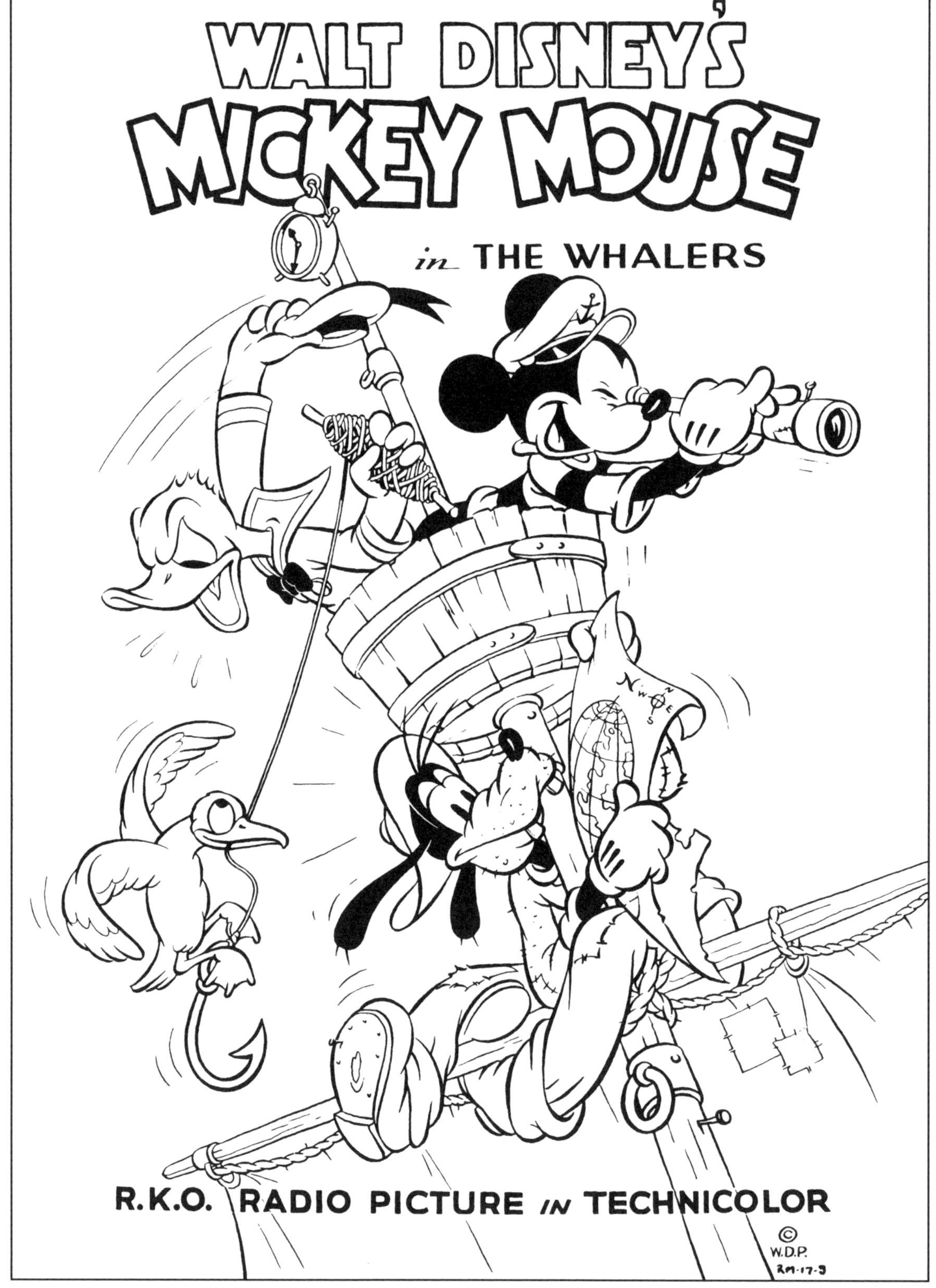

Mickey's and Goofy's comic strip whale trek was based loosely—*very* loosely—on this 1938 cartoon. In it, Goofy gets all the pre-Monstro thrills and chills... while Mickey struggles to empty a bucket of water (!). Poster art from theatrical release; art by Hank Porter, image courtesy Walt Disney Archives.

THE PLUMBER'S HELPER

JULY 7, 1938
–
DECEMBER 10. 1938

RICH MOUSE, POOR MOUSE

Back in 1937's "In Search of Jungle Treasure," Mickey risked his life in Africa to help Captain Churchmouse find his buried hoard—and was eventually rewarded with riches beyond imagination. Well-deserved riches, we say; but Mickey *stayed* rich in the serials that followed, and this caused a slight characterization crisis.

In past adventures, Mickey had won the day because he was resourceful, optimistic, brave, smart, and honest. Not because he was *rich*—that would have made things too easy, too boring. How dangerous is any conflict if one can just *buy* one's way out of it?

For a couple of stories, the authors tried not to make Mickey's wealth a factor in his success; but this didn't solve the long-term problem. Bringing Mickey to bankruptcy did! In "The Plumber's Helper," the stock market has crashed, and Mickey—who had given much of his wealth to charity, anyway—has now lost all his remaining savings. Gottfredson presses the reset button, and we return to the Horatio Alger hero who must pull himself up by his bootstraps.

The Depression-era background of this story will feel familiar to the present-day reader. Now as then, multitudes lose their assets and their jobs; in the struggle to make ends meet, Mickey is just one of the crowd. This profoundly human comic strip hero goes begging for the humblest jobs—something we could hardly imagine a Clark Kent ever doing. Note the touching scene of Mickey asking for a basic job in Horace's shop; his embarrassed friend must refuse the request, for he can't afford to pay Mickey enough.

Gottfredson's poignant images were part and parcel of period American culture. "The Plumber's Helper" dates from 1938, while John Steinbeck's *The Grapes of Wrath*—chronicling the similar struggle of a Depression-era family—was published in 1939. And though it's perhaps too much to call Mickey stories existentialist dramas, it's easy to compare the opening scenes of "The Plumber's Helper" with the bittersweet Gregory La Cava movie *My Man Godfrey* (1936), another tale of a rich man suddenly made poor.

Social symbolism aside, "Plumber's" narrative core is a detective story with a solid mystery plot. Mickey ends up infiltrating a gang of unlikely thieves—and we meet Detective Casey for the first time. Gottfredson finally promotes Mickey from free-roaming adventure seeker to quasi-official "police helper," a role that will be set in stone once Mickey befriends Chief O'Hara in "Mickey Mouse Outwits the Phantom Blot" (1939).

Art aficionados will notice that "The Plumber's Helper" is the last story in which Mickey retains his traditional 1930s look. Starting with the subsequent "Robinson Crusoe," Mickey's appearance will undergo a subtle restyling, accompanied by an equally subtle—but undeniable—shift toward a more cynical mood. "Plumber" can thus be considered the last appearance of the classic Mickey of the 1930s. Gottfredson's subsequent Mickey will be an equally great character, but a different person.

— Leonardo Gori and
Francesco Stajano

TELL ME--- YOU CAUGHT THE WHALE, OF COURSE---HAVE SOME MORE COCOA---MY, YOU LOOK HEALTHY---TRY SOME OF THAT MARBLE CAKE, TOO---HOW DO I LOOK?
UH-HUH! THANKS! DO I? THANKS! Y' LOOK SWELL!

HOW ABOUT THIS STOCK FAILURE? DID IT HIT Y' VERY HARD?
WELL, I STILL HAVE MY HOUSE, AND MONEY ENOUGH FOR NECESSITIES!

BUT, YOU--POOR DEAR! YOU MUST HAVE LOST EVERYTHING!
NOT QUITE! BUT, I HAVEN'T ANY RICHES TO WORRY ABOUT ANY MORE!

WELL, WHAT WILL YOU DO, NOW?
LOOKS LIKE I'LL HAFTA QUIT ROAMIN' --AND FIND A JOB!
WALT DISNEY

MUST YOU GO---SO SOON?
YEH, I GOTTA GO HOME AN' CLEAN UP A BIT BEFORE I HUNT FOR A JOB!

H'LO THERE, HORACE!
MICKEY! WELL, WELL, OLD SON--WHEN'D YOU GET BACK?

JUST NOW! AND, SAY---I NEED A JOB! HOW'S THINGS DOWN AT YOUR STORE?
HAW-HAW! SAME OLD KIDDER, AIN'T YUH? IMAGINE A ROOTIN', TOOTIN' ADVENTURER LIKE YOU SELLIN' PINK THREAD!

ALWAYS THE CARD! HAW-HAW-HAW!
HM-M! SOMEBODY BETTER TAKE ME SERIOUS ABOUT THIS!
WALT DISNEY

HIS FORTUNE PRACTICALLY WIPED OUT MICKEY IS TRYING TO FIND HIMSELF A JOB.

THESE PEOPLE OUGHTA HAVE SOMEP'N FOR ME!
EMPLOYMENT AGENCY
OFFICE HELP OUR SPECIALTY

YOUR PREVIOUS EXPERIENCE PLEASE!
WELL--I'VE TRAVELED QUITE A BIT---AFRICAN JUNGLE--SOUTH SEAS AN' ALL THAT! I'VE BEEN AN AIR PILOT AND--!
MISS SPINK

PARDON ME! WHAT WAS YOUR LAST POSITION?
I WAS ON A WHALING VOYAGE!

I SEE! NO PREVIOUS EXPERIENCE!
HUH?
MISS SPINK

FOR SEVERAL DAYS MICKEY HAS BEEN TRYING TO FIND A JOB, BUT HAS HAD NO LUCK......
GOSH! I NEVER THOUGHT IT'D BE SO HARD TO GET WORK!
Copr 1938 by Walt Disney Enterprises World rights reserved

AH, THERE'S A CHANCE NOW. THEY'RE ADVERTISING FOR MEN. I'LL SEE WHAT IT IS
SHORT ORDERS ETC.
MEN WANTED AT IRON ANVIL COMPANY

HEY, YOU-WHAT KIND OF A JOB ARE THEY OFFERING?
OH, JUST CARRYING LITTLE 300-LB. ANVILS FROM THE BOAT TO THE WAREHOUSE
MEN WANTED AT IRON ANVI

AND THE BOAT IS 3 MILES FROM THE WAREHOUSE! I'M STILL LOOKING FOR A JOB!
7-11
WALT DISNEY

HOW'S ABOUT BORRYIN' PART O' YER PAPER, CHUM?
HUH? OH--SURE!
The BUGLE

HELP YOURSELF! I'M ONLY READIN' THE EMPLOYMENT ADS!
LOOKIN' FER A JOB?

YEH! I S'POSE YOU'RE OUTA WORK, TOO!
YEP! BUT I DANG NEAR GOT A JOB YESTIDDY!
7-12

I ANSWERED AN AD AND THEY ALMOST TOOK ME! Y' GOTTER BE MIGHTY KEERFUL ABOUT LOOKIN' FER WORK!
The BUGLE
WALT DISNEY

MAYBE THERE'S A JOB OPEN HERE!
BUILDING -BY- HOPE-ITSTAYSUP CONSTRUCTION =CO=

WE JUST TOOK ON THE LAST MAN WE CAN USE! SORRY, PAL!

HULLO, MICKEY!
F' GOSH SAKES! HOW'D YOU GET A JOB?
JUS' WALKED IN AND ASKED FER IT!

JOBS ARE EASY TO GET, FUR AS I KIN SEE!
WALT DISNEY 7-13

WE NEED MEN! TO THE RIGHT MEN WE OFFER STEADY EMPLOYMENT! OLDTIME COMMERCIAL DAIRY
OH, BOY! WOTTA CHANCE!
7-14

YE START MILKIN' AT 4 A.M! YE'RE THROUGH BY 10 AND READY TO CLEAN TH' STABLES AND FEED THE COWS!
YES! WHAT'S NEXT?

THERE'S MINOR CHORES LASTING UNTIL THE 5 P.M. MILKING! THEN FEED, BEDDING, WASHING CANS, ETC. THET TAKES TILL ABOUT 10 O'CLOCK!
SORRY! I DON'T WANT THE JOB!

Y' ADVERTISE STEADY WORK, BUT THERE'S SIX HOURS WITH NOTHIN' TO DO BUT SLEEP!
WALT DISNEY

YES, SIR! BE RIGHT-- OOPS! THOUGHT IT WAS A CUSTOMER!
I JUST WANTA REST MY DOGS! THIS JOB-HUNTIN' IS WEARIN' 'EM OUT!
CANNED GOODS
Copr. by Walt Disney Enterprises 1938 World rights reserved

WHAT I CAN'T FIGGER IS WHY YOU PUT ALL YOUR DOUGH IN THAT BAD STOCK! YOU'RE NO SUCKER!
I DIDN'T SINK IT ALL! MOST OF IT WENT TO CHARITIES AND WHAT WAS LEFT, I INVESTED--- OR THOUGHT IT WAS AN INVESTMENT!
7-15

THE GUY SELLIN' THE STOCK WAS A FRIEND O' MINE AND--WELL-- I TRIED TO HELP HIM!

AND NOW YOU'RE THE GUY THAT NEEDS HELP-- AND WHERE Y' GONNA GET IT?
THAT'S JUST WHAT I WANTA KNOW!

PRETTY TOUGH TO BE BROKE! WISH I COULD DO SOMETHIN' FOR YOU!
IF I DON'T GET A JOB PRETTY SOON, Y' CAN LEND ME YOUR SHOULDER TO CRY ON!

SURE THING! AND ANY TIME YOU'RE STARVIN' I CAN LET Y' HAVE A SARDINE OR TWO!
OKAY-- I'LL REMEMBER THAT!
7-16

BOY WANTED
?

WHAT'S TH' IDEA? HERE Y' GOT A JOB AND BEEN KEEPIN' IT FROM ME!
HUH? UH--WHAT?
BOY WANTED
WALT DISNEY

HERE I AM NEEDIN' WORK AND YOU NEVER TOLD ME ABOUT **THIS** JOB!
GOSH, MICKEY---**YOU** WOULDN'T WANT THAT! IT'S JUST SOMEBODY TO WATCH THE STORE WHEN I'M OUT!
BOY WANTED

IT'LL ONLY PAY THREE DOLLARS A WEEK-- AND FREE LUNCHES!
HM-M! THE SALARY'S A BIT LOW TO **LIVE** ON! HOW ABOUT THE LUNCH?

CRACKERS AND CHEESE!
NO, THANKS! GUESS I BETTER LOOK SOMEWHERE ELSE!
SODA RACKERS
7-18

NOT VERY EXCITIN' WORK, BUT IT'S A **JOB**! THINK I'LL ASK THE LUCKY GUY HOW HE GOT IT!
EAT AT JOE'S NO COVER CHARGE
WALT DISNEY

I'M LOOKIN' FOR WORK! HOW DO Y' GET A JOB LIKE YOURS?
YUH JUST GIT DESPRIT AND THEN YUH TRY **ANYTHING**!
EAT AT JOE'S NO COVER CHARGE

HOW MUCH CAN Y' MAKE AT IT?
DOLLAR A DAY AND MEALS!
EAT AT JOE'S NO COVER

OH, GOSH! I COULDN'T LIVE ON THAT!

KNOW ANYTHING ABOUT TH' BANKIN' BIZZNUSS? I HEAR TH' THIRD NATIONAL NEEDS A TELLER!
THANKS, OL' BOY! I'M ON M' WAY!
EAT AT JOE'S NO COVER CHARGE
7-19

A STRANGER HAS GIVEN MICKEY A TIP THAT THE LAST NATIONAL BANK NEEDS A TELLER

HOPE I GET THERE 'FORE SOMEBODY BEATS ME TO IT!

FORGET-ME-NOT ICE CO.

ORGET-ME-NOT ICE CO.
SHUCKS! THAT DIDN'T GAIN ANY TIME!
ICE CO.
7-20

BOY! I HOPE---THEY HAVEN'T HIRED---SOMEBODY!
LAST NATIONAL BANK
1865
WALT DISNEY

OF COURSE, I DON'T KNOW ANYTHING ABOUT BANKIN', BUT I COULD LEARN!
LAST NATIONAL BANK

I HEARD Y' WERE LOOKIN' FOR A TELLER!
YES --- THAT'S RIGHT!

UH-- HOW ABOUT GIVIN' ME A CHANCE?
SORRY! YOU'RE NOT THE MAN WE WANT!

THE TELLER WE'RE LOOKING FOR IS THE ONE WHO SKIPPED WITH $60,000!
7-21

I MIGHT AS WELL GO HOME! EV'RY JOB I'VE BEEN AFTER'S HAD A JOKER TO IT!

JOE PIPER
FRIENDLY
PLUMBING
APPRENTICE DESIRED!
HUMPH! WONDER WHAT'S THE CATCH TO THIS ONE?

ANOTHER "DOLLAR A DAY, WITH MEALS," I S'POSE!
7-22

HECK--I'VE TRIED 'EM ALL! WHY NOT SEE THIS ONE THROUGH?
APPRENTICE DESIRED!
WALT DISNEY

MICKEY SEES A SIGN ASKING FOR A PLUMBER'S APPRENTICE. ALTHOUGH SKEPTICAL, HE DECIDES TO INVESTIGATE.

7-23

NO CATCH TO IT, SONNY, IF YOU'RE TH' RIGHT MAN! HAD ANY PLUMBING EXPERIENCE?
WELL- --NOT EXACTLY!

DO YOU KNOW ANYTHING ABOUT PLUMBING?
OH, YES! A LITTLE!

HOW MUCH!
UH-- TO TELL THE TRUTH-- VERY LITTLE!

FINE! BE HERE MONDAY, READY TO WORK!
!

MICKEY, ON HIS WAY TO WORK, MEETS MINNIE AND HAS A LITTLE TROUBLE EXPLAINING THE NATURE OF HIS NEW JOB.

MICKEY ARRIVES AT THE PLUMBING SHOP READY TO GO TO WORK, BUT FINDS THAT HIS BOSS HAS NO WORK TO DO!

7-28

MR. PIPER'S OUT RIGHT NOW! YES, I'LL TELL HIM AS SOON AS HE COMES IN, MR. DOODLESNIPE!

MR. DOODLESNIPE CALLED AND WANTS YOU TO COME OVER RIGHT AWAY!
Copr. by Walt Disney Enterprises 1938 World rights reserved

DOODLESNIPE? AH, YES-- I FIXED A LEAK FOR HIM YESTERDAY! SO HE WANTS ME AGAIN? THAT'S WHAT COUNTS, SONNY -- REPEAT CUSTOMERS!
8-1

YEH--EXCEPT THAT WHAT HE WANTS--HE SAYS THAT LEAK IS WORSE THAN BEFORE!

DON'T FORGET ANY TOOLS, SONNY! PEOPLE ARE ALWAYS BLAMIN' US PLUMBERS FOR THAT!
I'VE GOT 'EM ALL--- I HOPE!

SO DOODLESNIPE CLAIMS THAT LEAK I FIXED IS WORSE THAN BEFORE!
THAT'S WHAT HE SAID!
JOE PIPER
FRIENDLY
PLUMBING
8-2

CLEAR EXAGGERATION! THAT WAS A MIGHTY BAD LEAK--IN FACT, EXTREMELY BAD! I COULDN'T HAVE MADE IT WORSE!

THE MAN HAS NO GROUNDS FOR A KICK AT ALL!

YOU CALL YOURSELF A PLUMBER! LOOK AT THAT! LOOK AT IT!
CALM YOURSELF, MR. DOODLESNIPE! LET ME HANDLE THIS!
Copr. by Walt Disney Enterprises 1938 World rights reserved

VERY UNPLEASANT FELLOW! JUST ONE OF WHAT YOU MEET, SONNY, WHEN YOU'RE IN THIS---!
BUT THAT LEAK! HOW'RE WE GONNA FIX IT?

TAKE THIS TAPE AND BIND UP THE CRACKED PIPE! YOU'LL FIND IT ABOUT TWO FEET DOWN!
!

I'LL BE OUTSIDE! I SAW SOME OTHER LEAKS THAT NEED FIXIN' RIGHT AWAY!
WALT DISNEY
8-3

GOLLY! A SWELL INITIATION TO THE PLUMBIN' BUSINESS! I'M PRACTIC'LY DROWNED!

YOU WERE KINDA SLOW ON THAT JOB, SONNY! I FIXED A WHOLE MESS O' LEAKS WHILE YOU WERE DOWN THERE!
8-4

LEAKS, MY EYE, YOU BLANKETY-BLANK SO-AND-SO!
IS THIS A COMPLAINT, MR. DOODLESNIPE?

YOU'VE PLUGGED UP MY WHOLE LAWN-SPRINKLING SYSTEM!
!
WALT DISNEY

I'LL PROB'LY NEVER GET PAID FOR THAT DOODLESNIPE JOB! IT JUST SHOWS WHAT A TOUGH TRADE THIS IS!
Copr 1938 by Walt Disney Enterprises World rights reserved

JUST LIKE I TOLD Y' AT FIRST! STAY AN APPRENTICE AND YOU WON'T HAVE THE HEADACHES I'VE GOT!
WELL, I CAN'T SAY THIS IS MY LIFE'S WORK, BUT WHILE I'M AT IT I'D LIKE TO KNOW MORE ABOUT IT!

I USED TO BE THAT WAY--- UNTIL I BECAME A MASTER CRAFTSMAN!
8-5

ANYBODY CAN BE DOPEY ONCE IN A WHILE, BUT THAT GUY REALLY WORKS AT IT!
WALT DISNEY

GOOD MORNING! ANY BATHTUBS TODAY?
NO, THANKS!
Copr 1938 by Walt Disney Enterprises World rights reserved

THEN, HOW ABOUT SOME NICE FRESH IRON PIPE? ONLY 60 CENTS A YARD!
OH, IT'S YOU! TRYIN' TO WANGLE A LITTLE BUSINESS FOR YOUR BOSS, EH?

HE COULD CERTAINLY USE SOME MORE CUSTOMERS! AND THOSE HE HAS GOT, DON'T PAY THEIR BILLS!
HUMPH! HE AND I MUST HAVE THE SAME ONES!
8-6

JUST THE SAME, HE HANDS ME MY FIRST PAY ENVELOPE RIGHT ON TIME, WITHOUT A MURMUR!
MAYBE HE'S GOT A DARK AND SHADY SIDE-LINE!
WALT DISNEY

GOSH! THIS LOAFIN' AROUND IS AWFUL! WHY DOESN'T JOE PIPER COME IN WITH A JOB?

OH--HELLO, GOOFY!
I HEERED YUH WUZ WORKIN' AT PLUMBIN'! HOW D'YUH LIKE IT? ARE YUH GOOD AT IT?
Copr. by Walt Disney Enterprises 1938, World rights reserved

WELL, THERE'S A LOT TO LEARN! I DON'T KNOW MUCH ABOUT IT, YET!
OH! THEN I GUESS I BETTER BE GOIN'!

HOLD ON! WHAT'S THE IDEA?
WELL, I DID HAVE A JOB FOR YUH, BUT IF YUH DON'T KNOW MUCH, I CAN'T TAKE A CHANCE!
8-8
WALT DISNEY

WAIT A MINUTE! WHAT KIND OF A PLUMBIN' JOB DO Y' WANT DONE?
NEVER MIND! YUH SAID YUH DON'T KNOW MUCH--AND I WANT A GOOD JOB!

IT MIGHT BE SOMEP'N SIMPLE, ONLY YOU THINK IT'S TOUGH! TELL ME!
ALL RIGHT! KIN YUH FIX A BUSTED PIPE? IT'S PURTY BAD!

WHY, SURE! ANY KIND! AND IT'LL BE MIGHTY CHEAP TO YOU!
8-9

WELL, HERE IT IS! I DROPPED IT OUTEN MUH TOP FLOOR WINDER!
WALT DISNEY

WE GOT A LITTLE JOB, SONNY! BRING THE TOOLS--AND DON'T FORGET ANYTHING!
YES, SIR----NO, SIR!
Copr. by Walt Disney Enterprises 1938, World rights reserved
8-10

I'M THE PLUMBER, MISS!
SO I SEE! AND YOU'VE FORGOTTEN SOMETHING, AS USUAL, HAVEN'T YOU?

NO, MA'AM! I'VE GOT EVERY TOOL THIS JOB CALLS FOR!

MAYBE SO--BUT YOU'VE FORGOTTEN WHO SENT FOR YOU! IT WASN'T ME!
SLAM!

THIS MUST BE THE PLACE! ARE YOU THE LADY THAT---?
I AM! ALL MY CLOTHES IN THE TUB AND NOT A DROP OF WATER!
8-11
Copr. 1938 by Walt Disney Enterprises World rights reserved

AHEM-- ARE YOU SURE YOU HAVE--ER, PAID YOUR WATER BILL?
CERTAINLY! OF COURSE!

THEN, I WOULD SAY, THERE MUST BE SOMETHING WRONG!
IF NOT, WHY SHOULD I SEND FOR YOU?

GOSH! WITH ALL THOSE PIPES, IT'S GONNA BE TOUGH!
OH, NO --THAT MAKES IT EASIER! THERE'S BOUND TO BE WATER IN SOME OF 'EM!
WALT DISNEY

JUST SWITCHING A FEW CONNECTIONS DID THE TRICK! THERE'LL BE PLENTY O' WATER NOW!
I HOPE!
Copr. 1938 by Walt Disney Enterprises World rights reserved

HAVE YOU GOT IT FIXED, SO I CAN DO MY WASHING?
YOUR TROUBLE IS OVER, MA'AM! TURN 'ER ON, SONNY!

OMIGOSH! OIL!!
8-12

LIKE I ALWAYS SAID-- THESE PIPE SYSTEMS AIN'T PERFECTED YET!

HELLO, McKATZ! SURE THING! RIGHT UP MY ALLEY! YOU BET I'LL BE THERE!

THAT WAS McKATZ! HE'S THE MAN I'VE BEEN WAITING FOR! WE'RE THROUGH WITH PEANUT JOBS NOW, SONNY!
!
Copr. 1938 by Walt Disney Enterprises World rights reserved

THIS IS BIG-TIME STUFF! GET EVERYTHING ON THE TRUCK! I'VE GOT TO GO AND MAKE A PHONE CALL!
BUT-- MR. PIPER---!
8-13

WHAT THE HECK? WHO'S McKATZ--AND WHAT'S THE MATTER WITH THIS PHONE ALL OF A SUDDEN?
WALT DISNEY

I GUESS THAT'S EV'RYTHING, MR. PIPER!
NO--YOU HAVEN'T GOT A SAW! THAT'S VERY IMPORTANT!

FOR THE LIFE OF ME I CAN'T SEE WHY THIS JOB NEEDS SO MANY TOOLS!

YOU SEE, THIS IS A McKATZ JOB AND YOU NEVER KNOW JUST WHAT YOU WILL NEED!
WHO IS THIS McKATZ, ANYWAY?

A BIG CONTRACTOR, SONNY! HANDLES ONLY IMPORTANT WORK! PLAY BALL WITH HIM AND YOU'VE GOT A CHANCE TO PICK UP SOME REAL DOUGH!
JOE PIPER FRIENDLY PLUMBING
WALT DISNEY
8-15

YES, SIR! ANY TIME McKATZ LETS YOU IN ON A JOB, THERE'S MONEY IN IT!
SWELL, THAT'S WHAT WE NEED!
JOE PIPER FRIENDLY PLUMBING

WAIT A MINUTE, SONNY! DON'T DRIVE IN, YET!
HUH?
JOE PIPER FRIENDLY PLUMBING
8-16

CLICK!
F' GOSH SAKES! WHAT'S THE IDEA OF TAKIN' A PICTURE OF THE PLACE?

I ALWAYS DO ON THESE KIND O' JOBS! MAKES THE PLACE EASIER TO FIND NEXT TIME, Y' KNOW!

AH! THERE'S McKATZ, HIMSELF!
8-17

MY NEW APPRENTICE, McKATZ! HE'S ALL RIGHT!
HOW D' DO, SIR!
HOWDY!

YOU'D BETTER START IN THE BASEMENT! THEY WANT A BATH THERE, TOO!
GOOD! GET THE TOOLS, SONNY!
YES, SIR!

WHY THE APPRENTICE?
I TOLD YOU HE'S ALL RIGHT! AND HE'LL BE MIGHTY USEFUL LATER ON!

I'VE ONLY JUST MET HIM, BUT SOMEHOW I DON'T TRUST THAT GUY McKATZ!

HE MAY BE A BIG SHOT CONTRACTOR AND THIS MAY BE A SWELL JOB, BUT---!

OF COURSE, IF ANYTHING WAS WRONG, JOE PIPER WOULDN'T SUSPECT IT! HE'S TOO DARN DUMB!
8-18

I STILL DON'T TRUST THAT HELPER OF YOURS!
AW, HE WOULDN'T SUSPECT ANYTHING---HE'S TOO DUMB!

THIS IS THE KIND OF A JOB I LIKE! MIGHTY GOOD POSSIBILITIES HERE!
YES, SIR! I'VE BROUGHT IN ALL THE PIPE YOU WANTED!
Copr 1938 by Walt Disney Enterprises World rights reserved

THE OWNER MUST HAVE PLENTY O' DOUGH! McKATZ DOESN'T FOOL WITH ANY CHEAP PROPERTIES!

THAT'S THE THING TO REMEMBER, SONNY---KEEP AWAY FROM THE CHEAP STUFF!
YES, SIR! UH--HADN'T WE BETTER GO TO WORK?

WHAT'S THE IDEA? THE FIRST GOOD JOB I'VE HAD IN AGES AND YOU WANT TO GET IT DONE! TAKE IT EASY!
8-19

WELL, WE'RE JUST ABOUT FINISHED UP WITH THAT BATHROOM!
PLANS
Copr 1938 by Walt Disney Enterprises World rights reserved

GREAT GRIEF! DO Y' KNOW THAT WE PUT IN A TUB, AND THIS PLAN CALLS FOR A STALL SHOWER?
PLANS
8-20

YOU DON'T SAY? I MUST HAVE MISSED THAT, SOMEHOW!
WELL, WHAT'RE Y' GONNA DO? GOSH--WHY, THE OWNER'LL RAISE MERRY NED!

I SUPPOSE SO, BUT WHAT'S THE USE OF BORROWING TROUBLE IN ADVANCE?

WHEN WE FINISH THIS BATHROOM, WE'RE THROUGH HERE, AREN'T WE?
YEP! THIS WINDS IT UP!
Copr by Walt Disney Enterprises 1938 World rights reserved

HELLO, McKATZ!
HELLO, JOE! JUST DROPPED IN TO TELL YOU I'VE LINED UP A COUPLA NEW ONES, WHEN YOU'RE THROUGH!

SWELL, McKATZ! NICE GOIN'!
OKAY, JOE! I'LL TALK IT OVER WITH YOU-- -LATER!
!

JUST LIKE I TOLD YOU, SONNY--McKATZ IS THE MAN TO STRING ALONG WITH!
YEH-- I GUESS SO!
8-22
WALT DISNEY

CONFOUND IT! HERE COMES THAT PEST, DIBBLE!
DIBBLE? WHO'S HE?
Copr by Walt Disney Enterprises 1938 World rights reserved

HE'S SUPPOSED TO BE A BUILDING INSPECTOR, BUT HE'S JUST A FAULT-FINDER! NOTHING EVER SUITS HIM!

GOOD MORNING, MR. DIBBLE!
SO? THIS IS ONE OF YOUR JOBS, IS IT? LET ME SEE YOUR BUILDING PERMIT, PLEASE!

HUH? OH, YOU SAID PERMIT! I MUST'VE-- ---YES, I FORGOT ABOUT GETTING ONE!
8-23

I DECLARE, I DON'T KNOW WHAT'S THE MATTER WITH YOU, PIPER! NO OTHER PLUMBER GIVES ME SO MUCH TROUBLE!
8-24

YOU KNOW YOU'VE GOT TO HAVE A PERMIT FOR THESE INSTALLATIONS!
WELL-- -I JUST FORGOT, THAT'S ALL!

WELL, SEE THAT YOU GET ONE BEFORE I COME BACK TO INSPECT THE WORK!
OKAY, MR. DIBBLE, OKAY!

YOU SEE HOW HE IS? JUST LIKES TO MAKE TROUBLE! ABSOLUTELY UNREASONABLE!

YOU CAN GO HOME NOW, SONNY! I'VE GOT TO GO DOWN TO THE CITY HALL AND GET A PERMIT--JUST TO SATISFY THAT OLD BUILDING INSPECTOR!
OKAY, MR. PIPER!
MR. PIPER -FRIENDLY- PLUMBING

THAT INSPECTOR CAN'T BE SUCH A TOUGH GUY, IF HE PASSES JOE'S COCK-EYED WORK!
8-25

JUST THE FELLER I WANT TO SEE! I'VE GOT SOME NEWS Y' OUGHTA KNOW ABOUT!
YEH? TELL ME THE WORST!
WALT DISNEY

Y' SAY YOU'VE GOT SOME NEWS I OUGHTA KNOW? IS IT ABOUT MY JOB?
WELL, YES AND NO! NOT ABOUT YOUR JOB, DIRECTLY!

WELL, WHAT, THEN?
IT'S ABOUT YOUR BOSS-- MR. PIPER!
8-26

A PLUMBER WAS IN HERE LAST NIGHT AND HE TOLD ME THAT HE AND A BUNCH OF OTHER PLUMBERS ARE---
YES?

---CAMPAIGNING TO PUT PIPER COMPLETELY OUT O' BUSINESS!
OH, F' GOSH SAKES!

BUT WHY IN HECK SHOULD THE OTHER PLUMBERS WANT TO PUT PIPER OUTA BUSINESS?
WELL, IT SEEMS HE'S TOO DURN DOPEY, FOR ONE THING!

I HAFTA ADMIT THAT-- BUT I DON'T SEE WHERE IT CONCERNS THE REST!
THEY CLAIM HIS DUMB WORK INJURES THE GOOD NAME OF THE ENTIRE PROFESSION!
8-27

NONSENSE!
FU'THERMORE, FOR ALL HIS DUMBNESS, HE'S GETTIN' SOME FAT CONTRACTS THAT THE OTHER GUYS WANT! SO, THERE Y' ARE!

HM-M-M! SOMEP'N'S GOTTA BE DONE! I WAS TOO LONG GETTIN' THAT JOB, TO HAVE IT PULLED OUT FROM UNDER ME SO QUICK!
WALT DISNEY

WHAT'S THE TROUBLE, SONNY? WHY THE LONG PAN?
Copr. 1938 by Walt Disney Enterprises World rights reserved

I JUST HEARD THAT A BUNCH OF OTHER PLUMBERS ARE GOIN' TO TRY AN' PUT YOU OUTA BUSINESS!
WELL--WELL! WHAT'VE I DONE TO THEM?

WHY, UH--THEY SORTA CLAIM THEY'RE BETTER PLUMBERS, BUT YOU'RE GETTIN' THE BEST JOBS!
YEAH? THE BEST JOBS GO TO THE BEST MAN, SONNY! QUALITY WINS!
8-29

BESIDES-- WITH THE, ER-- CONNECTIONS I HAVE, I COULD EVEN SLIP A LITTLE AND STILL GET ALONG!
OH-- I SEE!
WALT DISNEY

DON'T YOU WORRY ABOUT US, SONNY! WHY, WE'RE JUST BEGINNING TO GET INTO THE BIG MONEY!
BRR-R-R-R R-RINGG..!!
8-30

HELLO! OH, McKATZ-- HOW ARE YOU? WHAT? THE WIDOW VAN DOUGH'S MANSION? BOY! YOU REALLY---AHEM--- YES, I'LL BE THERE, MR. McKATZ!

IS THAT A JOB AT MRS. VAN DOUGH'S PLACE?
YES! IT SEEMS THE CITY HAS CONDEMNED HER ANTIQUATED PLUMBING, POOR WOMAN!

IT'S OUTRAGEOUS! TEARING APART A FINE OLD MANSION LIKE THAT! FOR TWO CENTS I WOULDN'T TAKE THE JOB!
?
?
WALT DISNEY

THROUGH THE CONTRACTOR, McKATZ, PIPER GETS THE JOB OF MODERNIZING THE PLUMBING IN THE PALATIAL HOME OF THE WIDOW VAN DOUGH!
8-31

I PRESUME YOU KNOW JUST WHAT IS REQUIRED?
YES, MA'AM! I'VE GOT IT ALL DOWN!

I MUST SAY, IT'S A SHAME TO DISTURB A THING IN THIS BEAUTIFUL DWELLING!
OH, THANK YOU, MR. PIPER!

WHAT IGNORANT SCOUNDREL CONDEMNED YOUR PLUMBING, MA'AM?
SOME INSPECTOR NAMED DIBBLE, I BELIEVE!

DIBBLE! I MIGHT'VE KNOWN! I TELL YOU, MADAM, I HAVE INSTALLED SOME GEMS OF THE PLUMBING CRAFT-- --BUT HAVE I EVER SUITED DIBBLE? NO -- NEVER!
WALT DISNEY

THE WORK OF MODERNIZING MRS. VAN DOUGH'S PLUMBING GETS UNDER WAY.

WE'LL LAY THE NEW WATER PIPES FIRST!
OKAY! MR. PIPER!
RRR-RAT-A-TAT-A-TAT-A-TAT!

HEY--YOU! STOP THAT INFERNAL RACKET!

I'M SORRY, SIR-- BUT WE HAVE AN EXCAVATION TO DIG!
WELL, DIG IT SOMEWHERE ELSE!
SLAM!
9-1

IT DOESN'T MAKE SENSE TO ME, BUT TO BE OBLIGING, I'LL DO IT!
BRRRRR-RATATAT!
WALT DISNEY

HOW'S THAT RAIN GUTTER? WORN OUT?
I CAN'T QUITE SEE IT!

GOOD GRACIOUS! DID HE FALL?
NO, MA'AM---
9-2

---NOT YET!

THERE'S AS FINE A SINK AS I EVER INSTALLED! MRS. VAN DOUGH WILL BE PROUD OF THIS!
BUT, MR. PIPER -- YOU'VE MADE A MISTAKE!

YOU'VE GOT THE FAUCETS WRONG! THE HOT ONE'S ON THE COLD WATER PIPE AND---!
WELL, WELL--THAT WON'T DO! I COULD HARDLY EXPECT THE LADY TO REMEMBER IT EVERY TIME SHE USED THE SINK!

HM-M-M! I'M AFRAID WE'LL HAVE TO GO DOWN IN THE CELLAR AND CHANGE THE PIPE-LINES!
BUT--GOSH! WHY NOT CHANGE THE FAUCETS?
9-3

ANYBODY CAN THINK OF THE EASY WAY, SONNY! COME ON, LET'S GET DOWN CELLAR!
Y-YES, SIR!
WALT DISNEY

MICKEY AND HIS BOSS ARE NEARING THE END OF THEIR WORK IN THE PALATIAL VAN DOUGH MANSION.
9-5

A MIGHTY FINE BATH! YES, SIR-- ONE OF MY BEST!
YEH, IT LOOKS NICE!

THERE'S SOME WORK TO CLEAN UP DOWNSTAIRS! COME DOWN WHEN YOU'RE THROUGH!
OKAY, MR. PIPER!
Copr by Walt Disney Enterprises 1938 World rights reserved

OH, FOR PETE'S SAKE! HOW'S HE EXPECT ANYBODY TO GET UNDER THAT SHOWER? OF ALL THE DUMB TRICKS!

GOSH! AND HERE COMES DIBBLE TO INSPECT THE JOB! GOOD NIGHT!
WALT DISNEY

MR. DIBBLE, THE BUILDING INSPECTOR, ARRIVES TO LOOK OVER THE VAN DOUGH PLUMBING.
9-6

YOU'LL FIND EVERYTHING FIRST CLASS, MR. DIBBLE!
I HOPE SO! I NEVER KNOW WHAT TO EXPECT FROM YOU!

GREAT CAESAR, MAN! DID YOU IMAGINE YOU'D GET AWAY WITH THAT? JUST WHAT DID YOU MEAN IT TO BE--A FOOT BATH?

MR. DIBBLE, THAT'S A SHOWER! CAN I HELP IT IF I RAN SHORT OF PIPE AT THE LAST MINUTE?
YOU--- YOU--- OH-H!

OF ALL THE HOPELESS IDIOTS! JUST BECAUSE YOU HAD NO LONG PIECE OF PIPE, YOU EXPECT THIS THING TO PASS FOR A SHOWER!
SO! YOU WANT TO GET FUSSY, DO YOU?
Copr by Walt Disney Enterprises 1938 World rights reserved

GIVE ME THAT WRENCH!
CAREFUL, PIPER! D-DON'T LOSE YOUR HEAD!
?

I STILL SAY THIS IS A SHOWER!
CLANK! SQUEAK! CLONK!

WHAT'S WRONG WITH THAT?
PIPER-- YOU'RE IMPOSSIBLE!
9-7

TO CELEBRATE THE COMPLETION OF THE VAN DOUGH JOB, PIPER TREATS MICKEY TO SUPPER AND A MOVIE.

MICKEY SEES SOME STARTLING NEWS IN HIS MORNING PAPER AND HOT-FOOTS IT FOR THE PLUMBING SHOP.

9-12

MR PIPER IS QUESTIONED BY THE POLICE ABOUT THE VAN DOUGH ROBBERY.
9-15

SO YUH LEFT THE HOUSE ALL LOCKED UP SAFE AND SOUND, EH?
I CERTAINLY DID!

WHERE WERE YOU BETWEEN SEVEN AND ELEVEN P.M.?
I RESENT YOUR IMPLICATION! I WAS OUT TO SUPPER AND A MOVIE SHOW!

OH, YEAH? I S'POSE YUH KIN PROVE THAT!
I SURE CAN!

MY APPRENTICE WAS WITH ME AT THE TIME! HERE HE COMES NOW!
WALT DISNEY

THIS IS MY APPRENTICE! YOU MAY QUESTION HIM AS YOU LIKE!
OH-H! MICKEY IS YOUR APPRENTICE!
9-16

HOW ABOUT LAST NIGHT MICKEY? WERE YOU WITH PIPER BETWEEN SEVEN AND ELEVEN?
YES, SIR! HE TOOK ME TO DINNER AND A MOVIE!

DOES THAT SATISFY YOU ER--- GENTLEMEN?
MICKEY'S WORD IS ENOUGH FOR ME!
SORRY WE BOTHERED YUH!

NOW THAT THAT'S CLEANED UP, SONNY, WE CAN GET TO WORK! McKATZ HAS ANOTHER JOB FOR US!

MICKEY AND PIPER ARE NOW WORKING AT THE HOME OF AMBROSE PAUNCH, A BIG STOCK-BROKER.
9-17

WE'RE SURE LUCKY TO GET A JOB LIKE THIS! OLD MAN PAUNCH IS THICK WITH DOUGH!
I S'POSE SO!

I ALWAYS SAID SONNY, THAT McKATZ WOULD GET US INTO THE BIG-TIME STUFF!

HERE COMES McKATZ NOW!
YEH, YOU SAID THAT BEFORE!
Copr 1938 by Walt Disney Enterprises World rights reserved

NOW JUST WHAT IS THAT ALL ABOUT, I WONDER?
WALT DISNEY

MIGHTY MYSTERIOUS GUY, THAT McKATZ! ALWAYS WHISPERIN ABOUT SOMETHIN' OR OTHER!
9-19

WE'VE GOT TO HURRY THIS JOB SONNY! NO TIME TO LOSE!
WHY THE SUDDEN RUSH?

MR. PAUNCH IS GOING TO EUROPE-- HE'S LEAVING AT THE END OF THE WEEK!
WELL, WHAT TH' HECK? CAN'T WE WORK AFTER HE'S GONE?

WELL, UH-- McKATZ DOESN'T WANT US IN THE EMPTY HOUSE! TOO MUCH RESPONSIBILITY, ER-- **YOU** KNOW McKATZ --- THE SOUL OF HONOR--!

MICKEY AND PIPER ARE ON THE LAST LAP OF THEIR WORK IN THE AMBROSE PAUNCH HOME.
9-20

STEP ON IT -- I'M WAITING FOR THAT DRAIN PIPE!
WE'RE IN A PICKLE! THIS PIECE IS TOO LONG AND OUR HACK-SAW'S BUSTED!

THERE'S NO TIME TO GET ANOTHER! I'LL **MAKE** IT FIT!
!

THERE! YOU CAN'T STUMP AN OLD MASTER, SONNY!
BUT, GOSH-- NOBODY'LL STAND FOR **THAT!** YOU'LL ONLY HAFTA DO IT OVER!

OH, I DON'T KNOW! MAYBE IT WON'T EVEN BE NOTICED!
WALT DISNEY

DON'T WORRY ABOUT THE PAUNCH JOB! NOBODY'LL NOTICE THAT KITCHEN DRAIN PIPE!
IF THEY DON'T, IT'S A MIRACLE!
R-R-RRING!
9-21
Copr. 1938 by Walt Disney Enterprises World rights reserved

YES, MR. PAUNCH! I ONLY --- THAT'S JUST TEMPORARY YOU SEE! I FULLY INTEND--- **WHAT?**

SIR? THERE'S NO OCCASION FOR SUCH LANGUAGE! CALM YOURSELF MR. PAUNCH--- I'LL CHANGE IT TONIGHT!

I'M GOING BACK THERE--ER, A SLIGHT ALTERATION! YOU WON'T BE NEEDED!
OKAY! SEE Y' TOMORROW, MR. PIPER!
WALT DISNEY

THE BOSS MUST'VE WORKED AT MR. PAUNCH'S PRETTY LATE LAST NIGHT!
9-22

HE SHOULD'A KNOWN IN THE FIRST PLACE, HE'D HAFTA CHANGE THAT DRAIN PIPE!

WELL, FOR--- OMIGOSH!

HEY! DID Y' KNOW --THE --THE PAUNCH HOUSE WAS ROBBED LAST NIGHT?
HUH? NO! ARE YOU KIDDING?
WALT DISNEY

IT SAYS HERE, "ANOTHER MYSTERIOUS ROBBERY OCCURED LAST NIGHT--THIS TIME AT THE HOME OF AMBROSE PAUNCH---"
Copr 1938 by Walt Disney Enterprises World rights reserved

"---IN ADDITION TO VALUABLE JEWELRY, SEVERAL THOUSANDS IN BONDS WERE TAKEN! NO EVIDENCE OF HOW THE ROBBERS ENTERED WAS FOUND!"
9-23

YOU WERE WORKIN' THERE! HAVE Y' GOT ANY IDEA HOW IT COULD'VE HAPPENED?
NOPE! SOMETHIN' FISHY ABOUT THIS! WHO COULD---?

MR. PAUNCH COULDN'T HAVE DONE IT! HE WAS WITH ME ALL EVENING!

THE SAME NIGHT THAT MR. PIPER FINISHES HIS WORK IN THE PAUNCH HOUSE, THE PLACE IS ROBBED OF VALUABLE BONDS AND JEWELRY!
9-24

FIRST, MRS. VAN DOUGH WAS ROBBED, AND NOW, THIS!
TERRIBLE! MAKES ME LOOK LIKE A JINX ON MY CLIENTS!
Copr 1938 by Walt Disney Enterprises World rights reserved

I S'POSE YOU CAN'T TELL US ANYTHING ABOUT THIS, PIPER?
NOPE! SORRY! I WAS WORKING ON THE KITCHEN SINK ALL EVENING! MR. PAUNCH INSISTED ON WATCHING ME TO SEE THAT I DID THE WORK TO SUIT HIM!

YEAH, PAUNCH ALREADY TOLD US THAT! BUT IT'S MIGHTY QUEER HOW TWO CASES LIKE THIS COULD HAPPEN!

TWO MYSTERIOUS ROBBERIES, STILL UNSOLVED. HAVE OCCURRED IN THE LAST TWO HOUSES IN WHICH MICKEY HAS WORKED!
LOOKING FOR A SHOULDER TO CRY ON, MICKEY DROPS IN AT HORACE'S STORE.

9-26

AS TIME GOES ON, WITH NO FURTHER DEVELOPMENTS, MICKEY GRADUALLY FORGETS ABOUT THE ROBBERIES.

9-27

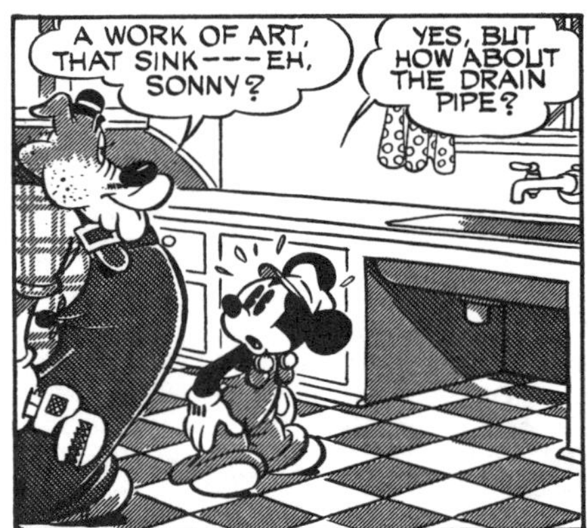

I DON'T SEE WHAT YOU'RE OBJECTING TO! AT LEAST, THE WATER CAN'T RUN ON THE FLOOR!
SH-H-H!- HERE COMES DIBBLE!

SO! ANOTHER ONE OF YOUR IDIOTIC STUNTS! ANY CHILD WOULD KNOW HE COULDN'T GET AWAY WITH THAT!

WHY, GREAT CAESAR, THE THING'S IMPOSSIBLE! IT'S AN INSULT TO MY INTELLIGENCE AS A BUILDING INSPECTOR!
IS THAT SO? WELL, UH-- --IS THAT SO?
9-29

IT'S ABSOLUTELY THE WORST JOB I EVER PUT MY OKAY ON!
WALT DISNEY

AREN'T WE GOING TO WORK TODAY, MR. PIPER?
TRUE HEARTS STORIES
Copr 1938 by Walt Disney Enterprises World rights reserved

HUH? OH, NO--- NOTHING TO DO TODAY!
BUT THAT SINK DRAIN! YOU KNOW- --THE ONE IN MR. POTTSGOLD'S HOUSE!
TRUE HEARTS STORIES
9-30

OF COURSE, I KNOW! BUT IT'S THE ONLY JOB WE'VE GOT! IF WE FINISH IT, WE'RE OUT OF WORK ENTIRELY---

---AND I CAN'T STAND IDLENESS!
?
!
TRUE HEARTS STORIES
WALT DISNEY

BUT, MR. PIPER! WE'VE GOT TO PUT A DRAIN PIPE UNDER THAT SINK AT MR. POTTSGOLD'S!
R-R-RINGG!!
TRUE HEARTS STORIES
Copr 1938 by Walt Disney Enterprises World rights reserved

WHO? OH-- MR. POTTSGOLD! OF COURSE- --I'LL GLADLY MAKE THAT LITTLE ALTERATION, BUT I WON'T BE ABLE TO GET THERE UNTIL THIS EVENING!

WHAT'S THE IDEA? WE'VE GOT NOTHIN' TO DO TODAY!
I KNOW--BUT WHEN I DO A JOB OVER, I ALWAYS DO IT IN MY SPARE TIME!
10-1

DON'T YOU SEE? IF I DID IT IN WORKING HOURS, I'D BE LOSING MONEY!
!
TRUE HEARTS STORIES
WALT DISNEY

EARLY IN THE EVENING PIPER, THE PLUMBER STARTS FOR THE POTTSGOLD HOUSE TO FINISH SOME INCOMPLETED WORK!

NEXT MORNING AS MICKEY LEAVES FOR THE PLUMBING SHOP

MICKEY ON HIS ARRIVAL AT THE PLUMBING SHOP FINDS THE POLICE WAITING TO TALK TO HIM!

10-5

YES, SIR--I'M QUITTIN' MY JOB TODAY! I'M NOT WORKIN' ANY LONGER FOR A GUY I THINK IS CROOKED!
HOLD ON, MICKEY! THIS IS NO TIME TO QUIT!
Copr by Walt Disney Enterprises
1938 World rights reserved

BUT I'M **CERTAIN** THAT PIPER HAS SOMEP'N TO DO WITH THESE ROBBERIES!
SO ARE WE--BUT WE CAN'T PROVE A **THING** ON HIM! THAT'S WHERE **YOU** COME IN!

DON'T Y' SEE? PIPER THINKS HE'S GOT YOU FOOLED COMPLETELY! **LET** 'IM THINK SO AND WE'VE GOT A CHANCE TO GET TH' GOODS ON HIM!

I'LL DO IT! FROM NOW ON I'M PIPER'S SHADOW!
THAT'S TH' STUFF, MICKEY! I THOUGHT WE COULD COUNT ON YOU!
10-6

OKAY, MR. CASEY! I'LL LET PIPER THINK HE'S FOOLIN' ME AND MAYBE I CAN GET SOME DOPE ON THESE ROBBERIES!
GOOD! WE'LL SCRAM BEFORE HE COMES IN. SO HE WON'T KNOW WE SUSPECT---
Copr by Walt Disney Enterprises
1938 World rights reserved

HOLD ON! I GOT A **BETTER** IDEA!

WE'LL STAY HERE AND PUT TH' HEAT ON 'IM! MAYBE HE'LL CRACK AN' SPILL SOMETHIN'!
10-7

LOOK HERE, YOU--YOU--POLICEMEN! YOU'VE GOT TO **DO** SOMETHING ABOUT THESE **ROBBERIES**! IF THEY'RE NOT **STOPPED**, THEY'LL **RUIN** MY **BUSINESS**!
WALT DISNEY

FINE POLICE WE HAVE IN THIS TOWN! **THREE** ROBBERIES IN A ROW AND NOTHING DONE ABOUT IT!
BUT, UH--MR. PIPER---!
Copr. by Walt Disney Enterprises
1938 World rights reserved

HOW DO YOU THINK **I** FEEL? EVERY HOUSE I WORK IN GETS ROBBED! MAKES ME LOOK LIKE A JINX OR--!
ER--YES, I SEE YOUR POINT!
10-8

MY BUSINESS IS SUNK! YOU'VE **GOT** TO GET THAT CROOK--DO YOU HEAR?
DON'T WORRY, PIPER---WE'LL GET HIM!
CLICK!

JUST AS I GET INTO THE **BIG** JOBS, **THIS** HAS TO HAPPEN!
YEH, IT'S PRETTY TOUGH, ALL RIGHT!
WALT DISNEY

ALTHOUGH CONVINCED THAT HIS BOSS IS CONNECTED WITH THE SERIES OF ROBBERIES, MICKEY HIDES HIS SUSPICIONS, HOPING THAT PIPER WILL GIVE HIMSELF AWAY!

10-10

PIPER'S CUP OF WOE SEEMS OVERFLOWING, WHEN HIS OLD FRIEND MCKATZ APPEARS A LITTLE DOUBTFUL OF HIM! MICKEY SHOWS NO INTEREST, BUT HE IS ALL EARS !

10-11

IN SPITE OF THE MYSTERIOUS ROBBERIES, PIPER GETS ANOTHER JOB FROM MCKATZ, THE BIG CONTRACTOR

RECENT DEVELOPMENTS HAVE CONFIRMED SOME OF MICKEY'S SUSPICIONS.
FOLLOWING UP A FURTHER HUNCH, HE PAYS A SURPRISE VISIT TO ONE OF PIPER'S CHIEF COMPETITORS.

10-15

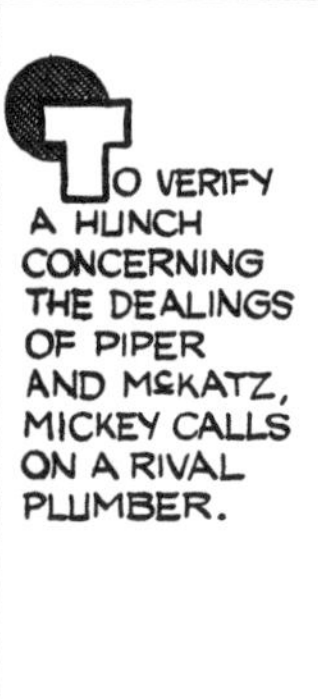

To verify a hunch concerning the dealings of Piper and McKatz, Mickey calls on a rival plumber.
10-17

WHAT I'M GETTIN' AT, MR. HIGGLESBY--YOU'VE BID ON SOME O' THESE JOBS, HAVEN'T YOU?
OF COURSE, I HAVE! BUT PIPER ALWAYS GOT 'EM, NO MATTER HOW LOW I BID!
Copr 1938 by Walt Disney Enterprises World rights reserved

JUST AS I THOUGHT! McKATZ HAS BEEN GIVIN' PIPER THE CREAM, REGARDLESS OF LOWER BIDS!
SURE HE HAS! BUT I STILL DON'T SEE WHAT YOU'RE AFTER!

JUST THIS, MR. HIGGLESBY! BY WORKIN' FOR PIPER, I'VE BEEN HELPIN' A GANG OF CROOKS! SINCE I FOUND IT OUT, I'VE BEEN TRYIN' TO GET THE EVIDENCE TO CONVICT 'EM!

NOW I KNOW THAT McKATZ GIVES PIPER ALL HIS BEST JOBS! YET PIPER'S A GOSH-AWFUL PLUMBER! WHAT'S THE ANSWER?
I GIVE UP! THIS IS ALL OVER MY HEAD!
WALT DISNEY

G'BYE, MR. HIGGLESBY! I DON'T THINK YOU'LL HAVE TO WORRY ABOUT PIPER VERY MUCH LONGER!
WELL, I DON'T KNOW EXACTLY WHAT YOU'RE UP TO, BUT I'M ALL FOR IT--AND SO IS EVERY OTHER HONEST PLUMBER!
EBENEZER HIGGLESBY PLUMBING CONTRACTOR

ONE THING SURE -- THE OBJECT OF THE GAME IS TO GET PIPER SET UP IN A RICH HOUSE!

LATER, THE HOUSE GETS ROBBED! BUT HOW? PIPER'S ALIBI IS FOOLPROOF EVERY TIME!
10-18

GUESS I'LL HAVE A WORD WITH MR. CASEY BEFORE I GO HOME!
P.D.
NO PARKING POLICE DEPT.

I'D LIKE TO SEE DETECTIVE CASEY, PLEASE!
SURE THING, ME LAD! GO RIGHT THROUGH THAT DOOR AND WAKE 'IM UP!
WANTED
REWARD
NOTICE
BAD GIRL
Copr 1938 by Walt Disney Enterprises World rights reserved

HELLO, MICKEY! DON'T TELL ME Y' GOT THE GOODS ON OLD PIPER ALREADY!
NO, BUT I'VE GOT AN IDEA HOW THE ROBBERIES COULD'VE BEEN WORKED!
10-19

Y' SEE, WE KNOW THAT PIPER, HIMSELF, COULDN'T HAVE BEEN THE THIEF! BUT HE COULD HAVE LET DIBBLE OR McKATZ IN THE HOUSE AND THEY'D PULL THE JOB!

SORRY, MICKEY! WE'VE ALREADY GRILLED THOSE GUYS AND THEIR ALIBIS ARE AIRTIGHT, TOO!
GOSH DARN! I THOUGHT I HAD SOMEP'N THERE!

GOSH! HOW CAN WE PROVE ANYTHING ON PIPER AND HIS PALS IF NONE OF 'EM ACTUALLY PULL THESE JOBS?
SURE, IT'S TOUGH-- BUT THAT'S WHERE WE'RE COUNTIN' ON YOU!
Copr 1938 by Walt Disney Enterprises World rights reserved

SOONER OR LATER PIPER'S BOUND TO MAKE A SLIP-- AND YOU'LL BE THERE TO TIP US OFF!
SOMEHOW, I DON'T FEEL RIGHT --I MEAN, DOIN' UNDER-COVER WORK WHILE PIPER PAYS ME! IT SEEMS SORT OF UNFAIR!

LISTEN, MICKEY! WHEN YOU'RE WORKIN' AGAINST CRIMINALS Y' GOTTA BEAT 'EM AT THEIR OWN GAME! Y' CAN'T LET LITTLE SCRUPLES STAND IN THE WAY OF A BIG PUBLIC SERVICE!
10-20

YEH, I GUESS YOU'RE RIGHT, MR. CASEY! OKAY--I'M NOT BACKIN' OUT!
THAT'S THE STUFF, KID!
WALT DISNEY

SEVERAL DAYS PASS UNEVENTFULLY. THERE ARE NO NEW ROBBERIES NOR ANY FURTHER CLUES TO THE OLD ONES!
10-21

THEN, ONE NIGHT, AT QUITTING TIME---!
LEAVE THE TOOLS IN THE BAG, SONNY! I'M GOING BACK TO WORK TONIGHT!
HUH? Y-YES, SIR!
Copr 1938 by Walt Disney Enterprises World rights reserved

BUT-- THAT JOB WE'RE ON- -- THERE'S NO RUSH TO---!
ARE YOU QUESTIONING MY RIGHT TO WORK OVERTIME IF I CHOOSE?
?

NO, SIR! NOT AT ALL --I ONLY---!
VERY WELL! I HAVE MY REASONS! YOU MAY GO HOME!

OH, BOY! WAIT'LL I TELL THE COPS ABOUT THIS!
WALT DISNEY

MR. CASEY! I GOTTA SEE Y' A MINUTE!
EH? WHAT'S ALL THE EXCITEMENT?
P.D.
POLICE DEPARTMENT

LOOK--PIPER'S GOIN' TO WORK TONIGHT--- AND THE JOB DOESN'T NEED NIGHT WORK--- HE'S UP TO SOMEP'N AND---!
YEH, WE ALREADY HEARD ABOUT IT, MICKEY!

WE GOT AN ANONYMOUS 'PHONE CALL TIPPIN' US OFF! LOOKS LIKE PIPER MAY BE GETTIN' THE OLD DOUBLE-CROSS FROM ONE O' THE GANG!
WELL-- F' GOSH SAKES!

ANYWAY, I'M STAKIN' OUT A SQUAD AROUND THE HOUSE WHERE PIPER'S WORKIN' TONIGHT! WE'LL NAB ANY THIEF RED-HANDED!
BOY! THAT'S ONE SHOW I'M NOT GOIN' TO MISS!
WALT DISNEY
10-22

ACTING ON AN ANONYMOUS TIP, THE POLICE HAVE SURROUNDED THE HOUSE WHERE PIPER IS WORKING AT NIGHT!
10·24

WE BEEN HERE THREE HOURS! THINK ANY-BODY COULD'A SNEAKED PAST US?
NAW, NOT A CHANCT! AN' CASEY'S GOT TH' FRONT COVERED!

THIS YEGG IS SURE SLOW! I COULD FRISK THE PLACE IN HALF THE TIME!
GOSH! HOPE HE DIDN'T ESCAPE SOME WAY!

NO DANGER O' THAT! WE---!
SH-H-H! THE DOOR--- SOMEBODY'S COMIN'!
WALT DISNEY

EXPECTING TO CATCH THE MYSTERIOUS ROBBER WITH HIS LOOT, THE COPS DISCOVER THAT IT IS PIPER LEAVING THE HOUSE!
10·25

WELL, IF IT AIN'T OUR OLD FRIEND, THE PLUMBER!
WORKIN' KINDA LATE, EH, PIPER?
ANY LAW AGAINST IT?
Copr. 1938 by Walt Disney Enterprises World rights reserved

NO-- SURE NOT!
PRETTY HEAVY BAG YUH GOT THERE! TOOLS, O' COURSE!
YES-- TOOLS, OF COURSE!

HAVE A LOOK! STICK YOUR NOSE IN IT--IT'S BEEN IN EVERYTHING ELSE!
TAKE IT EASY, MR. PIPER! THERE'S NO OFFENSE---!

---INSULTING A TAXPAYING CITIZEN---DARNED OUTRAGE---FINE STATE OF AFFAIRS!
WALT DISNEY

IT LOOKS LIKE PIPER'S PUT A FAST ONE OVER ON US AGAIN! GUESS I'LL GO HOME!
WELL, I'M STILL WATCHIN' THIS HOUSE! WE MIGHT NAB SOMEBODY, YET!
Copr. 1938 by Walt Disney Enterprises World rights reserved

THE FOLLOWING MORNING.
HM-M--- THAT'S FUNNY!
?
EH?

WHY, THERE WASN'T ANY ROBBERY WHERE Y' WORKED LAST NIGHT--ER--ULP--I MEAN---!
WHAT? JUST BECAUSE I'M IN A HOUSE, IT HAS TO BE ROBBED? DO YOU INSINUATE---?
10·26

NO--I JUST-- Y' KNOW Y' DID HAVE HARD LUCK IN THOSE OTHER HOUSES, AND I WAS AFRAID---!
YES, THAT'S TRUE! I'VE BEEN A VICTIM OF FATE BEFORE! BUT, SURELY, HONESTY MUST TRIUMPH IN THE END!
WALT DISNEY

BAFFLED FOR THE TIME BEING, THE POLICE LAY OFF PIPER AND AWAIT FURTHER DEVELOPMENTS.

MICKEY IS SURPRISED AND VAGUELY SUSPICIOUS WHEN PIPER TELLS HIM THEY ARE TO INSTALL A BATHTUB IN THE CITY BANK!

10-28

MICKEY AND PIPER ARE WORKING NIGHTS IN THE CITY BANK.
THEY ARE PREPARING TO INSTALL A BATHTUB IN THE BASEMENT FOR MR. SHECKELS, THE PRESIDENT!

1031

THE FOLLOWING MORNING, AS THE NIGHT WATCHMAN OF THE CITY BANK IS RELIEVED BY THE JANITOR.

11-4

MICKEY HAS TOLD DETECTIVE CASEY THE WHOLE STORY OF PIPER'S JOB IN THE CITY BANK.

11-5

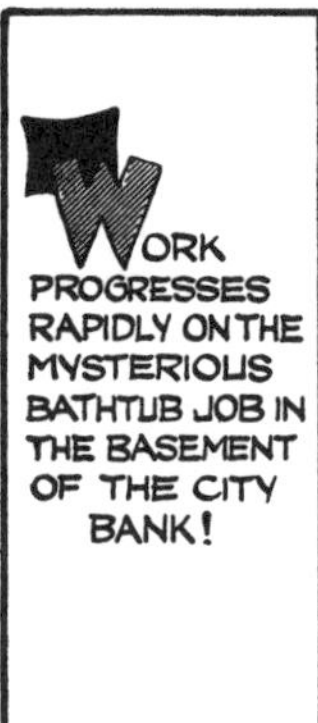
WORK PROGRESSES RAPIDLY ON THE MYSTERIOUS BATHTUB JOB IN THE BASEMENT OF THE CITY BANK!
11-7

A NEAT BIT OF CRAFTSMANSHIP! WE'RE ALMOST READY FOR THE TUB, ITSELF!
Copr. 1938 by Walt Disney Enterprises World rights reserved

SAY! HOW'LL WE CONNECT WITH THE CITY MAINS? WON'T WE HAFTA DO SOME EXCAVATING?
EH? OH, NO--- NO! THAT'S ALL BEEN DONE!

YES--THE EXCAVATING WAS DONE BEFORE WE CAME HERE! WE MUSTN'T TOUCH, ER--THAT IS, SOME MEN ALREADY TOOK CARE OF THAT---

---IN FACT, IT WAS DONE BY McKATZ'S MEN!
OH! I SEE!
WALT DISNEY

CONFOUND IT! THAT BATHTUB FOR THE CITY BANK SHOULD HAVE BEEN HERE LONG AGO!
WELL, DO WE HAFTA WAIT? WHY NOT USE ONE O' THESE?

YOU DON'T UNDERSTAND, SONNY! THIS BATHTUB IS UNIQUE---IT'S BEING BUILT TO ORDER IN McKATZ'S SHOP!
?
11-8

AH! HERE WE ARE AT LAST!
?

WHA--- WHAT'S THAT?
IT'S MR. SHECKEL'S BATHTUB, OF COURSE! WHAT DID YOU THINK?
WALT DISNEY

YOU--- YOU MEAN--THAT'S A BATHTUB?
OF COURSE IT IS! DESIGNED JUST AS SHECKELS WANTS IT!
11-9

WELL, GOSH---- HOW DO Y' GET IN IT?
IT'S A FOLDING TUB, SONNY! LOOK!

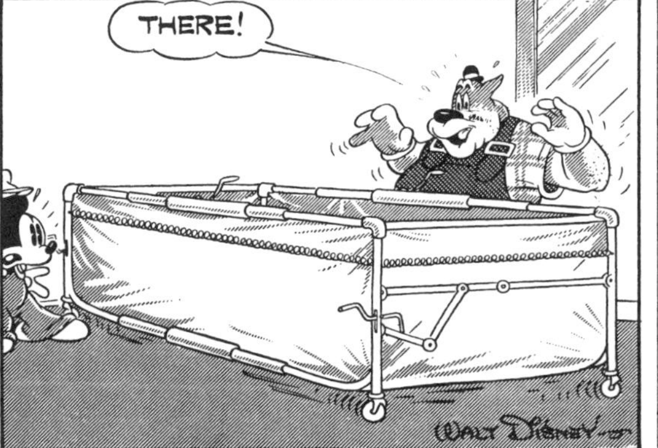
THERE!
WALT DISNEY

ISN'T IT-- KINDA LARGE!
I'VE ALREADY EXPLAINED TO YOU, HE DOESN'T WANT IT JUST TO BATHE IN! HE WANTS TO LEARN TO SWIM--IN PRIVACY!

MICKEY IS PLENTY SURPRISED TO DISCOVER THAT THE TUB FOR THE BANK PRESIDENT IS A GOOFY-LOOKING CANVAS AFFAIR!
11-10

IT'S AWFUL BIG AND CLUMSY! MUST BE A PRETTY AWKWARD JOB TO FOLD IT UP!
NOT AT ALL---

---JUST A TWIST OF THE WRIST!
HEY! WHAT TH'---!

THEN A FLICK OF THE FINGER--AND THERE YOU ARE!

SIMPLE, ISN'T IT? OF COURSE YOU SHOULD LOOK AT IT FROM THE OUTSIDE TO GET THE BEST EFFECT!
WALT DISNEY

THE PRESIDENT'S TRICK BATHTUB HAS BEEN CONVEYED TO HIS PRIVATE QUARTERS IN THE BANK BASEMENT.
11-11

YES, SIR! THAT'S JUST ABOUT THE FINEST FOLDING BATH I EVER SAW!

MAYBE SO! BUT I STILL DON'T GET THE IDEA WHY MR. SHECKELS WANTS IT TO FOLD UP!
I DECLARE, SONNY--- IT'S BEEN EXPLAINED TO YOU!

HE WANTS TO LEARN TO SWIM, WITHOUT TELLING HIS WIFE! IF SHE SHOULD COME IN, HE CAN FOLD THE TUB AND PUT IT OUT OF SIGHT!

WHY CAN'T YOU UNDERSTAND? CERTAINLY, THERE'S NOTHING UNUSUAL ABOUT THIS!
UH--NO--I S'POSE NOT! GUESS I'M JUST KINDA DUMB!
WALT DISNEY

YOU MEAN-- THE FAUCETS GO UP HERE? THEY WON'T BE ATTACHED TO THE TUB?
NOTHING WILL BE ATTACHED TO THE TUB, SONNY! SHECKELS COULDN'T FOLD IT THEN, COULD HE?
11-12
Copr. 1938 by Walt Disney Enterprises World rights reserved

ALL RIGHT! THEN, HOW'LL HE EMPTY IT, IF IT'S NOT CONNECTED TO THE DRAIN?
WHAT?

WHY, UH--- BRRHMPH! THAT'S SIMPLE --- DRAIN--- YOU SAID DRAIN, DIDN'T YOU? WELL, NOW---

---AS A MATTER OF FACT-- AHEM--THAT LITTLE PROBLEM SEEMS TO HAVE BEEN OVERLOOKED! GLAD YOU MENTIONED IT! I'LL HAVE TO-- ER, GIVE IT SOME THOUGHT!
WALT DISNEY

PIPER ALWAYS HAS AN ANSWER TO EVERYTHING, BUT---WHEN MICKEY ASKS HOW THE FOLDING BATHTUB CAN BE EMPTIED WITHOUT CONNECTING TO THE DRAIN- ----?!!

11-14

PIPER IS A LITTLE WORRIED ABOUT THE WATCHMAN'S SUSPICION OF MICKEY. NEXT DAY, IN THE SHOP, HE MAKES A CAUTIOUS TEST.

11-18

ACTING ON MICKEY'S INFORMATION, CASEY AND A SQUAD OF POLICE SPEED OFF TO THE CITY BANK!

SURROUND TH' PLACE, BOYS! DON'T LEAVE A LOOPHOLE FOR 'EM TO SLIP THROUGH!

TWO HOURS LATER.
BEGINS TO LOOK LIKE YOUR DOPE WAS A LITTLE BIT OFF, SON!
GOSH! I'D 'A SWORN TONIGHT WAS GOIN' TO BE THE BIG GETAWAY!
11-21

I'M GOIN' IN! IF THOSE GUYS ARE ACTUALLY WORKIN', I'LL COME OUT AN' TELL Y'!
WALT DISNEY

WITH THE POLICE WATCHING THE BANK FOR HOURS AND NO SIGN OF THE ROBBERS, MICKEY DECIDES TO INVESTIGATE.
11-22

PIPER MUST BE THERE YET -- HIS TRUCK'S STILL OUTSIDE!
I'LL JUST SORT O' DROP IN, AS IF I THOUGHT HE MIGHT NEED ME!
SIDE ENTRANCE CITY BANK
NIGHT BELL

ALL HE CAN DO IS CHASE ME OUT!
SIDE ENTRANCE CITY BANK
NIGHT BELL

WHERE THE HECK'S THAT WATCHMAN?

F' GOSH SAKES! IT'S NOT LOCKED!
SIDE ENTRANCE CITY BANK
NIGHT BELL
WALT DISNEY

DARN FUNNY--THE WATCHMAN LEAVIN' THIS DOOR UNLOCKED!
SIDE ENTRANCE CITY BANK
NIGHT BELL

HM-M-M! THERE AIN'T ANY WATCHMAN!
PAYING

NOW'S MY CHANCE TO SEE WHAT'S GOIN' ON IN THE BASEMENT!

G-GOSH ---EMPTY! THEY'RE GONE!
11-23
WALT DISNEY

MICKEY EXPECTS TO FIND PIPER IN THE BASEMENT WITH McKATZ AND DIBBLE---BUT THE ROOM IS EMPTY!

11-24

MICKEY FINDS THE BASEMENT ROOM EMPTY AND TRACES OF SMOKE HANGING IN THE AIR! HE THEN NOTICES DIRTY FOOTPRINTS LEADING ACROSS THE ROOM!

11-25

WITH SIREN SCREAMING, A HIGH-POWERED POLICE CAR ROARS THROUGH THE NIGHT, RACING AGAINST TIME!
WHEEOOO
11-28

WHAT DID YOU FIND IN THE BANK, ANYWAY, MICKEY?
I'M AFRAID YOU'D NEVER BELIEVE ME, SIR! IT'S TOO FANTASTIC!

WELL, HERE WE ARE!
I ONLY HOPE WE'RE NOT TOO LATE!
SKREEEE
WALT DISNEY

IS THIS WHERE THE STORM DRAIN EMPTIES?
THAT'S RIGHT!
Copr. by Walt Disney Enterprises 1938 World rights reserved
11-29

LOOK! THAT'S THE BOAT THE ROBBERS MEAN TO GET AWAY IN!
GUESS YOU'RE RIGHT, MICKEY! THEY---HUH?
HERE THEY COME!

PULL IN HERE, YUH MUGGS! STICK 'EM UP OR WE'LL BLOW THAT BATHTUB INTO TH' MIDDLE O' NEXT WEEK!
WALT DISNEY

FOLLOWING MICKEY'S TIP, THE POLICE HAVE BEEN ABLE TO NAB THE MOST UNUSUAL GANG OF BANK-ROBBERS THEY EVER ENCOUNTERED!
11-30

SMART GUYS, HUH? THOUGHT YUH COULD GET AWAY IN A TRICK BATHTUB!
HUMPH! THERE MUST'VE BEEN SOMEBODY BRIGHTER THAN YOU WORKIN' ON THIS JOB!
Copr. by Walt Disney Enterprises 1938 World rights reserved

WHAT? MY OWN APPRENTICE IN WITH THE COPS?
WELL-- DID Y' THINK I DIDN'T KNOW Y' WERE CROOKED?

THAT SETTLES IT--- YOU'RE FIRED!
WALT DISNEY

THEIR GETAWAY IN THE FLOATING TUB HAVING BEEN NIPPED BY MICKEY, THE FOUR BANK-ROBBERS ARE SAFELY IN CUSTODY OF THE POLICE!

12-1

BACK AT POLICE HEADQUARTERS THE COPS PREPARE TO PUT THE PRISONERS THROUGH THE THIRD DEGREE!

12-2

12-3

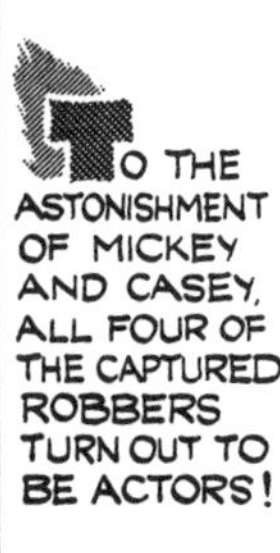

THE ACTOR-ROBBERS HAVE EXPLAINED HOW THEY GOT THE POSITIONS WHICH SERVED AS BLINDS FOR THEIR REAL OPERATIONS.

12-7

WELL--I S'POSE YOU BIRDS KNOW YOU'LL HAVE QUITE A FEW YEARS IN THE PEN!
YES, WE RATHER SUSPECTED IT!

AFTER ALL, WE OWE A DEBT TO SOCIETY--- AND LET IT NOT BE SAID THAT WE **REPUDIATE** THAT DEBT!

BUT OUR TIME SHALL NOT BE WASTED! WE'LL ORGANIZE A DRAMATIC CLUB!
12-8

SUCH A DRAMATIC CLUB AS **NO** PRISON HAS **EVER SEEN**!
HURRAH! BRAVO!
WALT DISNEY

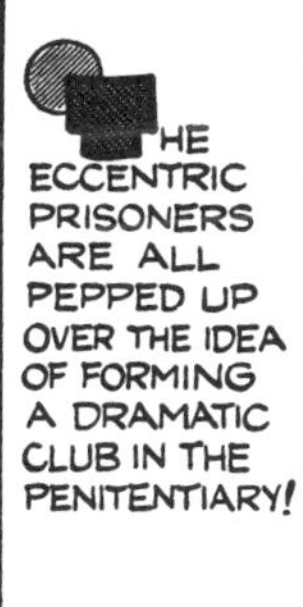
THE ECCENTRIC PRISONERS ARE ALL PEPPED UP OVER THE IDEA OF FORMING A DRAMATIC CLUB IN THE PENITENTIARY!
12-9

WE'LL GIVE THEM THE OLD CLASSICS!
"THE BELLS!"
"EAST LYNNE!"
ALL RIGHT, BOYS-- BREAK IT UP! AS FAR AS THE POLICE ARE CONCERNED, THIS CASE IS CLOSED!
Copr 1938 by Walt Disney Enterprises World rights reserved

OUR PLAYS WILL MAKE A **NAME** FOR THE PENITENTIARY!

WELL, ONE THING SURE -- YOUR AUDIENCE CAN'T WALK OUT ON YOU!
SIR?

BEFORE I GO, LET ME SAY THAT I HARBOR NO ILL WILL!
THAT'S DARN DECENT OF Y', MR. PIPER! THANKS!
12-10
Copr 1938 by Walt Disney Enterprises World rights reserved

NOT AT ALL! YOU WERE ONLY DOING YOUR DUTY AS YOU SAW IT! IF YOU CARE TO VISIT THE PRISON SOMETIME---

---I SHALL BE GLAD TO SEE YOU!
SURE, MR. PIPER! I'LL COME!

GOOD! AND DON'T FORGET TO BRING THE TOOLS, SONNY!
?
WALT DISNEY

From cartoon to comic—to cartoon (almost!): Gottfredson expanded *Mickey's Man Friday* (1935, left) into "Mickey Mouse Meets Robinson Crusoe" (1938), revamping Mickey's wardrobe in the process. The new design was then adapted *back to Mickey's Man Friday* for a planned remake (1940, right), though this film was never completed. Poster art by Tom Wood; model sheet attributed to Riley Thomson; images courtesy Walt Disney Archives.

Mickey Mouse Meets Robinson Crusoe -and- Unhappy Campers

December 12, 1938
–
May 20, 1939

ACCENTUATE THE NEGATIVE

Accepted social norms change and evolve over time. Never is this clearer than when we look today at Floyd Gottfredson's 1930s *Mickey Mouse* comic strips. While created to amuse prewar audiences of all colors, they casually contain exaggerated ethnic images that now feel insensitive to many.

As remembered by his peers, Gottfredson himself was no bigot. But like many old-time culture creators, he never fully grasped the impact of extreme ethnic humor—and past books in this series have shown us the results. Gottfredson insensitively drew Africans as humanized monkeys; he often gave them Southern-fried jargon to speak, likening them to American hillbillies. To be fair, Gottfredson did seem to realize that the results might offend. Consequently, he at times portrayed his bumpkin Africans as Mickey's rescuers and friends, as if trying to use positive elements to balance out the negative.

What to do, however, when one simply *couldn't* be positive? "Mickey Mouse Meets Robinson Crusoe" shows the quandary that resulted. If a *Robinson Crusoe* spoof were to accurately follow Daniel Defoe, it would require a Man Friday who was an ignorant jungle youth—and a cannibal tribe that could be nobody's friends. The roles, as usual, were given to Gottfredson's typical deep-South monkey figures. But while the results worked on paper, the characters were inescapably negative Black images.

To his credit, Gottfredson seems to have tried to counteract the problem. Alas, his solution was to make the white characters, too, into highly negative figures; perhaps in the belief that if everyone were embarrassing, no one would be. In practice, this did less to tame the awkwardness than to multiply it. Robinson Crusoe is now a cowardly, vainglorious white nebbish who repeatedly puts Mickey in harm's way. And as the climactic danger unfolds, an equally annoying crew of British scientists refuses to rescue our heroes.

As a final effort to tame his tale, Gottfredson posited that even in Mickey's world, the events were not "real." For one of only a few times in the Gottfredson canon, "Crusoe" is an adventure enacted not by Mickey in a genuine foreign clime, but by Mickey-the-actor in front of a Disney camera crew. If nothing else, this backhandedly explains the natives' hillbilly lexicon. They're Americans playing comedic parts, not real jungle-dwellers.

In the end, however, no complex explanation can save Gottfredson's story from itself. Even if the adventure isn't "real," even if it mocks all ethnic groups equally, "Robinson Crusoe" is something of a misstep—its vibe so negative that Gottfredson later seemed to want to undo its effects. After years of turning jungle natives into American Southerners, he would never do so again after this. And when we next heard from Friday...

But *that* is an entirely *different* sad story. [DG]

HIS PLUMBING EXPERIENCE NOW A THING OF THE PAST, MICKEY IS ON HIS WAY HOME.
12-12

POOR OLD PIPER! HE WASN'T SUCH A BAD EGG!

GUESS I OUGHTA GO IN AND SEE MINNIE! SEEMS LIKE AGES SINCE---
Copr 1938 by Walt Disney Enterprises World rights reserved

--- NO I WON'T! I'LL GO HOME FIRST AND GET CLEANED UP!

MICKEY MOUSE! YOU COME IN HERE, RIGHT THIS INSTANT!
WALT DISNEY

MICKEY IS STOPPED BY MINNIE, AS HE PASSES HER HOUSE!
12-13

I WAS GOIN' TO CLEAN UP A LITTLE AND COME BACK LATER!
NEVER MIND THAT! YOU COME IN RIGHT NOW AND EXPLAIN YOURSELF!

THE IDEA! THAT SILLY PLUMBING WORK! WHAT EVER MADE YOU TAKE IT IN THE FIRST PLACE? YOU DIDN'T HAVE TO!
WELL--IT WAS SOMEP'N TO DO! AND QUITE EXCITIN', AS IT TURNED OUT!
Copr 1938 by Walt Disney Enterprises World rights reserved

NOBODY'S BEEN ABLE TO GET HOLD OF YOU FOR DAYS!
WELL, WHO WANTS ME?

THE STUDIO DOES! THEY'VE GOT A NEW PICTURE READY FOR YOU!
OH, BOY!
WALT DISNEY

YOU HURRY AND CALL THE STUDIO! MR. DISNEY'S BEEN TRYING ALL DAY TO GET YOU!
Copr 1938 by Walt Disney Enterprises World rights reserved

HELLO, WALT-- THIS IS MICKEY! I HEAR YOU'VE GOT A NEW PICTURE FOR ME!
YES--WE'RE GOING TO MAKE "ROBINSON CRUSOE!" THINK YOU'D LIKE TO WORK IN IT?
12-14

YOU BET I WOULD! WHAT DO I PLAY-- NOT CRUSOE?
NO--NOR FRIDAY, EITHER! IT'S A GOOD PART, THOUGH! SEE MacCORKER ON THE LOT TOMORROW--- HE'LL GIVE YOU ALL THE DOPE!

HOT DAWG! A "ROBINSON CRUSOE" PICTURE!
THAT'LL KEEP YOU OUT OF MISCHIEF FOR AWHILE, YOU REPROBATE!

MICKEY ARRIVES AT THE STUDIO, ALL SET TO STUDY HIS PART IN A NEW PICTURE!
12-15

MORNIN', MICKEY! GLAD TO SEE YOU ON THE LOT AGAIN!
THANKS, POPS! I'M GLAD TO BE HERE!
STAGE 5

HI, THERE, GOOFY! HOW'RE Y' DOIN'?
HUH? OH, HULLO, MICKEY! UH-- I'M FEELIN' KINDER LOW!
STAGE 3

WHAT'S THE MAIN TROUBLE?
WELL, THEY GOT ME IN A PITCHER WHERE I'M CO-STARRED WITH A GRASSHOPPER----

--- AND THUH DURN CRITTER'S STEALIN' ALL THUH LAFFS, GAWRSH-DING IT!
!

WELL, I'VE GOTTA FIND THE DIRECTOR AND GET MY SCRIPT! WE'RE DOIN' "ROBINSON CRUSOE!"
WHUT'S THAT? I NEVER HEARD OF IT!
STAGE 3

OF COURSE YOU HAVE! EVERYBODY KNOWS IT! JUST STOP AND THINK A MINUTE!

IS THAT THUH YARN ABOUT THUH SHIPWRECKED GUY WHAT LIVED ON A ISLAND AND ---?
SURE! THAT'S IT!

JUST WHAT I THOUGHT! NEVER HEARD OF IT!
!
WALT DISNEY
12-16

MICKEY GETS HIS SCRIPT FROM MacCORKER, THE DIRECTOR, AND FINDS A QUIET CORNER TO READ IT!
12-17

WHAM!
BANG!
CLATTER!
BANG!
SCENE 3-A PROD M-23

GET A MOVE ON, YOU GUYS!
COMIN' RIGHT UP!
GANGWAY!
SCENE 3-A PROD M-23

BOY! I CAN'T WAIT TO GET STARTED!

GOOD! SEE THAT YOU'RE HERE MONDAY FOR REHEARSAL, THEN!
OH-- H'LO, MAC! SURE, I'LL BE HERE-- DON'T WORRY!
WALT DISNEY

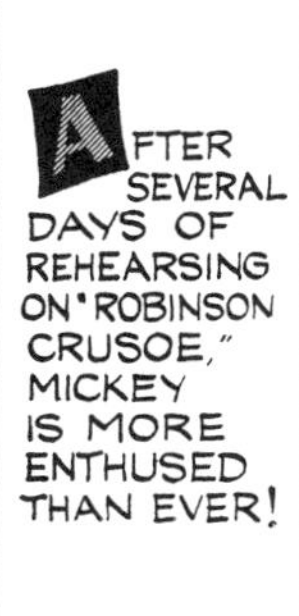
AFTER SEVERAL DAYS OF REHEARSING ON "ROBINSON CRUSOE," MICKEY IS MORE ENTHUSED THAN EVER!
12-19

SO YOU LIKE IT, DO YOU, MICKEY?
I'LL SAY! IT OUGHTA BE A SWELL PICTURE, MAC!

WHY NOT? I'M DIRECTIN' IT, AIN'T I?
WELL, I STILL SAY IT'LL BE GOOD!

OKAY, WISE GUY! I HOPE YOU GET SEASICK TOMORROW!
TOMORROW? ARE WE GOIN' ON LOCATION, MAC?
CUTTING ROOM No 4
NO SMOKIN

YOU GUESSED IT! ENTIRE COMPANY'S ON THE YACHT AT NINE O'CLOCK!
OH, BOY! I'M NOT MISSIN' THAT BOAT!

EARLY NEXT MORNING, MICKEY IS ON HIS WAY TO THE PIER TO JOIN THE "ROBINSON CRUSOE" COMPANY, GOING ON LOCATION.

HELLO, MAC! EV'RYBODY HERE? HOW SOON DO WE LEAVE? WHEN DO WE START SHOOTIN'?
WHOA! SLOW DOWN, OR YOU'LL BE AT THE PREVIEW, ALREADY!

A COUPLE OF HOURS LATER, THE YACHT DROPS ANCHOR OFF ABALONE ISLAND.
12-20

WELL, HERE WE ARE, MICKEY!
YEH! GOOD OLD ABALONE! WHERE ALL THE DESERT ISLAND PICTURES ARE MADE! BOY— WHAT A WILD, PRIMITIVE PLACE!
Copr 1938 by Walt Disney Enterprises World rights reserved
PREPARATIONS ARE BEING COMPLETED FOR SHOOTING THE FIRST SCENES OF "ROBINSON CRUSOE"

MAKE SURE THAT STUFF ON THE RAFT CAN'T SLIP!
AND WATCH THOSE REFLECTORS! DON'T LOSE ANY LIGHT!
IT'S ALL TIGHT, CHIEF!
OKAY, CHIEF!
Copr 1938 by Walt Disney Enterprises World rights reserved

A SHORT TIME LATER!
12-21

READY, THERE?
ALL READY!
CAMERA READY?
OKAY!
SOUND OKAY?
OKAY!
OKAY!
"MAC"
SCRIPT
WALT DISNEY

WITH EVERYTHING FINALLY SET FOR THE OPENING SCENE, "ROBINSON CRUSOE" IS NOW UNDER WAY!

A
S THE STORM ABATES A LITTLE, MICKEY SIGHTS A SMALL ISLAND JUST AHEAD. HE AND CRUSOE ANXIOUSLY HOPE FOR THE TIDE TO CARRY THEM IN!

A
FEW HOURS LATER, MICKEY AND CRUSOE ARE DELIGHTED TO SEE THAT THEIR RAFT IS BEING CARRIED TOWARD THE BEACH!

12-27

A
LTHOUGH MICKEY AND CRUSOE ARE WASHED ASHORE, THE RAFT, WITH ALL THEIR SUPPLIES, IS CARRIED OUT AGAIN! JUST AS THEY BEMOAN THIS LOSS, A HUGE WAVE ROLLS IN!

12-28

WELL, AT LEAST WE'RE ON DRY LAND! WONDER WHAT KINDA PLACE IT IS?
DEAR ME! I--I HOPE THERE AREN'T SAVAGES ABOUT!

I DON'T B'LIEVE ANYBODY LIVES HERE AT ALL! Y' CAN'T HEAR A SOUND!
DOUBTLESS YOU'RE RIGHT! WE'RE PROBABLY ALONE, UH-- PROBABLY!

HARK! I HEAR FOOTSTEPS!

HA! HA! NOTHIN' BUT A LITTLE BUNNY!
AND WE THOUGHT WE WERE IN DANGER!
THUMPITY!
THUMP!
WALT DISNEY
12-29

FUNNY HOW SCARED WE WERE BY THAT LITTLE RABBIT!
HA-HA! THAT WAS VERY AMUSING!

I VERILY BELIEVE WE VISIONED A LION WAS UPON US!

AR-R-ROUCH!
BONG
HUH?
12-30

WHA-WHAT WAS THAT?
I'M NOT--CERTAIN! BU-BUT IT WASN'T A RABBIT!
WALT DISNEY

AS NIGHT APPROACHES, MICKEY AND CRUSOE ARE WORRIED ABOUT SLEEPING AMID THE DANGER OF WILD ANIMALS.
12-31

I'VE GOT IT! WE'LL SLEEP UP IN THIS TREE!
OH, DEAR- --I FEAR ME I'LL NEVER SHUT AN EYE!

'TWILL NEVER DO! I SHAN'T GET A WINK UP HERE!
BUT IT'S THE SAFEST PLACE, MR. CRUSOE!

AFTER ALL-- I'M NO BIRD-- Z-Z-- TO BE- Z-Z- ZZ- Z-Z-
BOY! HE CAN'T SLEEP, EH?

HELP! THE RAFT'S SINKING!
WALT DISNEY

MICKEY IS HAVING QUITE A TIME TRYING TO TEACH CRUSOE TO SLEEP IN A TREE, SO AS TO BE SAFE FROM WILD ANIMALS.

MICKEY DOES NOT KNOW WHAT TO MAKE OF IT, AS AN APPARENTLY FRIENDLY TIGER CARRIES HIM DOWN FROM THE TREE!

MICKEY VOICES THE FEAR THAT IT MAY BE A LONG TIME BEFORE THEY ARE RESCUED FROM THE ISLAND AND THE THOUGHT DISTRESSES CRUSOE NO END

1-9

UH-- WHAT'S THE IDEA, MR. CRUSOE?
GOING TO BUILD A BOAT--- TO GET AWAY IN!

THAT'S A PRETTY BIG JOB, SIR! DON'T Y' THINK WE OUGHTA FIX A PLACE TO LIVE IN FIRST?

YOU'RE RIGHT, I FEAR! WE'RE DOOMED TO THIS PLAGUEY EXISTENCE! WE SHALL HAVE TO MAKE THE BEST OF IT. CURSE THE LUCK!
YES, SIR! LET'S GET RIGHT TO WORK ON OUR STOCKADE!
1-12

CRUSOE IS FINALLY CONVINCED THAT THERE IS NO ESCAPE FROM THE ISLAND, AND WORKS WITH MICKEY, BUILDING A STOCKADE TO PROTECT THEM FROM WILD ANIMALS.
Copr 1939 by Walt Disney Enterprises World rights reserved

MANY DAYS HAVE WE WORKED AT THIS AND NEITHER MAN NOR BEAST HAS BEEN SEEN!
ALL THE SAME, IT'S BETTER TO BE READY, IF THEY DO COME!
1-13

PERHAPS SO--- BUT THIS CEASELESS TOIL IS VERY WEARISOME! IT DEPRESSES ME GREATLY!

AS I SAID BEFORE-- ALL THIS, AH-- FRENZIED PREPARATION FOR DEFENSE---! AFTER ALL-- WHAT DO WE FEAR?
NOTHIN'--- IF WE'RE READY!
Copr 1939 by Walt Disney Enterprises World rights reserved

WE ARE MEN AND HAVE FIREARMS! SHOULD DANGER COME-- LET US FACE IT CALMLY!
YEH--AND LET'S BE ABLE TO SEE IT COMIN'! THAT'S WHY WE NEED THIS LOOKOUT!
1-14

ROWR-R-R!!
MUST BE A LION AROUND!
OH, MY STARS!

GOOD GRIEF! AND THIS FENCE NOT FINISHED!

THE ROAR OF A LION IN THE WOODS NEARBY FIRES CRUSOE WITH A BURST OF ENERGY AND HE FRANTICALLY FINISHES THE STOCKADE!

THERE, EGAD! I DEFY ANY CURSED BEAST OF PREY TO GET IN!
YEH--THE ONLY TROUBLE IS---
Copr. 1939 by Walt Disney Enterprises World rights reserved

---WE CAN'T GET OUT, EITHER! YOU FILLED IN WHERE OUR GATE WAS GONNA BE!
1-16

HORRORS! TRAPPED BY OUR OWN HAND! WE SHALL STARVE! WE SHALL PERISH! OH, WOEFUL DAY!
WALT DISNEY

THE CASTAWAYS HAVE FINALLY COMPLETED THEIR STOCKADE AND ARE ABLE TO BREATHE EASIER!
NOW, IF I BUT HAD SOME RAIMENT TO REPLACE THESE RAGS!
Copr. 1939 by Walt Disney Enterprises World rights reserved

YEH, I NEED CLOTHES, TOO! LET'S SEE IF THERE'S ANY IN THE STUFF WE BROUGHT ASHORE!

NOT A GARMENT IN THE WHOLE LOT! NAUGHT BUT A MESS OF WORTHLESS HIDES!
WORTHLESS? Y' MEAN THESE SWELL GOATSKINS?

BUT--BUT WE NEED CLOTHING!
AND WE'RE GONNA HAVE CLOTHIN'! HERE--JUS' TRY THIS FOR SIZE!
1-17
WALT DISNEY

THINK YOU TO MAKE GARMENTS FROM THESE CRUDE SKINS? WHY, THEY'LL BE--PREPOST'ROUS!
MAYBE SO---BUT THEY'LL BE PANTS!

I DREAD TO THINK WHAT MRS. CRUSOE WOULD SAY! SHE'S SO VERY FUSSY ABOUT MY WARDROBE!

HERE Y' ARE, SIR! TRY ON YOUR NEW SUIT!
1-18
Copr. 1939 by Walt Disney Enterprises World rights reserved

I MUST CONFESS, 'TIS--ER--QUITE ADEQUATE!
HOT DAWG! IT MAY NOT BE STYLISH, BUT IT SURE COVERS THE SURFACE!

MICKEY AND CRUSOE ARE CONGRATULATING THEMSELVES ON THE SAFETY OF THEIR STOCKADE, WHEN SUDDENLY A SECTION OF THE WALL BEGINS TO BULGE!

1-20

An elephant forces his way into the stockade, followed by a lion and tiger! Mickey and Crusoe scurry to safety on the lookout tower!
SMOKED FISH
MOLASSES

GOOD GRIEF-- OUR FOOD---!
Copr. 1939 by Walt Disney Enterprises World rights reserved

---THE BRUTES ARE EATING EVERYTHING! THEY'LL RUIN US!
AND--F'R PETE'S SAKE, LOOK AT THE ELEPHANT--!
1-23

---HE'S TRYIN' TO GET IN THE HOUSE!
GAD!
WALT DISNEY

HOW IN-- WHAT GOES ON---?
IT'S THAT- ---DARNED-- ELEPHANT!
1-24

HE'S SHAKIN' THE---?!!
HELP!!

OMIGOSH!

As the elephant jerks his head loose from the hut door, he shakes Mickey and Crusoe out of the tree!

'TIS THE END!
1-25

EH?

HE'S GOT ME! HELP! HE'S CARRYING ME OFF!
Copr. 1939 by Walt Disney Enterprises World rights reserved.

OF ALL THE---UG- GLUG--G- OWW!
WALT DISNEY

MICKEY AND CRUSOE FIND THAT THE ANIMALS ON THE ISLAND ARE, FOR SOME UNKNOWN REASON, AS TAME AS HOUSE CATS!

1-27

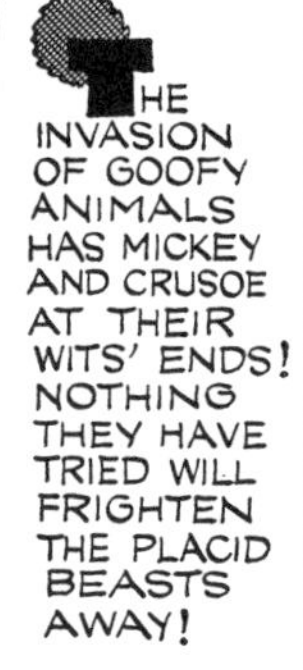

AFTER ALL ELSE HAS FAILED TO DRIVE THE ANIMAL PESTS AWAY, CRUSOE TURNS THE TRICK BY MAKING FACES AT THEM!

1-30

THEIR STOCKADE REPAIRED AND THE NEW SCARECROW ON GUARD AGAINST THE ANIMALS, MICKEY AND CRUSOE SET OUT TO EXPLORE THE ISLAND.

1-31

EXPLORING THE ISLAND, MICKEY AND CRUSOE ARE TERRIFIED TO DISCOVER THE PRINT OF A HUMAN FOOT!

AFTER FINDING THE HUMAN FOOTPRINT, MICKEY AND CRUSOE TURN BACK, EXPECTING EVERY MOMENT TO HAVE A HORDE OF SAVAGES SPRING OUT AT THEM!

R-3

FLEEING FROM THE MENACE OF SAVAGES, MICKEY AND CRUSOE ARE AMAZED TO FIND ONE PARKED ON THEIR FRONT STEP!

R-4

Copr. 1939 by Walt Disney Enterprises World rights reserved

FINDING A NATIVE IN THEIR STOCKADE WAS SURPRISE ENOUGH FOR MICKEY AND CRUSOE, BUT WHEN HE SPOKE---!!?
R-6

YOU--YOU WERE SAYING-- SOMETHING---?
AH SHO' NUFF WUZ, BOSS! AH SEZ, WHEN D' WE EAT?

MY WORD!
SEE THAT? HE DOES SPEAK ENGLISH!
WHUT'S FUNNY 'BOUT IT? AIN'T Y' ALL TALKIN' DAT WAY, TOO?

THIS IS ALL BESIDE THE POINT! SOMETHING MUST BE DONE, BEFORE THE REST OF THE SAVAGES ARE UPON US!

LAWSY MASSA, BOSS! IS SAVAGES A-COMIN'? DEN LET'S US GIT AWAY F'UM YERE FAST!
Distributed by King Features Syndicate, Inc

TU'N MUH LOOSE! IF DEY'S SAVAGES A-COMIN', I'SE GWINE ELSEWARD!
HOLD ON! WE DON'T KNOW ABOUT ANY SAVAGES! IT'S JUST A MISTAKE!
R-7

ARE YOU REALLY ALONE HERE? NO OTHER RASCALS ARE HIDING ABOUT?
DAT'S RIGHT, BOSS! I'SE D' ONLY RASCAL DEY IS!

PHEW--WHAT A RELIEF! THE CREATURE'S HARMLESS!
WELL, WHERE'D Y' COME FROM AND WHAT'RE Y' DOIN' HERE? HAVE Y' GOT A NAME?
SHO'! MAH NAME'S FRIDAY! AND SAY--- WHEN D' WE EAT?

FRIDAY? HOW'D Y' GET THAT NAME?
DEY GAVE IT TO ME WHEN AH WUZ BO'N, ON ACCOUNT OF AH'VE HAD BAD LUCK ALL MAH LIFE!
HUH !!?

SO FAR, ALL MICKEY AND CRUSOE HAVE LEARNED FROM THE NATIVE IS THAT HE IS ALONE AND HIS NAME IS FRIDAY!
R-8

Y' STILL HAVEN'T TOLD US WHAT YOU'RE DOIN' HERE---NOR WHERE Y' CAME FROM!
DAT'S VERY SIMPLE, BOSS! HERE'S HOW 'TIS--- YO' SEE, IT'S DISAWAY---

---AH HAPPENS T' LIVE NEX' DO'---AN' IT SEEMED LAK' AH OUGHTA BE NEIGHBO'LY AN' DRAP IN FO'-- AHEM--FO' A MESS O' VITTLES! DAT'S ALL!
Distributed by King Features Syndicate, Inc

POPPYCOCK! THERE'S NO PLACE NEXT DOOR--- NOR WITHIN MILES--- --IF ANY!
CERTAINLY NOT! DID Y' EXPECT US TO BELIEVE THAT YARN?

WELL-- LAWZY, BOSS-- --DAT WUZ ONLY MAH FUST TRY! EFFEN YO' HAIN'T B'LEEVIN' IT, AH KIN TELL YO' SOME DIFF'RUNT ONES!

ALL EFFORTS FAIL TO FIND WHERE FRIDAY CAME FROM--- HE TELLS A DIFFERENT STORY EVERY TIME!
R-9

NEVER HAVE I HEARD SUCH BOSH! THE CREATURE'S A **MASTER** AT PREVARICATION!
THANK YO', BOSS---THANK YO'!
Copr. 1939, by Walt Disney Productions.

WELL, LET'S FORGET HOW HE GOT HERE! WE CAN USE AN EXTRA PAIR OF HANDS, SO WHY NOT LET 'IM STAY?

DAWG-**GONE**, MAN-- YO' SHO' TUK D' WORDS RIGHT OUTEN MAH MOUF! YERE AH **STAYS**!
HM-M! THINK YOU THE RASCAL WILL EARN HIS SALT?
WELL --O' COURSE, FRIDAY, Y' UNDERSTAND YOU'LL HAFTA **WORK** FOR YOUR KEEP!

OH-OH! DAT SETTLES IT--- YERE AH **GOES**!
WALT DISNEY

Y' MEAN YOU'RE **LEAVIN'**, RATHER THAN DO A LITTLE WORK FOR US?
YASSUH-- YO' SEE, AH BEEN RAISED KINDER DELICATE AND---!
R-10

Y' LIKE TO **EAT** THOUGH, DONTCHA? Y' WOULDN'T EXPECT US TO SHARE OUR **FOOD** UNLESS---!
!

SAY NO MO', BOSS--- I'SE YO' MAN! YO' SHOULD'A MENTIONED DAT **FOOD** BEFO'! WHEN D' WE EAT?
PRETTY SOON! WHADDYA LIKE?

KIN AH HAVE **HIM**?
Distributed by King Features Syndicate, Inc

DID YOU HEAR THAT? THIS SAVAGE---- THIS **DEPRAVED** WRETCH--- ACTUALLY WANTS TO **EAT** ME!
WELL, AH NEVER ET NOBUDDY AND AH KINDER LAK' TO SEE HOW HE TASTE! DIDN'T **'SPECK** HE'D 'LOW IT--AH JES' **ASKED**, DAT'S ALL!

AREN'T YOU ASHAMED? WANTIN' TO EAT PEOPLE--WHY, THAT'S **TERRIBLE**! HOW'D Y' LIKE IT IF SOME CANNIBALS WANTED TO COOK **YOU** FOR DINNER?
LAWSY, BOSS-- AH **WOULDN'T** LAK' IT! AND DAT REMINDS MUH, DEY'S CANNIBALS AFTER MUH, RIGHT NOW!

EH? WHAT'S THAT?
SHO'! DEY WUZ ON MUH TRAIL--- A WHOLE SLATHER OF 'EM, BUT AH FOOLED 'EM AND COME IN YERE!

GREAT GUNS!
'S ALL RIGHT, BOSS-- DEY AIN'T LAK'LY FOUND MUH **YET**! DEY'S POWAHFUL SLOW, DEM BABIES IS-- YASSUH!
WALT DISNEY
R-11

MICKEY AND CRUSOE ARE VERY ALARMED WHEN FRIDAY TELLS THEM THAT CANNIBALS ARE FOLLOWING HIM! HOWEVER, SEVERAL HOURS PASS WITH NO SIGNS OF THEM.

R-13

ANOTHER ONE OF YOUR YARNS, EH? TRYIN' TO TELL ME YOU TRAINED A PARROT TO HERD GOATS!
BUT AH HAVE, BOSS! AH DONE TOLE YO' DIS YERE FOWL'S MAH HELPER!

JES' YO' WAIT! SEE 'AT BUCK STRAYIN' OFF DERE?
YEH-- I SEE HIM!

AWK---WHAR YO' THINK YO'RE GWINE, YO' LOP-EARED BAG O' BONES? SQUAWK--AWK!
R-16

SQUAWK--- GIT BACK DAR, 'FO' AH PULVERIZE YO'---AWK!
WELL, I'M A MONKEY'S UNCLE!
YASSUH!
WALT DISNEY

TO MICKEY'S COMPLETE AMAZEMENT, FRIDAY HAS ACTUALLY TRAINED A PARROT TO HERD GOATS!

YASSUH--DAT 'ERE FOWL DONE EASE D' RIGORS O' MAH LABOR QUITE CONSID'ABLE! YASSUH!
YEH-- I COULD SEE THAT!
Copr 1939, by Walt Disney Productions World rights reserved

WELL--Y' STILL HAFTA CARRY WATER FOR 'EM, AND IT'S TIME RIGHT NOW! BETTER GET GOIN'!
OH, AH GOT DAT ALL TOOKEN KYAR OF, TOO!

NOW, LOOK HERE-- DON'T TRY TO TELL ME THE PARROT DOES THAT, TOO!
NO, SUH! BUT 'AT WATER'S A-COMIN' UP--- YERE 'TIS NOW!
Distributed by King Features Syndicate, Inc.

F' GOSH SAKES! WHAT NEXT?
JEST ANUDDER ASSISTANT AH BEEN TRAININ'!
WALT DISNEY
R-17

AT DINNERTIME, CRUSOE HEARS OF FRIDAY'S LABOR-SAVING DEVICES WITH SOME SKEPTICISM.
R-18

IT'S A FACT, SIR! THEY'RE REALLY CLEVER!
HUMPH! WISH HE WAS CLEVER ENOUGH TO GET A DECENT MEAL! BEANS--CORN-CORN-BEANS! GAD, WHAT I'D GIVE FOR A ROAST CHICKEN!
SLUP! SLUP! GULP!
Copr 1939, by Walt Disney Productions World rights reserved

LISTEN-- THERE'S PLENTY OF WILD DUCKS ON THE ISLAND! LET'S GO HUNTING!
A MOST SAVORY IDEA, EXCEPT--- IS IT SAFE TO LEAVE OUR HABITATION UNGUARDED?

WE'LL LEAVE FRIDAY HERE--HE KNOWS HIS JOB WELL ENOUGH NOW! ANYWAY, HE'LL PROB'LY TRAIN A SQUIRREL TO WASH DISHES OR SOMEP'N, WHILE WE'RE GONE!

SEE THAT YOU GUARD THE PLACE WELL, YOU RASCAL!
REST YO' MIND AT EASEMENT, BOSS! JES' BRING BACK PLENTY O' DEM ROASTED DUCKS, 'ATS ALL!
Distributed by King Features Syndicate, Inc

SEEKING A CHANGE OF DIET, MICKEY AND CRUSOE LEAVE THEIR MAN, FRIDAY, AT THE STOCKADE AND GO DUCK HUNTING. THEY RETURN, WELL PLEASED AT THEIR SUCCESS.

MICKEY AND CRUSOE ARE AMBUSHED BY CANNIBALS, BUT FRIDAY'S SIZZLING FEET ENABLE HIM TO ESCAPE!

CAPTURED BY CANNIBALS. MICKEY IS TAKEN BEFORE THE KING, WHOSE MILD MANNER AND SEEMING FRIENDLINESS KEEPS MICKEY GUESSING.

HM-M-M! AFTER DUE CONSIDERMENT AND COGITATERIN', AH BEGINS TO HAB MAH DOUBTS!
UH-- DOUBTS---?
©Copr. 1939, Walt Disney Productions World Rights Reserved

IN FACK--- AH KIN SEE DAT YO' WON'T DO! TOO BAD!
CLAP! CLAP!!

Y' MEAN-- I'M NO GOOD TO EAT?
WHAT AH MEAN, IS---
2-27

---DAT YO' AIN'T NO GOOD FO' NUFFIN' ELSE BUT! PUT 'IM BACK IN D' PANTRY, DARWIN!
YOWSAH, YO' MAJESTY!

SMALL FRY KIN KEEP A BIT! YO NEXT, SOURPUSS -- HIS MAJESTY DESIAHS YO' COMP'NY!
OH-H DEAR-- HE WON'T LIKE ME! I-I'M NOT WELL-- -I'D DISAGREE WITH HIM!

YOU SAID, YOURSELF THE KING IS, ER-- DELICATE! HE'D NEVER BE ABLE TO---!
AW, BUTTON YO' MOUF! D' KING'LL MEK' UP 'IS OWN MIND!

AH! AM DIS D' OTHAH SPECIMEN, DARWIN?
YOWSAH, YO' MAJESTY!
2-28

WELL, SINGE MAH WHISKAHS, EFFEN HE AIN'T JEST WHAT D' DOCTAH ORDERED!
ALACK! OH, WOE IS ME!
WALT DISNEY

MAN, I'SE SHO' JUBILATED TO HAVE YO' AMONGST US! 'DEED AH AM!

BUT, YOUR MAJESTY! SURELY YOU- --YOU CAN FIND BETTER THINGS TO EAT THAN ME! I-I JUST KNOW I'LL TASTE TERRIBLE!
SO YO' AIN'T HANKERIN' TO BE DUNKED IN A SOUP KITTLE, EH? WELL, LISTEN, MAN---

---MAH PLANS CONCERNIN' D' INTERMEJIATE FUTURE DOES NOT INCLUDE EATIN'! I'SE GOT OTHAH IDEAS!
Y-YOU HAVE?
3-1

AT THE SAME TIME, MICKEY IS ALSO MAKING OTHER PLANS!
IF THOSE APES'LL LEAVE ME ALONE A WHILE, THEY'RE GONNA FIND AN AWFUL VACANT ROOM HERE!
WALT DISNEY

WHILE MICKEY STRUGGLES TO FREE HIMSELF CRUSOE IS WITH THE CANNIBAL KING. TO CRUSOE'S GREAT RELIEF, THE KING DOES NOT INTEND TO EAT HIM!

CRUSOE DISCOVERS WHY HIS LIFE IS TO BE SPARED--- THE KING WANTS TO GET RID OF HIS WIVES AND PRESENTS THEM ALL TO HIM!

MICKEY HAS FREED HIMSELF AND IS ABOUT TO RELEASE CRUSOE, WHEN HE HEARS ONE OF THE GUARDS COMING!

WHEN MICKEY DECIDES TO ESCAPE HE REALLY MEANS IT!

AFTER ALL MICKEY'S VALIANT EFFORT TO REACH THE STOCKADE AND GET GUNS, HE FINDS A PARTY OF NATIVES WAITING FOR HIM!

WHEN THE CANNIBALS ANCHOR MICKEY WITH A BIG CHAIN AND PADLOCK, THINGS BEGIN TO LOOK PRETTY BAD.

TO FORESTALL ANY CHANCE OF THE PRISONERS ESCAPING, THE KING HAS A GUARD CHECK UP EVERY FEW MINUTES.
MICKEY, HOWEVER, CONTRIVES A PLAN TO FOOL HIM!

OH-- MY WORD!

?
?

EH? WHERE AM I?
LOOK, MAN-- JUS' WHUT YO' A-DOIN', ENNYHOW?
3-13

I--I MUST HAVE BEEN SLEEP-WALKING! YOU KNOW-- YOU CLOSE YOUR EYES AND HOLD OUT YOUR ARMS--VERY INTERESTING!

LIKE DIS? WHY DERE'S NUFFIN TO IT!
DON' MAKE NO SENSE TO ME!

WHITE FOLKS MIGHTY DUMB!
YO' SED IT!
WALT DISNEY

CRUSOE HAS BEEN GONE TWO DAYS AND MICKEY IS PRETTY WORRIED.

WHAT COULD'A HAPPENED? HE SAID HE'D BE BACK AN' RESCUE ME!

OH-OH--THAT LOOKS BAD! THEY'RE GETTIN' READY FOR A FEAST!
3-14

HERE Y' ARE! BUT WHAT--?
ALAS, MICKEY-- 'TIS NO USE! I SAT ON A STUMP AND PONDERED FOR TWO DAYS---

---AND NOT ONE PLAN OF RESCUE COULD I THINK OF! WE'LL JUST HAVE TO REMAIN PRISONERS!
WALT DISNEY

I'LL BE DOGGONED IF I'M GOIN' TO SIT AROUND WAITIN' TO BE COOKED! THERE MUST BE A WAY TO GET RID O' THIS DARNED PADLOCK!
IT LOOKS HOPELESS TO ME!

WHERE'D THEY EVER GET THE BLAME THING, ANYWAY?

I'D LIKE TO BUST IT ON THE--- HUH!!?
3-15

GOOD GRIEF! SUPPOSE THE GUARD HAD SEEN IT?
!
CLICK!
WALT DISNEY

BY ACCIDENT, MICKEY GETS THE PADLOCK OPEN, BUT CRUSOE, IN A SUDDEN PANIC SNAPS IT SHUT AGAIN!

ALL MICKEY'S STRUGGLES ARE OF NO AVAIL---THE STUBBORN PADLOCK REFUSES TO OPEN.

AS MICKEY MAKES HIS ESCAPE THROUGH THE WINDOW, A GUARD COMES IN JUST IN TIME TO STOP CRUSOE FROM FOLLOWING.

ESCAPING FROM THE CANNIBAL VILLAGE AND INTO THE JUNGLE, MICKEY IS SURPRISED TO DISCOVER THEIR EX-SERVANT, FRIDAY.

Y' SAY YOU WERE BACK IN THE VILLAGE, TOO?
YASSUH, BOSS! NOT PREZACKLY IN DAR, BUT KINDER LURKIN' 'ROUND D' EDGES, YO' MIGHT SAY!
3-20

WHAT WAS THE BIG IDEA?
WELL--AH SORTA WANTED TO SEE HOW Y'ALL WUZ GITTIN' 'LONG!
DEN AH GOT TO WATCHIN' D' PREPAREMENTS FO' D' BIG FEAST AND---!

FEAST? WHEN'S THIS GOIN' TO BE?
TONIGHT! DIDN'T YO' KNOW, BOSS?

SHO'! TONIGHT'S WHEN DEY GWINETER DINE OFFEN MISTAH CRUSOE!
!
WALT DISNEY

FRIDAY BREAKS THE NEWS THAT THE CANNIBALS INTEND TO PUT CRUSOE IN THE POT THAT NIGHT!

THAT'S RIGHT--I REMEMBER NOW! THE KING WARNED HIM THAT THE FEAST WOULD BE AT THE NEXT FULL MOON!
---WHICH AM TONIGHT!
3-21

IT'S JEST AN OLD CUSTOM WID DEM BABIES! WHEN D' MOON GIT FULL, DEY AIM TO DO LIKEWISE!
WELL, THEY WON'T GET AWAY WITH IT! CRUSOE'S GOT TO BE RESCUED--SOMEHOW!

HECK! IF WE DO GET FREE, WE'LL ONLY BE CAUGHT AGAIN! WE CAN'T GET OFF THE DOGGONE ISLAND!

LOOKY, BOSS--IF Y'ALL WANTS TO LEAVE, WHYN'T YO' TAKE DAT SAILIN'BOAT WHAT AM ANCHORED OFF-SHO'?
WH-WHAT?!!
WALT DISNEY

DAT'S WHUT AH SAID, BOSS! DEY'S BEEN A SAILIN'BOAT LAYIN' OFF SHO' FO' D' PAST SEBEN, EIGHT WEEKS!
NOW LOOK, FRIDAY---THIS IS NO TIME FOR YOUR TALL STORIES!
3-22

WE'VE GOT TO THINK OF A WAY TO RESCUE CRUSOE--IN A HURRY!
WELL--OF CO'SE, EF YO' DON'T WANNA USE DAT 'ERE SAILIN'BOAT---!

COME ON! LET'S SETTLE THIS RIGHT NOW!
YASSUH!

DAR SHE AM, BOSS!
WELL, F'R---HOT DOG!
WALT DISNEY

The discovery of a ship anchored off the island fills Mickey with new hope. He hastily builds a big fire as a signal.

Deep gloom descends over Mickey when the mysterious ship completely ignores his signal fire.

Friday has managed to smuggle a few guns and supplies out of the stockade and hide them from the cannibals.

With the aid of Friday's trained parrot and some odds and ends, Mickey hopes to get Crusoe out of his perilous fix!

Night falls, and in the cannibal village the natives prepare a sumptuous feast!

FRIDAY'S TRAINED PARROT AND THE WEIRD GET-UP OF MICKEY AND FRIDAY ARE ENOUGH TO SCARE THE CANNIBALS OUT OF THEIR WITS!

STOP! OR WE'LL PERFOLATE YO!
TRY AN' STOP US, BIG BOY!
4-6
Copr. 1939, Walt Disney Productions World Rights Reserved

GAD! ARE WE ACTUALLY SAFE?
YES, SIR! WE'RE OUTA RANGE, NOW!
HOT DAWG!

GREAT GUNS! WE'RE LOST AGAIN!
Distributed by King Features Syndicate, Inc.

JUST AS MICKEY'S PARTY THINK THEY ARE SAFE, A HUGE CANOE SUDDENLY APPEARS! HEAVILY MANNED, IT GAINS QUICKLY ON THE LITTLE BOAT!
LAWZY---WE'S GONERS!
THERE'S JUST ONE CHANCE---!
Copr. 1939, Walt Disney Productions World Rights Reserved
4-7.

BAM!
Distributed by King Features Syndicate, Inc.

HOT DOG! THEY WON'T GET FAR THAT WAY!
BRAVO! WELL SHOT, MICKEY!
YASSUH, AH NEVAH HEERED NO MUSIC SO SWEET AS DAT 'ERE BAM!
WALT DISNEY

FINALLY ESCAPING FROM THE LAST OF THE CANNIBALS, MICKEY AND HIS COMPANIONS HEAD FOR THE MYSTERIOUS SHIP!
SHIP AHOY! WE WANT TO COME ABOARD!
AHOY! RIGHTO---WE'LL LOWER A LADDER!
Copr. 1939, Walt Disney Productions World Rights Reserved

WELCOME, GENTLEMEN---!
4-8
Distributed by King Features Syndicate, Inc.

WELCOME, IN THE NAME OF THE QUEEN!
AND CONGRATULATIONS! YOU HAVE MADE OUR SCIENTIFIC VOYAGE A COMPLETE SUCCESS! BRAVO!

SAFELY ABOARD THE SHIP, MICKEY'S PARTY IS WARMLY GREETED BY TWO ECCENTRIC SCIENTISTS WHO ARE IN CHARGE. THEY ARE ON AN EXPEDITION TO STUDY UNUSUAL LIFE IN REMOTE PARTS OF THE WORLD!

NEXT MORNING. OUTFITTED WITH NEW CLOTHES FROM THE SHIP'S STORES, MICKEY AND CRUSOE BEGIN TO FEEL MORE LIKE THEMSELVES.

THE FINAL SCENE OF "ROBINSON CRUSOE" HAS BEEN SHOT AND THE COMPANY PREPARES TO LEAVE THE ISLAND LOCATION.
MAKE IT SNAPPY, BOYS! LET'S GET GOIN'!
4-13

HOW'D I DO, MAC?
Y' DID ALL RIGHT, SON! IT SHOWS THAT A CLASSY DIRECTOR CAN GET RESULTS OUT OF ANYBODY!

OH, BOY, I'M NEARLY HOME --- AND, BELIEVE ME, WHEN I GET THERE I'M GOIN' TO STAY PUT --- FOR A WHILE!
WALT DISNEY

IT'S ABOUT TIME I CAUGHT UP WITH SOME O' MY READIN'!
4-14

SLAM!
H'LO, UNCA MICKEY!
MAMA SAID WE COULD COME AN' STAY WITH YOU!
UH-- YEH?

FINE, BOYS! IS THERE ANY, UH-- SPECIAL OCCASION FOR THIS VISIT?
OH, NO, UNCA MICKEY ---NOTHIN' SPESHUL!
WE JUST CAME TO SEE Y'---THAT'S ALL!

I LIKE UNCA MICKEY, DON'T YOU?
I SURE DO--DON'T YOU?
HMMM-M-M!
WALT DISNEY

H'YA, MICKEY, OL' KID, OL' SOCKS! HOW YUH FEELIN'?
FINE, GOOFY! WHAT'S ON YOUR MIND?
4-15

OH, NUTHIN' ATALL! I JES' COME OVER TO SEE HOW YUH WUZ! YUH'RE LOOKIN' FINE, MICKEY!
THANKS! I SEEM TO BE GETTIN' A LOT OF ATTENTION- -- MY NEPHEWS ARE VISITIN' ME, TOO!

YES -- HEH-HEH- -- WE'RE HERE, TOO!
HA-HA! ISN'T THAT FUNNY?
WELL, WHADDYA KNOW--- AIN'T THET SOME COINCERDENCE?
?

NO DOUBT ABOUT IT--- SOMEP'N DEFINITELY IS UP!

B-Z-Z---
B-Z-Z---
B-Z-Z--!
WONDER WHAT THEY'RE UP TO?
Copr 1939, Walt Disney Productions
World Rights Reserved
4-17

LET US MAKE YOU COMFY, UNCA MICKEY!
HERE Y'ARE MICKEY!
REST YOUR HEAD, UNCA MICKEY!

HERE'S THUH VACATION SECTION FOR YUH!
Distributed by King Features Syndicate, Inc.

IS HE FIXED UP NICE, NOW?
YEP---HE'S THUH PITCHER O' SOLID COMFORT, B'GAWRSH!

POP CORN

WELL, WE SURE FIXED MICKEY UP GOOD AN' COMF'TABLE!
NOW LET'S ASK HIM TO TAKE US TO CAMP PHOOEY!
Copr 1939, Walt Disney Productions
World Rights Reserved
4-18

MICKEY, WILL YUH--ER I MEAN--ARE YUH--ER--HOW YUH FEELIN'?
FINE! I WAS FEELIN' LIKE GOIN' TO CAMP PHOOEY FOR SOME REST...

--BUT YOU'VE MADE ME SO COMFORTABLE I'M GOIN' TO STAY RIGHT WHERE I---

---AM!!?
Distributed by King Features Syndicate, Inc.

GOSH, I'D LIKE TO TAKE YOU ALL OUT TO CAMP PHOOEY, BUT MY JALOPY'S NOT BIG ENOUGH! IF WE ONLY HAD A TRAILER OR SOMETHIN'---!

?
4-19

HEY, WHAT'S THE BIG IDEA?
GOOFY SAID THE CHICKENS COULD USE OUR HOUSE IF---

---WE USE THEIRS!
Distributed by King Features Syndicate, Inc.

Copr 1939, Walt Disney Productions
World Rights Reserved

HEY, MICKEY--- I'M AFEERED WE WENT AND LOADED HER TOO HEAVY!

4-20

NOPE! ABSOLUTELY NOT! THERE JUST ISN'T **ROOM** TO TAKE PLUTO WITH US!
4-21

LATER
MY GOSH! WONDER WHAT THAT CROWD'S DOIN' IN FRONT O' THE HOUSE!

OUR PAL PLUTO
WE WANT PLUTO
PLUTO SHOULD COME CAMPING, TOO
MICKEY IZ UNFAIR

HEH-HEH! SHUCKS, BOYS --I WAS ONLY FOOLIN'! WE MAY BE A LITTLE CROWDED, BUT WE'LL **FIND** A WAY TO TAKE HIM ALONG!
OUR PAL PLUTO

TO CAMP PHOOEY

PLUTO

4-22

PLUTO

C'MON OUT, Y' LAZY MUTT--- Y' NEED **SOME** EXERCISE!
PLUTO
Distributed by King Features Syndicate, Inc.

OH, BOY--- WE'LL SURE HAVE SOME FUN WHEN WE GET TO THE CAMPSITE!
Copr. 1939, Walt Disney Productions World Rights Reserved

4-24

!
WALT DISNEY

HEY, MICKEY--- STOP TH' CAR! A GOSH DARN GOAT JUST ET OUR BROOM!

HEY, YOU! QUIT EATIN' MY BROOM!
4-25

WISE GUY, HUH?

WALT DISNEY

LET'S STOP AN' GO FISHIN', UNCA MICKEY!
WE'RE GOIN' TO THE CAMP SITE AND WE'RE NOT STOPPIN' FOR ANYTHING!
4-26
Copr. 1939, Walt Disney Productions World Rights Reserved

BAM

?
Distributed by King Features Syndicate, Inc.

---AND DON'T FORGET, KIDS-- THE LIMIT IS ONE FISH!
Copr. 1939, Walt Disney Productions
World Rights Reserved

4-27

!

4-28

GOSH! WHAT'S WRONG WITH PLUTO?
GRR-R-GR-R!
Copr. 1939, Walt Disney Productions
World Rights Reserved
4-29

LOOK! A WILD ANIMAL!

S-STEADY, NOW, GOOFY!
I'LL GIT 'IM RIGHT BETWEEN TH' EYES!

BANG
BANG

Copr 1939, Walt Disney Productions
World Rights Reserved

HEY, GOOFY--STOP WHEN Y' GET TO A GOOD PLACE! I WANTA HANG OUT THE WASHIN'!
5-1

OUR CLOTHES--- WHERE ARE THEY?
WE HUNG 'EM UP, UNCA MICKEY!
Distributed by King Features Syndicate, Inc

!
WALT DISNEY

GAWRSH! LOOKIT ALL THUH WILD DUCKS!
NEVER MIND THE DUCKS! KEEP DRIVIN' WHILE I TAKE IN THE WASH!

WELL, I CAN'T HELP THINKIN' O' DUCKS WHEN ALL WE EVER HAVE TO EAT IS BEANS!
YEAH-- BEANS!

WHAT'RE WE HAVIN' FER SUPPER T'NIGHT ---BEANS?
NO---

---DUCKS!

CAN PLUTO SLEEP IN THE TRAILER TONIGHT? IT'S STARTING TO RAIN!
LET IT RAIN--- HIS DOG HOUSE IS DRY! ANYHOW, HE'D MAKE IT TOO CROWDED IN HERE!

Copr 1939, Walt Disney Productions
World Rights Reserved
5-3

PLUTO

GOSH, GOOFY, ARE Y' SURE Y' TOOK THE RIGHT DETOUR?
DURN RIGHT I DID!
5-4

THIS TUNNEL'S A SHORT CUT, MICKEY--- IT'LL SAVE A LOTTA TIME!

GOSH, WE'VE BEEN IN THIS TUNNEL TWO HOURS!
LOOK, THERE'S A LIGHT---WE MUST BE GETTIN' OUT!

!
!
!
6000 FT BELOW SURFACE LEVEL

HEY, GOOFY, BETTER LET THOSE APPLES ALONE! THAT BULL DOESN'T LOOK FRIENDLY!

AW, BULLS DON'T HURT YUH! I READ A BOOK ABOUT A BULL AN' ALL HE DID WUZ SMELL FLOWERS!
5-5

I'D LIKE TO GET TH' GUY THAT WROTE THAT BOOK!

IF YOU'RE GOIN' TO DRAG THAT CONTRAPTION ALONG BEHIND, YOU'VE GOTTA PUT A RED FLAG ON IT!
PLUTO
5-6

GOOD NIGHT! A BULL'S CHASIN' US, AN' IT SURE AIN'T FERDINAND!
!
PLUTO

STEP ON 'ER, MICKEY --- I THINK WE'RE GAININ'!

SPEEDIN' NOW, HUH? THIS TIME YUH GET A TICKET!

GOSH, GOOFY---WHAT A TRAFFIC JAM! WE'LL NEVER GET TO THE SITE!
5-8
Copr 1939, Walt Disney Productions World Rights Reserved

LEAVE IT T' ME, MICKEY--- I'LL FIX IT!

THE FINANCE COMPANY IS LOOKIN' FOR THUH GUY WHO'S BEHIND IN HIS PAYMENTS!

GOOD NIGHT, MICKEY
GOOD NIGHT, GOOFY!
G' NIGHT!
G' NIGHT!
5-9

CRASH

SHE WON'T FALL DOWN AGIN, I BETCHER!
BANG
BAM
BANG

NEXT MORNING.
ZZZZ
ZZZZZZ
ZZZZZ

HEY, GOOFY, WHY'RE 'Y' STOPPIN'?
IT SORTA LOOKS LIKE WE'RE STUCK IN THE MUD!
Copr 1939, Walt Disney Productions World Rights Reserved
5-10

IT'S NO USE! WE'LL SPEND THE NIGHT HERE AND GET HER OUT IN THE MORNING!

FRESH CONCRETE
Distributed by King Features Syndicate, Inc.

HEY, GOOFY, HOW'D Y'EVER GET ON THIS ROAD?
I ASKED A FARMER!
5-11

WHAT'D HE SAY?
HE DIDN'T SAY NUTHIN'---HE JUST POINTED THIS WAY!

WE'LL SEE HIM WHEN WE GET BACK TO THE MAIN ROAD!
JUST SHOW ME THAT FARMER!

THAT'S HIM!

!
!

NICE WORK, GOOFY! NOW SHE'S A SIDE CAR!
5-12

B-B-BUT, OFFICER---!
THE LAW'S TH' LAW! TRAILERS BELONG ON TH' REAR!

CHEER UP, GOOFY---ONLY A HUNDRED MILES MORE TO THE SITE!

HURRAY! WE'RE NEARLY THERE!
WHOOPEE!
WHEE!

HERE'S A GOOD PLACE! LET'S CAMP UP HERE FOR THE NIGHT!
OH, BOY! WHAT A SIGHT WE'LL SEE IN THE MORNING!

?
?
?
?
5-13

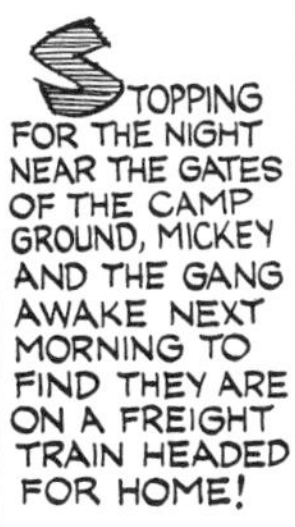
STOPPING FOR THE NIGHT NEAR THE GATES OF THE CAMP GROUND, MICKEY AND THE GANG AWAKE NEXT MORNING TO FIND THEY ARE ON A FREIGHT TRAIN HEADED FOR HOME!

FER GAWRSH SAKES! HOW'D WE GIT HERE?
YOU MUSTA DRIVEN ONTO THIS FLAT CAR IN THE DARK! NOW, HOW'RE WE GONNA GET OFF?
BAW! WE WANNA GO CAMPIN'!

GREAT JUMPIN' WOMBATS! SO HOBOES IS TRAVELIN' IN STYLE, NOW!
HONEST, WE'RE NOT HOBOES! WE WERE ON A CAMPIN' TRIP AND KINDA GOT ON HERE BY MISTAKE!

WELL, TH' NEXT TIME YUH TRY TO STEAL A RIDE HOME, THINK UP A BETTER YARN! YER GETTIN' OFF HERE---SEE!
UH-HAW!
YES, SIR! THANKS! HERE IS WHERE WE LIVE!
BAW! WE DIDN'T GET TO THE CAMP!
5-15
WALT DISNEY

AW, UNCA MICKEY, WHY CAN'T WE GO BACK TO THE CAMP?
YOU PROMISED TO TAKE US, UNCA MICKEY!
PLUTO
5-16
Copr. 1939, Walt Disney Productions World Rights Reserved

LISTEN, BOYS---I DID TAKE Y'! IT WAS GOOFY'S FAULT, GETTIN' ON THAT FREIGHT TRAIN THAT BROUGHT US HOME! PESTER HIM IF Y' WANTA GO AGAIN!

YER RIGHT, MICKEY! IT WUZ MY FAULT THUH KIDS MISSED THUH CAMP AN' I'M GONTER MAKE AMENDS, B'GAWRSH!

YES, SIR! YOU TAKE US BACK AGIN AN' THIS TIME I WON'T PARK ON NO FREIGHT TRAIN!
WALT DISNEY

FOR THE HUNDREDTH TIME--- I'M NOT GOIN' TO MAKE THAT TRIP TO THE CAMP GROUNDS AGAIN!
AW-W---!
PLEASE-- UNCA MICKEY!
Copr. 1939, Walt Disney Productions World Rights Reserved
5-17

NO! AND IT'S HIGH TIME Y' PUT YOUR MINDS ON SOMETHIN' ELSE! GO GET ME A STORY AND I'LL READ TO Y'!
WELL-L--- ALL RIGHT!

AND I HOPE THAT'S THE LAST I HEAR OF CAMPIN' TRIPS!

OMIGOSH!
BUT YOU SAID YOU'D READ US A STORY!
YOU PROMISED, UNCA MICKEY!
HIGHLIGHTS OF CAMP
The STORY OF CAMP PHOOEY
Come TO CAMP PHOOEY
Your CAMP
CAMPING
TO SEE
Distributed by King Features Syndicate, Inc

BR-R-R-R
R-RI-NNNG!
FOR THE LAST TIME--NO!! I CAN'T TAKE ANOTHER TRIP TO THE CAMP SITE!
BAW!
WAW!
THE STORY OF CAMP PHOOEY
Come to CAMP PHOOEY
YOUR CAMP
the CAMP
CAMPING
What TO SEE
CAMP
5-18

TELEGRAM FER MICKEY MOUSE!
THAT'S ME!
TELEGRAM
Copr. 1939, Walt Disney Productions
World Rights Reserved

IT'S FROM YOUR MOTHER! SHE SAYS TO COME HOME----
?
?

---THEY'RE GONNA TAKE Y' TO CAMP PHOOEY!
YIPPEE!
WHEE!
Distributed by King Features Syndicate, Inc.

BOY, IT'S SURE SWELL--YOUR FOLKS TAKIN' Y' TO THE CAMP! IT JUST MAKES EV'RYTHING HUNKY-DORY AND---!
YEH! YEH ---CAN WE GO NOW?
Copr. 1939, Walt Disney Productions
World Rights Reserved
5-19

G'BYE, UNCA MICKEY!
WELL! G'BYE! HAVE A GOOD TIME!

WELL, S'LONG, MICKEY! SEE YUH LATER!
HEY---WHERE DO Y' THINK YOU'RE GOIN'?

I'M GOIN' WITH THE KIDS' FOLKS! THEY'LL NEED AN EXPERIENCED GUIDE THET KNOWS TH' WAY----AN' I'M IT!
WALT DISNEY

SINCE ALL MY VISITORS LEFT, THIS PLACE IS TOO QUIET TO BE NATURAL!
Copr. 1939, Walt Disney Productions
World Rights Reserved
5-20

GOSH, WHAT A RAINY NIGHT! I'M GLAD I DON'T HAVE TO BE OUT IN IT!
BRRR-R-R-R-R-RING

WHO? POLICE CHIEF O'HARA--AND Y' WANTA SEE ME?
YES, MICKEY! WE'VE GOT A MYSTERY THAT'S BAFFLED THE WHOLE FORCE! HOW'D YOU LIKE TO TRY YOUR HAND AT HELPING US?
WALT DISNEY

BOY-OH-BOY---A MYSTERY! AND THE CHIEF SOUNDED PRETTY WORRIED, TOO! HOT DOG!
Distributed by King Features Syndicate, Inc.

MICKEY MOUSE OUTWITS THE PHANTOM BLOT

MAY 22, 1939
–
SEPTEMBER 9, 1939

PHANTOMS, FEARS AND FORESHADOWING

Ruthless, silent, efficient; covered from head to toe in a sinister black cloak, the Phantom Blot is arguably Gottfredson's most menacing villain. Witness the ominous way he stalks his prey. He silently appears in the back seat of a taxi; stealthy as a ghost, he pins a threatening handwritten note on Chief O'Hara; with astonishing cheek, he abducts a victim straight from the police station.

The Blot's elaborate deathtraps are genuinely scary. Their Rube Goldberg mechanisms are triggered by the victim's involuntary cooperation, adding the suspense of torture—and the torture of suspense!—to an already-threatening setting. Even the usually brave Mickey starts shaking when he reads the Blot's first warning note.

In "Mouse history" context, recurring baddie Pegleg Pete is often a figure of fun; a gallery of more menacing one-shot villains—from Professor Triplex to Dr. Vulter—are ferocious, but hardly haunting. By contrast, the Blot is truly mesmerizing. The felon's all-covering black mantle means he could be anyone: we and Mickey are left to wonder whether bit players, such as anonymous policemen or store managers, might turn out to be the deadly criminal. Curiously, the Blot's actual facial features—as revealed at story's end—*do* bear some resemblance to a bit-part shopkeeper seen earlier. More significantly, though, the Blot's face may remind the alert reader of Gottfredson's boss!

Detective Casey, here making his second appearance, is now "demoted" to a dumber role with the introduction of the smarter, more experienced Chief O'Hara. But even O'Hara is incapable of unraveling the mystery behind the Blot's obsession with cheap cameras. It will take a fearless and resourceful Mickey to get to the bottom of this puzzle—risking his life several times in the process.

So effective, so gripping is this spy story that beyond its bad guy, its *structure* influenced later Mickey talents. Romano Scarpa, Gottfredson's foremost artistic heir, loved the "Blot" story when he read it as a teenager—and built one of his most famous Mickey masterpieces, "Kali's Nail" (1958), on a very similar plot. Here too, a spy hides a secret formula in a shipment of goods that he must then steal back from retailers. Scarpa's treatment is original, but the homage is still recognizable.

When Gottfredson's "Blot" is not foreshadowing later Mickey stories, it is anticipating other world events. Mickey leads us to a secret underground hideout he once built, knowing "it would be handy some day"; an ominous 1939 echo of the bomb shelters that—thanks to World War II—many readers would soon come to know all too well. Meanwhile, "Blot"'s adrenaline-pumping action scenes, from a motorboat ride to a car chase, look ahead to classic James Bond movies. Risky business for a secret agent; even riskier for a Mouse!

— Francesco Stajano and Leonardo Gori

GOSH, I CAN'T IMAGINE WHY THE CHIEF O' POLICE WANTS TO SEE ME ON A NIGHT LIKE THIS!
5-22
Copr. 1939, Walt Disney Productions World Rights Reserved

ANYWAY, HE SAID IT'S A MYSTERY THEY CAN'T SOLVE, SO THAT SOUNDS LIKE FUN!

WOW--I'M GETTIN' SOAKED!
HEY--TAXI!

VACANT
HULLO, MICKEY! CLIMB UP FRONT AND TELL ME WHAT BRINGS Y' OUT IN THIS WEATHER!
OH--HELLO, JOE! I'M BOUND FOR POLICE HEADQUARTERS!
TAXI

SO, YOU'RE WANTED BY THE COPS, EH? I OUGHTA MAKE Y' RIDE IN THE BACK!
HAVE A HEART, JOE---I NEED COMPANY!

FUNNY THING--THE CHIEF O' POLICE WANTIN' TO SEE Y' TONIGHT!
YEH, IT IS KINDA MYSTERIOUS. PROB'LY NOTHIN' IMPORTANT, EITHER!
5-23
Copr. 1939, Walt Disney Productions World Rights Reserved

NAW! NOTHIN' UNUSUAL EVER GOES ON IN THIS BURG!
YOU SAID IT! WELL, G'NIGHT, JOE!

AHA!
POLICE HEADQUARTERS
ENTRANCE

GR-R-R!
POLICE HEADQUARTERS
WALT DISNEY

AH, HERE Y' ARE, MICKEY---I'VE BEEN WAITIN' FOR YE!
I CAME AS FAST AS I COULD, MR. O'HARA! WHAT'S ON YOUR MIND?

ER--LET'S GO--AHEM--INTO A PRIVATE ROOM!
HELLO, MR. CASEY--HOW ARE Y'?
H'LO!
5-24

SHH-H!-DON'T SAY A WORD TILL EVERYTHING'S LOCKED FAST AND TIGHT!
BUT, GOSH---WHO CAN GET INTO POLICE HEADQUARTERS?
CLICK!

LISTEN, MICKEY! THIS--THIS "PHANTOM" WE'RE AFTER CAN POP UP ANYWHERE ---AT ANY TIME!
PH-PHANTOM!?

POLICE CHIEF O'HARA HAS CALLED MICKEY INTO HIS OFFICE FOR A VERY MYSTERIOUS CONFAB. HE LOCKS ALL DOORS AND TAKES UNUSUAL PRECAUTIONS.

NOW THAT WE'RE ALONE, I'LL EXPLAIN THE SET-UP! YE SEE, THIS "PHANTOM" KNOWS CASEY AND ALL OUR **REGULAR** DETECTIVES---
CLICK!
5-25

---BUT HE'D NEVER SUSPECT **YOU**! THAT'S---**EH!!?**
OH--PARDON **ME**, CHIEF! FORGOT Y' WAS BUSY!

AS I WAS SAYING--- BEFORE--- **WHAT TH'--?**
'SCUSE **ME**, CHIEF--- SAY--DID Y' HEAR THE ONE ABOUT THE TWO IRISHMEN--

ALL RIGHT, CASEY! Y' KNOW **DARN** WELL WHAT MICKEY'S HERE FOR, SO YE MIGHT AS WELL SIT IN ON IT!
THANKS, CHIEF! HOPE I'M NOT BUTTIN' IN!

AS I STARTED TO TELL YE, THE BIRD WE'RE AFTER IS WISE TO CASEY AND OUR OTHER SNOOP-HOUNDS! **ALSO**, HE'S TOO SLICK FOR 'EM!
5-26

IZZAT SO? LISTEN, CHIEF, I CAN---!
QUIET! THE TRUTH IS, MICKEY, WE'RE COMPLETELY STYMIED!
WHAT SORT OF GUY **IS** THIS CROOK?

HE CALLS HIMSELF THE "**BLOT!**" AND HE'S ALWAYS TOGGED OUT TO LOOK SOLID, DEAD BLACK, WITH ONLY HIS EYES SHOWIN'! HE'S PLENTY WEIRD, **I'M** TELLIN' YE!

AND TO SHOW HE'S NOT JUST CLOWNIN' FOR TH' FUN OF IT, HERE'S A LOVE NOTE HE SENT US!

My dear
Why be so cruel and heartless? Put your men on some other case, where they have a CHANCE to live! Be humane!
WOW!
WELL, HE DIDN'T SCARE **ME** ANY!

BOY--THIS "BLOT" SURE SOUNDS LIKE A DANGEROUS CHARACTER!
DON'T LET THAT WARNIN' FOOL YOU--HE'S JUST A CRACKPOT, THA'SALL!
5-27

CRACKPOT MY EYE! HE'S THE SMARTEST THIEF WE EVER RAN UP AGAINST!
YEAH---WELL, WHYN'T HE SWIPE SUMPIN' BESIDES **CAMERAS?** IS **THAT** SMART?
?
?

Y'MEAN--THAT'S **ALL** HE EVER TAKES?
RIGHT! HE'S PASSED UP CASH, JEWELS AN' **EVERY**THING --TO GET CAMERAS!

AND WHAT'S HE **DO** WITH 'EM? SMASHES 'EM AND THROWS 'EM AWAY! DON'T THAT **PROVE** HE'S A LOONY DOPE?
IF **YOU** COULD EVER CATCH HIM, **THAT'D** PROVE IT!

THE POLICE HAVE ASKED MICKEY'S AID IN TRYING TO SOLVE A MOST UNUSUAL AND BAFFLING SERIES OF ROBBERIES COMMITTED BY AN ELUSIVE CROOK WHO CALLS HIMSELF THE "BLOT." THIS THIEF STEALS ONLY CAMERAS --NOTHING ELSE!

THE LIGHTS IN THE POLICE CHIEF'S OFFICE SUDDENLY GO OUT! THERE IS A SCUFFLE IN THE DARK AND WHEN THE LIGHTS GO ON AGAIN MICKEY HAS DISAPPEARED!

BY TOPPLING OVER THE TABLE TO WHICH HE IS TIED, MICKEY NARROWLY ESCAPES FROM THE "BLOT'S" DEATH-DEALING DEVICE!

EXTRY! ALL ABOUT THE BIG CAMERA ROBB'RY!
MUGGINS' DEPARTMENT STORE ON EAST MAIN ST. I'LL GO OVER AND HAVE A LOOK!
G-5
Copr. 1939, Walt Disney Productions World Rights Reserved

OH -- SPECIAL INVESTIGATOR, EH? WELL, THIS IS JUST ANOTHER MYSTERY LIKE ALL TH' OTHERS HAVE BEEN!

LOOKS LIKE HE HAD TO SCRAM BEFORE HE COULD GET THE REST OF THESE!
OH, NO--THEY'RE A DIFFERENT BRAND---

---Y' SEE, THE "BLOT" ONLY GOES AFTER JUST ONE MAKE!
! ! ?

IF THE "BLOT" ONLY STEALS THIS ONE MAKE OF CAMERA -- MAYBE IT'S GOT SOME VALUABLE PART OR---
HARDLY! THE WHOLE THING SELLS FOR ONLY THIRTY CENTS!
G-6
Copr. 1939, Walt Disney Productions World Rights Reserved

GOSH! THAT MAKES IT EVEN TOUGHER TO FIND A MOTIVE!
WELL, THAT'S YOUR JOB! I'M ON A MORE IMPORTANT CASE--- MICKEY MOUSE HAS BEEN KIDNAPED!

YEH? WHAT MAKES THAT MORE IMPORTANT THAN TRYIN' TO SOLVE THIS BUSINESS?

ANYWAY, WHO, UH---
HEY! I'M MICKEY MOUSE!
WHY, OF COURSE-- -- SO Y' ARE!
Distributed by King Features Syndicate, Inc.
WALT DISNEY

WELL, SINCE YOU'RE NOT KIDNAPED, AFTER ALL, I'D BETTER CALL THE CHIEF AND TELL HIM! HE THINKS THE "BLOT" HAS YOU!
HE DID HAVE ME, BUT I GOT LOOSE! NEVER MIND THE CALL -- I WANT TO TALK TO THE CHIEF, MYSELF!
G-7
Copr. 1939, Walt Disney Productions World Rights Reserved

--- AND, LISTEN, MR. O'HARA, I'VE GOT A COUPLA HUNCHES I'D LIKE TO TRY OUT, SO I MAY NOT BE AROUND FOR A WHILE!
OKAY, MICKEY- -- JUST WORK YOUR OWN WAY! ONLY TAKE EVERY PRECAUTION!

NOW, TO GET THOSE BUSTED CAMERAS AND EXAMINE 'EM WHERE I WON'T BE INTERRUPTED!

HM-M-M! NO SIGN OF ANYTHING UNUSUAL ON THIS ONE!

FAILING TO GET ANY CLUES FROM THE BROKEN CAMERAS, MICKEY STARTS OUT TO LOOK FOR THE "BLOT," HIMSELF!

MICKEY HAS CONCOCTED A NEW SCHEME, THE SUCCESS OF WHICH DEPENDS ON LURING THE "BLOT" INTO A CHASE!

ARMED WITH CAMERAS OF THE MAKE THE "BLOT" IS AFTER, MICKEY HOPES TO ATTRACT HIS ATTENTION AND LURE HIM INTO A CHASE.

MICKEY'S PLAN TO LEAD THE "BLOT" INTO CHASING HIM SUCCEEDS ONLY TOO WELL!

ALTHOUGH MICKEY PURPOSELY LED THE "BLOT" INTO A CHASE, HE DID NOT MEAN IT TO BE QUITE SO CLOSE!

PLANNING TO DROP OUT OF SIGHT AND WORK FROM UNDER COVER, MICKEY INTENDS TO FOOL THE "BLOT" BY A COMPLETE AND MYSTERIOUS DISAPPEARANCE!

Receiving a note saying that Mickey has been kidnaped and warning her not to inform the police, Minnie instantly goes straight to headquarters!

Rushing Minnie and Casey out, Chief O'Hara locks himself in and goes to work on the code in the Mickey-kidnap note.

Realizing that the code message in Mickey's "phony" kidnap note must be kept secret, Chief O'Hara tells Minnie they need do nothing about it!

NOW THAT WE KNOW MICKEY HAS **NOT** BEEN KIDNAPED, LET'S GO BACK TO THE NIGHT HE TRICKED THE "BLOT" INTO A MERRY CHASE!

CONFOUNDING THE "BLOT" BY AN AMAZING DISAPPEARANCE, MICKEY HAS DROPPED FROM SIGHT INTO A SECRET TUNNEL UNDER HIS BACK YARD!

SECURE IN A SECRET HIDEOUT BENEATH HIS REAL HOME, MICKEY PREPARES TO GIVE THE BAFFLING CAMERA MYSTERY EVERYTHING HE'S GOT, DETERMINED TO FIND THE SOLUTION!

MICKEY LEAVES HIS SECRET HIDEOUT DISGUISED AS AN OLD MAN. HE FEELS HIS GET-UP MUST BE A SUCCESS WHEN PLUTO ANGRILY CHASES HIM OUT OF THE YARD!

While waiting for a reply cable from the camera manufacturers, Mickey decides to investigate the warehouse where the shipments are landed!

Snooping around the waterfront, Mickey is startled by bumping into the "Blot." He tries to cover his confusion, counting on his disguise to get him out of the jam.

FORGETTING HIMSELF FOR AN INSTANT, MICKEY TIPS HIS HAT TO THE "BLOT" AND EXPOSES HIS DISGUISE!

THE "BLOT" HAS RIGGED MICKEY UP ON A RAFTER IN SUCH A WAY THAT IF HE FALLS ASLEEP AND TUMBLES OFF HE WILL HANG HIMSELF!

MICKEY IS IN ONE AWFUL FIX! TO FALL OFF THE RAFTER MEANS SURE DEATH BY HANGING! AND THE "BLOT" HAS DOPED HIM WITH SLEEPING POWDERS!

DOPED WITH SLEEPING POWDERS AND FACING CERTAIN DEATH IF HE FALLS, MICKEY MANAGES TO CATCH HIS COAT ON A NAIL. SUSPENDED THERE, HE SLEEPS OFF THE EFFECT OF THE DRUG.

STILL HANGING PRECARIOUSLY BY HIS COAT COLLAR ON A NAIL, MICKEY SUCCEEDS IN WORKING HIS HANDS IN FRONT OF HIM AND GETTING A KNIFE FROM HIS POCKET!

UNABLE TO GET RID OF THE NOOSE THE "BLOT" PUT AROUND HIS NECK, MICKEY STARTS FOR HOME, ONLY TO BE PINCHED AS AN ATTEMPTED SUICIDE! POLICE CHIEF O'HARA COMES TO HIS RESCUE.

MICKEY LEAVES THE POLICE CHIEF'S OFFICE, FULL OF RENEWED PEP AND DETERMINED THAT THE "BLOT" HAS BEEN GETTING AWAY WITH THINGS LONG ENOUGH!

ALL RIGGED OUT IN THE VERY LATEST IN DISGUISES, MICKEY PURSUES HIS INVESTIGATIONS DOWN AT THE MAMMOTH DEPARTMENT STORE!

MICKEY HUSTLES BACK TO HIS ROOM.

FINDING THAT A MYSTERIOUS CRIME WAS REPORTED THE SAME DAY THE FIRST SHIPMENT OF "LITTLE KORKER" CAMERAS ARRIVED, MICKEY NOW FEELS THAT HE IS GETTING SOMEWHERE!
HE RUSHES BACK TO THE POLICE DEPT!

HI, CASEY!
HULLO--- WHAT TH' DICKENS---?!!
7-20

LOOK, MR. O'HARA ---I'M ON A HOT CLUE, SO DON'T SLOW ME DOWN! HOW MANY CAMERAS HAVE BEEN STOLEN ALTOGETHER?
WELL, WELL --- YE SURE ARE BUSY THESE DAYS! I'LL GET THOSE FIGURES FOR YE!

---TO DATE, THE NUMBER STOLEN IS 237!
237-- THANKS!
SWISH!

BACK IN MICKEY'S LAB AGAIN.
THE ORIGINAL LOT WAS 250 CAMERAS--- THAT LEAVES JUST THIRTEEN TO BE FOUND!
THAT SETTLES IT--FROM NOW ON IT'S A RACE WITH THE "BLOT" FOR THOSE THIRTEEN CAMERAS!

MICKEY REALIZES THAT HIS ONLY CHANCE OF SUCCESS LIES IN BEATING THE "BLOT" TO THE LAST 13 CAMERAS!
7-21

THESE SALES SLIPS SHOW THE NAMES OF EVERYBODY THAT BOUGHT ONE OF THE CAMERAS ---
Copr. 1939, Walt Disney Productions World Rights Reserved

---FROM WHICH I CHECK OFF THE STOLEN ONES ACCORDIN' TO THE POLICE REPORT---

---AND IT GIVES ME THE NAMES OF THE MISSING THIRTEEN! HOT POTATO! NOW TO GET AFTER 'EM!

WELL? WHAT D' YE WANT?
WHY--UH-- I HAPPEN TO BE MAKING A COLLECTION OF, ER---ODD CAMERAS! I HEARD YOU HAD A SPECIMEN HERE!
WALT DISNEY

SO YE COLLECT ODD CAM'RAS, DO YE?
THAT'S RIGHT! AND I'M READY TO BUY THE "LITTLE KORKER" YOU OWN!
7-22

IT COST ME THUTTY CENTS, NEW! WOULD YE BE WILLIN' TO PAY--- SAY, THREE DOLLARS?
WELL, AHEM-- THAT'S A BIT STEEP --- BUT I GUESS MAYBE I COULD---!

YEAH? WELL, YE DON'T SWINDLE ME, MISTER! THERE'S SUMPIN' MIGHTY VALLYBLE ABOUT THEM CAM'RAS, OR THIS HERE ROBBER GUY WOULDN'T BE AFTER 'EM---

--- SO I'M KEEPIN' MINE 'TIL I FIND OUT WHAT I GOT!
SLAM!!
OUCH! I'M NOT MAKIN' SUCH A HOT START!
WALT DISNEY

ARMED WITH A LIST OF NAMES, MICKEY IS TRYING TO BAG THE LAST 13 CAMERAS BEFORE THE "BLOT" CAN GET TO THEM! SO FAR, HE HASN'T HAD MUCH LUCK!

ONLY TEN CAMERAS LEFT ---AND NO WAY TO TELL WHICH ONE CONTAINS THE KEY TO THE MYSTERY! THE "BIG BLOT" AND MICKEY, AS THE "LITTLE BLOT," RACE AGAINST TIME!

SIX MORE CAMERAS NABBED, BUT STILL THE RIGHT ONE HASN'T TURNED UP!

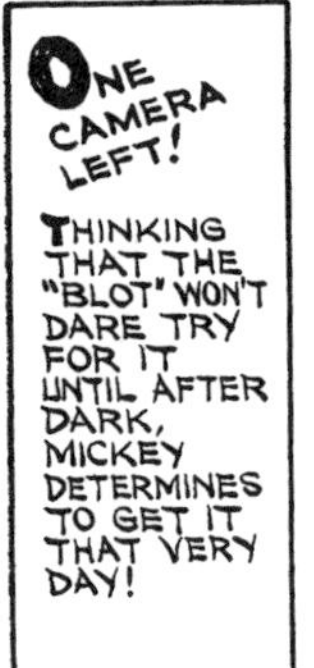

LEARNING THAT THE OWNER OF THE LAST REMAINING CAMERA LIVES OUT IN THE COUNTRY, MICKEY LOSES NO TIME IN GETTING THERE!

ALL RIGHT, MR. PERKINS --- THIS NIECE Y' GAVE THE CAMERA TO --- WHERE DOES SHE LIVE?
26 ELM ST! 'COURSE I DON'T KNOW IF SHE'S STILL GOT IT --- AWFUL ROUGH ON TOYS, THAT CHILD ---!
GAS
8-3

---ANYWAYS, YE KIN ASK HER MA--THAT'S MY SISTER---THOUGH, WHY YE WANT A WUTHLESS CAM'RA, I DON'T KNOW----!

ELM STREET--- ABOUT ONE CHANCE IN A MILLION THAT DARN CAMERA STILL EXISTS! 22 --24---!

---GOOD GOSH! CAN THAT BE-- IT IS! I'VE GOT IT!!
LOOKIT THE BIRDIE, PLEASE!
WALT DISNEY

---BUT, LISTEN, LITTLE GIRL---YOUR UNCLE SILAS SENT ME! HE'S LETTING ME BUY THE CAMERA-- --SEE, HERE'S TH' MONEY!
NO! IT'S MINE ---MINE! DON'T WANT NASTY OLD MONEY!
8-4

COME NOW, TOOTSIE--- WHADDYA SAY WE GO IN AND TALK TO MAMA?
NAME'S NOT TOOTSIE ---MA'S NOT HOME, SHE'S TO AUNT GUSSIE'S ---AND THIS IS MY OWN CLICK-BOX!

LOOK, THEN---LET'S GET IN TH' CAR AND RIDE OVER TO AUNT GUSSIE'S!
NO! NO! YOU LEMME 'LONE! MA DON'T 'LOW ME TO RIDE 'CEP'N I KNOW PEOPLE!
ICE CO

AND, PERFECTLY RIGHT, TOO! YOU'RE A GOOD CHILD--YES-- HEH-HEH---ALWAYS MIND MAMA---!
STICKLEVILLE ICE CO.
PAT PAT!
WALT DISNEY

HE TRIED TO TOOK MY CLICK-BOX, HE DID!
HEH-HEH! Y' SEE, THE CHILD DOESN'T UNDERSTAND--- I WAS BUYING HER UNCLE ---ER, I MEAN-HIS CAMERA SEE---!
ICE
GRR G-R-R
8-5

GO 'WAY! DON'T WANT NASTY OLD MONEY!
GOOD GOSH! AM I GOIN' TO LOSE THIS THING AFTER ALL I'VE BEEN THROUGH?

I'LL BE DARNED IF I AM!
HEY

HELP! POLICE!
ROBBERS!
KIDNAPERS!
WALT DISNEY

WITH THE LONG SOUGHT CAMERA FINALLY IN HIS POSSESSION, MICKEY BEATS A HASTY RETREAT FROM STICKLEVILLE'S ANGRY BUT MISUNDERSTANDING CITIZENS!

AFTER FINALLY GETTING THE CAMERA THAT CONTAINS THE MYSTERIOUS HIDDEN PAPER, MICKEY IS AGAIN OUTWITTED BY THE "BLOT!" THE VILLAIN FORCES MICKEY'S CAR OFF THE ROAD, CRASHING IT INTO A TREE!

Copr 1939, Walt Disney Productions
World Rights Reserved

Copr 1939, Walt Disney Productions
World Rights Reserved

Distributed by King Features Syndicate, Inc.

AGAIN CAPTURED BY THE "BLOT," MICKEY IS FORCED INTO ANOTHER OF THE VILLAIN'S INFERNAL DEVICES!

WOW! WHAT A PICKLE! A BURNING CANDLE IS GIVING MICKEY THE HOT FOOT, BUT TO MOVE HIS FOOT WILL FIRE THE GUN OVERHEAD!

DROPPING ONE LEG OF THE STOOL THROUGH A KNOT HOLE, MICKEY OVERTURNS IT, BARELY ESCAPING THE BULLET MEANT FOR HIM!

Copr 1939, Walt Disney Productions
World Rights Reserved

JUST AS HE IS FREEING HIMSELF FROM ONE OF THE "BLOT'S" DEADLY DEVICES MICKEY SUDDENLY FINDS HIMSELF FALLING THROUGH A TRAP DOOR!

ESCAPING MIRACULOUSLY FROM ONE TRAP AFTER ANOTHER, MICKEY IS GROGGY BUT STILL DETERMINED TO KEEP AFTER THE "BLOT!"

MAKING HIS GETAWAY IN A STOLEN SPEEDBOAT, THE "BLOT" IS AMAZED TO DISCOVER MICKEY CLINGING TO AN AQUAPLANE ATTACHED TO THE STERN!

THROWN LOOSE FROM THE "BLOT'S" SPEEDBOAT, MICKEY LANDS IN ANOTHER BOAT WHICH STARTS OFF CARRYING HIM THROUGH THE WATER AT A RIOTOUS PACE!

UNKNOWN TO THE "BLOT," WHO IS MAKING HIS ESCAPE IN A PLANE, MICKEY GRABS PART OF THE PLANE AND HOISTS HIMSELF ABOARD!

Apparently making a safe get-away in a seaplane, the "Blot" is suddenly startled when the plane starts to turn out of his control!

Meanwhile, at police head-quarters, Detective Casey is ready to present his complete case to Chief O'Hara!

Out over the sea the "Blot" finds his plane mysteriously turning back toward land!

With the "Blot" unable to control its course, Mickey forces the seaplane to turn back!

DETECTIVE CASEY IS ABOUT TO CLINCH HIS CASE AGAINST THE "BLOT" WITH THE FINGERPRINT RECORD FROM WASHINGTON!

MICKEY, HIDDEN ON THE PLANE'S TAIL IS STEERING THE SHIP DOWNWARD IN HOPE OF FORCING A LANDING!

SEEING THE "BLOT" BAIL OUT OF THE FALLING PLANE, MICKEY TAKES A QUICK CHANCE AND JUMPS AFTER HIM!

WHILE MICKEY BRINGS DOWN THE "BLOT" IN A BLOODLESS AIR BATTLE, CHIEF O'HARA IS STILL SIZZLING OVER CASEY'S BLUNDER!

The "BLOT'S" confession tells of being the agent for a foreign syndicate which was after a secret formula being taken to America! On shipboard he high-jacked the messenger of the valuable paper!

THE MIRACLE MASTER

SEPTEMBER 11, 1939
–
JANUARY 13, 1940

"—WELL, I'LL BE DARNED! I DON'T KNOW IF I DREAMED ALL THAT, OR—"

The "it was all a dream" ending is the archetypal comics-writing cop-out: most typically a sign that the storyteller can't figure out how to solve plot problems. Yet this cop-out has become such an industry standard that we are unfazed when we see it used today. That said, it might have been a slap in the face when 1940 readers saw it employed by Gottfredson in "The Miracle Master"; it was the first (and last) time he used it in a story that he plotted.

Gottfredson may have succumbed to the cliché because—like many of its victims—he had written himself into a corner. Mickey and a genie have spent over half the story trying to magically improve Mickey's cynical hometown when the genie suggests they return to his own impoverished homeland. Here in "Genieland," the genie lives with his family in a giant rusty lamp/house amid charlatan "sleight-of-hand" magician beggars. As Mickey tries to better these people's lives, things get more confusing for both the Mouse and the narrative.

Perhaps this is because, by the time we get to Genieland, "The Miracle Master" has already made its point. We have seen a stubborn, jaded modern community—Mouseton—hurt itself by refusing to accept magical gifts. No subsequent, similar sequence could possibly speak more profoundly. In Genieland, Gottfredson tries to prove that greed and distrust know no race or creed; but his strictly gag-format approach, teeming with flighty-women jokes, undermines any seriousness his point might have.

Moreover, the illogic of the Genieland arc is prone to more scrutiny in the immediate wake of the Mouseton arc's social commentary. The genie's people are supposedly immortals—but how *can* they be, if they are incapable of real magic? Gottfredson needed a real Miracle Master to get out of this one.

The larger story, however, is still significant in that it introduced genuine fantasy to the *Mickey Mouse* daily strip. In previous serials, Gottfredson had taken pains to give solid, rational explanations for all of the fantastic, seemingly otherworldly phenomena Mickey encountered. "The Miracle Master" marked the first time Gottfredson eschewed reality and simply ran with the idea of genuine magic. Considering he had spent an entire decade working against the concept, it's no wonder Gottfredson had trouble resolving Mickey's encounter with the bona-fide supernatural. Concluding that none of it was real to begin with may have been the only viable option for him at this stage.

In a way, "The Miracle Master" is a fitting coda to the Gottfredson of the 1930s. A fresh decade demanded more challenging, unconventional situations for Mickey—calling for Gottfredson to retool his style as he penned them. And the majority of these would be adventures that neither Mouse nor artist could just dream his way out of. After all, this world ain't magic!

— Thad Komorowski

Y' AIN'T HEARD ABOUT MINNIE? WHY, SHE'S GONE IN FOR ANTIQUES--- CURIOS AN' SUCH! SAKES ALIVE, IT'S A **RAGE** WITH HER!
GOSH! WHAT'LL SHE THINK OF NEXT?
9-11

I S'POSE IT'S A GOOD HOBBY IF Y' KNOW WHAT YOU'RE GETTIN', BUT MINNIE **DOESN'T**! BOY--THEY CAN SELL HER ANYTHING!

GUESS WOMEN ARE LIKE THAT--- ALWAYS A LITTLE DUMB OR FOOLISH! THEY WALK INTO SOMETHIN' WITH THEIR EYES OPEN, BUT---!

BLAWW-W!
HEY, YOU!
HONK!
SCREE-EE-E---!
BEEP-EEP-EEP!
TWEE-EE-EET!
HONK!

YUH DARN **DOPE**!
WAKE UP!
DUMBBELL!
HONK!
BEEP!
Distributed by King Features Syndicate, Inc.

DARN IT! THAT'S PROB'LY MINNIE WANTIN' ME TO GO SHOPPIN' WITH HER FOR SOME OF HER PRECIOUS ANTIQUES!
R-R-R-R-R-R-R

YES, MINNIE, THIS IS- ---**WHAT**?!! WHAT'S **WRONG**---?
OH, MICKEY---**QUICK**! COME **RIGHT AWAY**--- DON'T LOSE A **MINUTE** ---**HURRY**- --**HURRY**--
9-12

GOSH! SOMETHIN' TERRIBLE'S GOIN' ON---

---HOPE I GET THERE---IN TIME!

MINNIE! WHERE **ARE** Y'? WHAT'S HAPPENED?

LOOK! ISN'T IT **EX**-QUISITE? REAL, **GENUINE** HEPPLEDALE! I'M SO **THRILLED**--- I JUST **HAD** TO CALL YOU--!!
WALT DISNEY

I MUST TEACH YOU SOMETHING ABOUT ANTIQUES! CAN YOU GUESS WHAT THIS BEAUTIFUL PIECE COST?
YOU MEAN--- Y' HAD TO **PAY** FOR ---FOR THAT STEPLADDER?
9-13
Copr 1939, Walt Disney Productions World Rights Reserved

SILLY GOOSE! IT'S AN **EXTREMELY** RARE EXAMPLE --CAN'T BE DUPLICATED!
CAN'T BE VERY COMFORTABLE, EITHER, I'LL BET!

E-E-EEK! DON'T YOU **DARE**! THE IDEA--THINKING THAT'S TO **SIT** IN! SUCH IGNORANCE!
HUH? I'M SORRY, MINNIE! I'VE BEEN SITTIN' IN CHAIRS FOR YEARS---NEVER KNEW IT WAS WRONG!

DON'T GET FUNNY---I'M **TRYING** TO TEACH YOU SOMETHING! DO YOU SEE THIS OLD HAND MIRROR?
YEH, DON'T TELL ME--I KNOW---

---IT'S **VERY** RARE AND Y' MUSTN'T **LOOK** IN IT! I LEARN FAST!

TO PROVE THAT MINNIE CAN'T TELL A GENUINE ANTIQUE FROM A BOGUS, MICKEY GOES TO AN OLD JUNK SHOP, LOOKING FOR SOMETHING TO FOOL HER WITH.

SOMET'ING TO LOOK OLD AND HISTORICS, YOU SAID! I ASK YOU --DOES **THAT**---?
NEVER MIND --IT'S WHAT I WANT! HOW MUCH?
NO SALE
9-18

SEVEN DOLLARS IT COST ME, FIVE I'M ASKING--- I'LL TAKE THREE-FIFTY!
HERE--TAKE IT **QUICK**, OR YOU'LL BE PAYIN' **ME!**

BOY, WILL I HAVE FUN WITH MINNIE WHEN I MAKE A THREE-FIFTY LAMP LOOK LIKE A PRECIOUS ANTIQUE!

ALL I GOTTA DO IS TAKE OFF THE WIRIN' AND --SAY--- IT'S **EXACTLY** LIKE A PICTURE FROM "ARABIAN NIGHTS!" IF I DON'T LOOK OUT I'LL BELIEVE MY OWN GAG!
WALT DISNEY

YES, SIR---A LITTLE "DE-MODERNIZING" AND I'LL BET I CAN KID MINNIE INTO THINKIN' THIS IS A RARE OLD ORIENTAL LAMP!
9-19

WONDER IF IT REALLY LIGHTS!

HUH?
OUCH!

DID--DID SOMEBODY SPEAK?
WALT DISNEY

GOSH! I MUST BE CUCKOO--- THINKIN' I HEARD VOICES IN THAT LAMP!
9-20

OF COURSE, IT COULDN'T BE! ALL I DID WAS TO PLUG IT IN LIKE THIS AND---

CUT IT OUT!!!

IT **D-DID** TALK---I **S-S-SWEAR** IT DID!

I'M SOME DOPE! BUY A LAMP TO KID MINNIE THAT IT'S AN OLD ANTIQUE--- THEN KID **MYSELF** THAT IT TALKS!
9-21

JUST VIBRATIONS FROM A SHORT IN THESE WIRES, THAT'S ALL!

OF COURSE! EMPTY! I ALMOST THOUGHT I HAD A **MAGIC** LAMP--- ONE O' THE KIND THAT Y' RUB---

---AND SAY SOMEP'N LIKE--- **ALI-GA-ZAM, ALI-KA-BOOBLA--- LET THE GENIE APPEAR!**

DIDST THOU CALL, MASTER?
WALT DISNEY

THY HUMBLE SERVANT, OH, MASTER!
UH-- ULP---!
9-22

WHAT? HE SWOONS?
PLOP!

COME, MASTER-- THAT'S ONLY FOR WEAKLINGS AND WOMANKIND!

WHO--WH-WHAT ---B-BUT--- ARE YOU **REAL?**
WHY, CERTAINLY! THAT IS, I THINK SO--- UNLESS I'M DREAMING!

HERE--- PINCH ME!
WALT DISNEY

Y-YOU **ARE** --REAL?
OF COURSE --UNLESS I'M DREAMING! GO AHEAD --PINCH ME AND SEE!
9-23
Copr. 1939, Walt Disney Productions, World Rights Reserved

OUCH! YES, IT'S ME ALL RIGHT!

NOW, WHAT IS MY GRACIOUS MASTER'S BIDDING TO THIS HUMBLE SLAVE OF THE LAMP? WHY DIDST CALL ME?

OH, I DIDN'T! I--I MEAN, IT--IT'S NOTHIN' ---JUST A SORT OF A MISTAKE, I GUESS---!
SO! I AM CALLED TO CHASE THE WILD GOOSE! THOU RUB THE MAGIC LAMP, BUT WANT **NOTHING!**
Distributed by King Features Syndicate, Inc.

MY GREAT AND NOBLE MASTER IS IN ALL THINGS MOST WISE! HE IS INDEEDLY A VERY FOUNT OF WISDOM---

---EXCEPT THAT HE SEEMETH TO BE A HALF-WIT!

BUT, MASTER--I DON'T UNDERSTAND! MANY LONG CENTURIES I HAST BEEN IN THE LAMP, UNDISTURBED! THEN SUDDENLY I AM CALLED--- TO NO PURPOSE!
WELL--UH, GOSH! I DIDN'T KNOW IT WAS A MAGIC LAMP--- NOBODY BELIEVES SUCH THINGS ANY MORE!
9-25
Copr 1939, Walt Disney Productions
World Rights Reserved

WHAT! DOST MEAN TO SAY THE WORLD HATH BECOME AN ABYSM OF IGNORANCE--- AND BLACK SUPERSTITION?

TELL ME ONE THING! ARE THERE-- COULD THERE BE PERSONS WHO DOUBT --- MIRACLES?
WELL, YES--- Y' SEE--- PRACTIC'LY EVERYONE'S LIKE THAT!

NO! OH, NO! PARDON, MASTER, BUT I MUST SIT DOWN--I'M ALL UNNERVED! WHAT A WORLD THOU HAST HERE! WHAT A WORLD!
WALT DISNEY

YEA, VERILY--'TIS A SAD STATE THY WORLD HATH COME TO! NO FAITH IN MIRACLES OR GENIES--OR ANY SUCH COMMONPLACE MAGIC! A DARK, DARK AGE!
?
9-26

BUT, SURELY, THOU ART DIFFERENT--THOU OWNEST THE LAMP! COULDST THOU DOUBT ME, THY SERVANT?
WELL, I--- THIS IS KINDA NEW---I DON'T KNOW WHAT TO THINK!

I HAVE IT! LET THOU ORDER UP A FEW SIMPLE MIRACLES AS PROOF!
MIRACLES?

PARDON MY ASKING FOR EASY ONES! IT HATH BEEN SOME THOUSAND YEARS SINCE I HAVE WORKED AND I MAY BE A BIT RUSTY!

SO, IF YOU DON'T MIND--NOTHING FLASHY! JUST TURNING SOME FRIEND INTO A TOAD, OR SOMETHING LIKE THAT!

PLEASE, MASTER--- ORDER SOME LITTLE MIRACLE, JUST TO CONVINCE THYSELF!
AW-W, SHUCKS--- I CAN'T B'LIEVE---!

COME, MASTER --- ONE LITTLE MIRACLE--- JUST A SAMPLE!
WELL, OKAY--- HERE GOES! LET THIS SCREWDRIVER TURN INTO A-A --AN ICE CREAM CONE!
9-27

!
SNAP!
PLING!

IT--IT'S REAL!
THOU FAILED TO STATE THE FLAVOR--- HOPE THOU LIKEST VANILLA!
WALT DISNEY

I'LL BE DOGGONED! I JUST ASKED FOR IT AND A REAL ICE CREAM CONE APPEARED--- LIKE MAGIC!
'TIS BUT CHILD'S PLAY FOR THE SLAVE OF THE LAMP!
9-28

S'POS'N I CALLED FOR SOMETHIN' ELSE --- WOULD IT WORK AGAIN?
ART THOU NOT THE MASTER? COMMAND!

ALL RIGHT! LET A- A RABBIT--A WHITE RABBIT APPEAR--- RIGHT THERE!

BOY--I'VE REALLY GOT SOMETHIN' HERE!
SNAP!
PLING!
WALT DISNEY

GOSH, IT WORKED AGAIN! I CALLED FOR A RABBIT TO APPEAR ---AND THERE HE IS!
WHAT DOST EXPECT WHEN THOU CALLEST FOR A RABBIT?
9-29

HE'LL NEED FOOD! LET'S SEE--- GIVE HIM A NICE HEAD OF CABBAGE!

WH- WHAT---!!?
SNAP!
PLING!
?
?

NO-NO-NO! THAT'S NOT IT! CHANGE HIM BACK! CHANGE HIM BACK!

DOST NOT KNOW THY MIND? THE LAMP WORKED JUST AS ORDERED!
PHEW! I CAN SEE Y' GOTTA BE KINDA-- CAREFUL OF THE THING!
WALT DISNEY

WHAT WISHEST THOU, NOW, O, MASTER?
LET'S SEE! I'D LIKE A NICE SOFT CHAIR--- AND THEN-- I'LL TAKE A HAMBURGER!
9-30

WOW! SOME SERVICE!

AH!
PLING!

?
POP!

WH- WHAT'S THE IDEA?
PARDON, MASTER --- THY HUMBLE SERVANT NEARLY FORGOT THE ONIONS!
PLING!
WALT DISNEY

GEE, IT'S GREAT TO HAVE A MAGIC LAMP AND GET ANYTHING Y' WANT---!
10-2

---BUT I DON'T FEEL VERY GOOD-- IN FACT---I'M AFRAID I'M GONNA BE SICK!

OH-H---I WISH I HADN'T EATEN ALL THAT STUFF!

F' GOSH SAKES! SOMEP'N'S WRONG WITH ME-- I FEEL---!!

JUST HUNGER, NO DOUBT! REMEMBER, THOU HAST EATEN NOTHING!
WELL, I'LL BE DARNED!
WALT DISNEY

THIS MAGIC IS GREAT STUFF, BUT I SEE WHERE IT CAN BE OVERDONE! TAKE THESE EATS AWAY!
STRANGE PERSONS, THOU MORTALS! EVERY MASTER OF THE LAMP HATH BEGUN BY ORDERING FOOD--- THEN FOUND IT MORE THAN HE COULD EAT!
10-3

MORTALS ARE SO SLOW TO THINK OF THE REALLY IMPORTANT THINGS THEY COULD DO FOR THEMSELVES!
POP!

FOR INSTANCELY- --THOU PAYEST MONTHLY TRIBUTE TO SOME LANDLORD FOR THIS WOODEN TENT?
UH, YES-- THAT'S RIGHT!

AND DOUBTLESS SOME FINANCE PERSONS EXACT TRIBUTE FOR THE CAMEL THOU RIDEST?
YEH, THEY DO-- IN A WAY! BUT, WHERE'S THE MAGIC COME IN?

DOST NOT SEE, MASTER? GIVE BUT THE WORD, AND ALL THESE PERSONS CAN BE READILY BOILED IN OIL!

THE IDEA! TALKING ABOUT BOILING PEOPLE IN OIL! WHY, THAT--IT'S AWFUL!
STILL, THERE BE PERSONS WHO SHOULD BE BOILED IN OIL! WHAT'S THE USE OF A MAGIC LAMP IF---?
10-4

IT'S FOR GOOD THINGS, LIKE-- WELL---LET THERE BE FRESH FLOWERS STREWN OVER THIS ROOM!

XX FLOUR
XX FLOUR
XX FLOUR
XX FLOUR
SNAP!
HEY!
KA-HUK! KA-HAWF!

VERILY, MASTER- --THOU CALLEST FOR THE STRANGEST THINGS!
XX FLOUR
XX FLOUR
WALT DISNEY

A NICE MESS-- FLOUR ALL OVER THE PLACE! WELL, AT LEAST I DON'T HAFTA SWEEP IT UP!
X X FLOUR
X X FLOUR
10-5

HAVE THIS ROOM TIDY AND CLEAN AS A WHISTLE--- MAKE IT LIKE NEW!

HOT DOG- --THERE SHE GOES!
X X FLOUR

WELL, F'R---!!?
HAST FORGOT THE ROOM ART LIKE NEW---AND THE VARNISH NOT DRY YET??
R-RIP-P!

IF Y' MUST BE SO DOGGONE LITERAL, BRING ME A NEW PAIR O' PANTS---AND THIS TIME I DO MEAN NEW!
WALT DISNEY

DEEPLY REGRETFUL, O, MASTER, THAT THY UNWORTHY SLAVE HATH BLUNDERED!
OH, THAT'S ALL RIGHT--I GUESS IT'S NOT YOUR FAULT! I CAN SEE THIS MAGIC STUFF'S KINDA TRICKY BUSINESS!
10-6

I'VE GOT AN IDEA FOR SOME FUN! I'LL PULL SOME TRICKS ON PLUTO!

LET PLUTO APPEAR, RIGHT IN THIS ROOM!

WHAT DASTARDLY CREATURE DARETH CALL UPON PLUTO, LORD OF THE UNDERWORLD!?
Distributed by King Features Syndicate, Inc.

N-NO--I DIDN'T CALL YOU---I JUST C-CALLED FOR P-PLUTO!
I AM PLUTO --LORD OF ALL UNDER THE EARTH!
WHO BRINGETH ME FORTH SHALT SUFFER FOR IT!
10-7

IT'S-- IT MUST BE S-SOME MISTAKE! YOU SHOULD BE ---P-PLUTO'S A DOG!

NO! NO! I MEAN-- VANISH! VANISH!!
GRR-R-- ARR-R-- AR-RRH!

VERY TIRING, THESE QUICK CHANGES, MASTER! WOULDST THOU'D MAKE UP THY MIND?
WHOOSH!
POP!

DOGGONE THIS GENIE! I GOTTA MAKE IT CLEAR THAT WHEN I WANT PLUTO I DON'T MEAN A FIRE AN' BRIMSTONE GUY OUT OF A GREEK MYTH!
10-9

LOOK! PLUTO'S THE NAME OF MY DOG --AND I WANT HIM HERE!
VERY GOOD, MASTER!
YOUR HUMBLE SLAVE SHALT TRY AGAIN!
BONG!

BONG!
BONG!
!
!

HEY--- STOP!!
BONG!

?
?
?
?
?
WALT DISNEY

WHAT'S TH' IDEA-- --GOIN' BACK INTO THE LAMP? I WASN'T THROUGH YET!
10-10

HEY! CAN Y' HEAR ME?
KNOCK! KNOCK! KNOCK!

ARE Y' IN THERE?

SHUCKS! I FORGOT Y' HAFTA RUB IT! ALI-GA-ZAM, ALI-KA-BOOBLA --- LET THE GENIE APPEAR!

I SAID-- LET THE GENIE APPEAR!

GOSH DARN! I'VE LOST ALL MY MAGIC!
WALT DISNEY

JUST THINK--ALL TH' SWELL MAGIC I WAS DOIN' WITH THIS LAMP AND NOW IT WON'T WORK AT ALL!
10-11
Copr 1939, Walt Disney Productions World Rights Reserved

WELL, IT WAS FUN WHILE IT LASTED!

NEXT MORNING

HO-HUM!
MAYBE I DREAMED IT ALL AND THE LAMP NEVER WAS MAGIC!

CAN'T DO ANY HARM TO TRY AGAIN! ALI-GA-ZAM, ALI-KA-BOOBLA ---LET TH' GENIE APPEAR!

AT THY SERVICES, O MASTER!
HOT DOG! I DIDN'T DREAM IT---IT'S TRUE!

HOW COME Y' POPPED RIGHT OUT THIS MORNIN' AS SOON AS I RUBBED THE LAMP, AND---?
WELL? DIDST NOT CALL ME?
10-12

YEH, BUT I CALLED Y' LAST NIGHT AND COULDN'T GET A **PEEP** OUTA Y'!
AH, BUT THAT WAS AFTER WORKING HOURS!

WORKIN' HOURS? Y' MEAN TO SAY---?
CERTAINLY! WE GENIES ONLY WORK FOUR HOURS DAILY!

YOU SEE---WE HAVE NEVER BECOME SUFFICIENTLY CIVILIZED TO **HAVE** TO WORK MORE!

BUT, GOSH---IF Y' ONLY WORK FOUR HOURS A DAY, Y' MIGHT QUIT JUST WHEN I NEED Y' MOST--MAYBE WITH A MIRACLE HALF-FINISHED!
THOU DOST NOT UNDERSTAND! 'TIS NOT NECESSARY THAT I BE PRESENT FOR MIRACLES TO WORK!
10-13

I MIGHT EVEN MAKE MYSELF INVISIBLE---

---LIKE THIS!
!
POP!

BUT STILL, THY EVERY WISH WOULD BE GRANTED! SUCH AS, FOR INSTANCE---

---SUPPOSE THOU WANTED THY MORNING SHOWER! PRESTO!
YOW!!
WALT DISNEY

HEY! CUT IT OUT! TURN IT OFF!
Copr. 1939, Walt Disney Productions
World Rights Reserved
10-14

I DON'T TAKE A SHOWER IN THE BEDROOM, Y' DOPE!
VERY SORROWFUL, MASTER! 'TWAS ONLY TO SHOW THE POWER OF THE LAMP, WHEN I AM NOT VISIBLE!

EVEN WERE I **INSIDE** THE LAMP, THY WISHES WOULDST STILL BE HONORED!
YEH? WELL, THEN, GET BACK IN THERE, RIGHT NOW!

I WISH I WAS DRESSED AND DOWN AT THE BREAKFAST TABLE!
Distributed by King Features Syndicate, Inc.

HOT DOG! IT WORKS LIKE MAGIC!
THUMP!
WALT DISNEY

WITH THE DISCOVERY THAT THE GENIE CAN GRANT WISHES WITHOUT COMING OUT OF THE LAMP, MICKEY FEELS POSSESSED OF VAST NEW POSSIBILITIES!

YEH, THIS IS GONNA GIVE ME A CHANCE TO SURPRISE PEOPLE WITH SOME REALLY FANCY EYE-OPENERS!
10-16

LOOK AT THE SWELL BREAKFAST I JUST HAD-- WITHOUT SO MUCH AS HAVIN' TO FRIZZLE AN EGG! AND NOW---

---NOW, THE DISHES ARE WASHED AND BACK IN THE CUPBOARD--- PRESTO!

HEY! Y' DON'T HAFTA BE SO IMPULSIVE ABOUT IT!
CRASH!
WALT DISNEY

THE POWER OF MIRACLES- --IT'S ALL MINE! WITHOUT EVEN CALLING THE GENIE, I CAN DO **ANYTHING**! I CAN AMAZE HORDES OF PEOPLE---
10-17

---I CAN TURN THIS RUG INTO A ROSE BUSH--JUST LIKE **THAT**!
SNAP!

THERE YOU ARE, LADIES-- REAL ROSES-- **OUCH**--- WITH GENUINE THORNS---

---AND--**WOW**--- ABSOLUTELY AUTHENTIC BEES! WHY, THERE'S NO LIMIT--HEY, TAKE IT EASY, MR. BEE ---TO MY POWER--!
WALT DISNEY

TICKLED TO DEATH WITH THE SEEMINGLY UNLIMITED MAGIC OF THE LAMP, MICKEY GAILY CALLS UP ONE THING AFTER ANOTHER!

NOW, LET'S HAVE A CANARY BIRD --**PRESTO**!
PLING!
SNAP!
10-18

TWEET! TWEET!
NO---MAKE IT A WHOLE **FLOCK** O' CANARIES! ATTABOY!
Copr. 1939, Walt Disney Productions
World Rights Reserved

TWEET! TWITTER! TWITTER! TWEET!
OVER HERE, WE'LL HAVE A NICE ORANGE TREE! **AH**!

AND THERE-- A MARBLE FOUNTAIN!

NOW---LET IT PLAY **MUSIC**! **YIPPEE!!**
WALT DISNEY

PROUD OF HIS SUCCESS AS A MAGICIAN, MICKEY CALLS OUT THE GENIE TO VIEW HIS CREATIONS!

HOW'S ABOUT IT? PRETTY SNAZZY WORK, DON'T Y' THINK?
IF THOU'LT PARDON ME, MASTER--ALL THIS ORDINARY TRASH--I FAIL TO SEE A REASON---!
10-19

TRASH, IS IT? I'D LIKE TO SEE YOU DO ANY BETTER! HERE, I'LL SHOW Y'A REAL TRICK--WATCH THIS!

BR-R-R-R-RINGG-G G-ALING-ALING!
LET THERE BE--HUH? WHAT'S THAT BELL? I DIDN'T ORDER ANY BELL TO RING!

OH--IT'S THE 'PHONE! HEH-HEH! I SORTA FORGOT WE HAD SUCH COMMONPLACE THINGS!
WALT DISNEY

RIGHT IN THE MIDST OF HIS FUN WITH THE LAMP, MICKEY IS SUDDENLY BROUGHT DOWN TO EARTH BY A 'PHONE CALL!

OH, HELLO, MINNIE! WHAT'S ON YOUR MIND?
LISTEN, MICKEY---I JUST PICKED UP THE MOST GORGEOUS FOOTSTOOL---
10-20

---IT MUST BE AGES OLD---AND YOU'D NEVER GUESS HOW CHEAP I GOT IT---

---OF COURSE, I KNOW YOU'RE NOT INTERESTED IN ANTIQUES, BUT REALLY---
CLICK!

---THIS PIECE IS SO EXCEPTIONAL, I JUST WISH YOU WERE HERE TO SEE IT!
WALT DISNEY

---HONESTLY, MICKEY, I WISH YOU COULD SEE THIS ANTIQUE! WHY DON'T YOU COME ON OVER, NOW?
10-21

RIGHT NOW, MINNIE?
YES, IF YOU AREN'T DOING---!!?
EEEEK!!

GOOD HEAVENS, YOU SCARED ME! HOW IN THE WORLD--? WHY, I THOUGHT YOU WERE ON THE 'PHONE A MINUTE AGO!
SURE---I WAS!

NOW, MICKEY! YOU CAN'T BE AT YOUR HOUSE ONE MINUTE AND HERE THE NEXT--AS IF YOU HAD A MAGIC LAMP, YOU KNOW!

BUT S'POS'N I DID HAVE A---!
MICKEY MOUSE! TAKE THAT BUTTERY LOOK OFF YOUR FACE AND STOP TRYING TO FILL ME WITH FAIRY TALES!

HONEST, MINNIE, THIS IS A MAGIC LAMP! NO KIDDIN'--- WAIT'LL Y' SEE TH' STUNTS I CAN DO!
NOW, MICKEY, YOU KNOW I HATE PARLOR TRICKS! ANYHOW, I ASKED YOU OVER TO SEE THE ANTIQUE FOOTSTOOL I BOUGHT!
10-23

MM-MUMBLE --M-MBLE---!

HUH? WHAT FOOTSTOOL, MINNIE?
WHY, THAT ONE THERE---!!? OH-H-- MERCY!!

IT LOOKS ANTIQUE, ALL RIGHT--- KINDA WOBBLY IN TH' LEGS, AN' ALL---!
YOU'RE NOT FUNNY! AND TAKE THAT REPTILE BACK WHERE YOU GOT IT FROM --THIS INSTANT!
WALT DISNEY

OF ALL THINGS! BRINGING A NASTY OLD TURTLE INTO MY HOUSE, JUST FOR A SILLY TRICK!
WHADDYA MEAN-- TRICK? DIDN'T I CHANGE IT BACK TO A FOOTSTOOL AGAIN? DOESN'T THAT PROVE IT'S REAL MAGIC?
10-24

OH, OF COURSE! SO IS PULLING RABBITS OUT OF A HAT AND ALL THAT KIND OF NONSENSE---!
BUT, I TELL Y', THIS IS DIFFERENT! IT'S THE LAMP---!

OH-- YOU AND YOUR OLD LAMP! FOR MY PART I PREFER TRAINED SEALS!
A MATTER OF TASTE, THAT'S ALL! BUT IF THAT'S THE WAY Y' FEEL ---

EE-E-E-K!

GIVE 'EM WHAT THEY ASK FOR, I ALWAYS SAY!
NOW, THAT'S ENOUGH! YOU'RE CARRYING YOUR OLD TRICKS ENTIRELY TOO FAR!
WALT DISNEY

THE IDEA! SHOWING OFF YOUR CIRCUS TRICKS IN MY HOUSE! TURTLES AND SEALS ALL OVER THE ROOM---!
BUT I MADE 'EM VANISH, DIDN'T I? DON'T Y' BELIEVE, NOW, I'VE GOT HONEST-TO-GOSH MAGIC?

NO, I DON'T AND I NEVER WILL! IT'S JUST SOME OF YOUR HOCUS-POCUS!
WILL Y' B'LIEVE ME IF I SUSPEND THIS OLD CROCK UP IN THE AIR?
10-25

EEEK! DON'T YOU DARE USE MY PRECIOUS ANTIQUE FOR YOUR TRICKS! PUT IT DOWN!
AS YOU WISH, MADAM!
CRASH!

OH-H-- I KNEW IT! YOU CLUMSY, BUNGLING LITTLE WRETCH---YOU'VE DESTROYED FOREVER MY PRICELESS VASE! OH-H--I'M SPEECHLESS!!

WHY ALL THE FUSS? NOTHIN'S HAPPENED TO YOUR VASE!
WALT DISNEY

Y' SEE, MINNIE --- THERE'S YOUR VASE AS GOOD AS EVER!
WELL, **NO MORE** OF THESE STUNTS! I SUPPOSE THEY'RE JUST ILLUSIONS, BUT THEY LOOK TOO REAL! THEY SCARE ME!
10-26

MINNIE, THIS **IS** A **REAL** MAGIC LAMP-- NOT A TRICK! CAN'T I CONVINCE Y' **SOME** WAY?
SILLY-- CERTAINLY NOT! WHO IN THIS DAY AND AGE **COULD** YOU EXPECT TO BELIEVE SUCH NONSENSE?

THAT'S JUST WHAT **I** SAID AT FIRST! THEN--A **MIRACLE** HAPPENED --- RIGHT BEFORE MY EYES!
INDEED? AND MAY I ASK **WHO** SHOWED YOU THIS SO **CONVINCING**-- MIRACLE?

IT WAS THE GENIE, **HIMSELF!** YOU KNOW-- THE ONE WHO LIVES IN THE LAMP!
MICKEY MOUSE --ONE MORE WORD AND **I'M** GOING TO CALL A DOCTOR!
WALT DISNEY

I CAN SEE THERE'S ONLY ONE WAY TO CONVINCE **YOU**! I'M GOIN' TO CALL THE GENIE OUT! ALI-GA-ZAM---
MICKEY DO YOU **FEEL** ALL RIGHT? DOES YOUR **HEAD** HURT OR ANYTHING?
10-27

---LET THE GENIE APPEAR!

WHO **IS** THIS FEMALE UNBELIEVER-- ---?
--THIS WITLESS DOUBTER OF MINE EXISTENCE ?
EEE-E-E-K!

QUICK--- SHE'S FAINTED! **WATER!**
PLOP!

MY GOSH --**RAIN**!
WALT DISNEY

---WHAT-- WHAT HAPPENED?
YOU FAINTED--THEN, WHEN I CALLED FOR WATER, THAT DOPEY GENIE MADE IT RAIN! QUICK--AN UMBRELLA!
10-28
Copr 1939, Walt Disney Productions World Rights Reserved

THERE WE ARE --- IT'S ALL RIGHT, NOW!

ALL RIGHT, IS IT? LOOK AT MY FLOOR!
PARDON, MASTER-- MIGHT THY "DOPEY" SERVANT SUGGEST THOU TURNEST OFF THE RAIN?
HUH? **OH**-- YEH---!
Distributed by King Features Syndicate, Inc.

SORRY, MINNIE --- I SHOULDA THOUGHT---!
DON'T SAY **ONE WORD**! THIS IS THE **LAST STRAW**! LEAVE MY HOUSE **INSTANTLY** --AND TAKE YOUR --YOUR **STOOGE** WITH YOU!
AND DON'T **EVER** COME BACK!
WALT DISNEY

POOR MINNIE! A REAL SHOWER OF RAIN INSIDE HER LIVING-ROOM IS THE LAST STRAW!
10-30

THAT'S ENOUGH! GET OUT-- AND STAY OUT! I'LL NEVER SPEAK TO YOU AGAIN!
ALL RIGHT -- YOU'LL BE SORRY! I COULDA DONE BIG THINGS FOR Y'!

NO, YOU DON'T! TRYING TO SNEAK OUT AND LEAVE ME WITH THIS MESS! YOU "HOCUS-POCUS" THE WATER OUT OF HERE!

THERE Y' ARE, MINNIE --- GOOD AS NEW!
JUST AS I THOUGHT --- NOTHING BUT A CHEAP, THEATRICAL TRICK! NOW, GO!
SNAP!

BOY! WHEN MINNIE WANTS TO BE STUBBORN, Y' MIGHT AS WELL GIVE UP!
A VERY UNPLEASANT FEMALE! IF I MIGHT SUGGEST -- BOILING IN OIL ---?
SLAM!
WALT DISNEY

MY! MY! I WONDER WHO THE DISTINGUISHED-LOOKING FOREIGNER IS WITH MICKEY?
MINNIE MOUSE
10-31

GOOD MORNING, MICKEY! TEE-HEE --- I DON'T THINK I'VE HAD THE HONOR OF MEETING THE GENTLEMAN- --- TEE-HEE!
MINNIE MOUSE

MISS CLARABELLE, ALLOW ME TO PRESENT---!
OHHHHHHH- --MERCY- ---!!

POP!
GUESS YOU BETTER DISAPPEAR 'TIL I REVIVE HER! IT LOOKS LIKE THE LADIES CAN'T TAKE IT!
WALT DISNEY

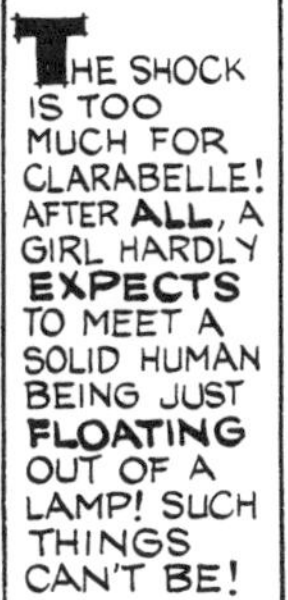
THE SHOCK IS TOO MUCH FOR CLARABELLE! AFTER ALL, A GIRL HARDLY EXPECTS TO MEET A SOLID HUMAN BEING JUST FLOATING OUT OF A LAMP! SUCH THINGS CAN'T BE!

YOU'RE ALL RIGHT NOW, CLARABELLE- --COMIN' ALONG FINE!
BUT--BUT I'M SURE--I SAW SOME CREATURE ---COMING FROM A LAMP--!?
11-1

Y' HAD QUITE A FALL --- GUESS IT JARRED YOUR HEAD A LITTLE!
THAT MUST HAVE BEEN IT! LAN' SAKES--I'M GLAD IT WASN'T REAL! LIKE TO HAVE SCARED THE WITS OUT OF A BODY!

SHE'S GONE NOW --- YOU CAN APPEAR AGAIN! TOO BAD YOU'RE SO UPSETTING TO STRANGERS!

OH, BOY--HERE COMES GOOFY! WONDER HOW HE'S GOIN' TO TAKE IT?
WALT DISNEY

HI YA, MICKEY, OL' KID, OL' SON!
H'LO, GOOFY! SAY, I WANT Y' TO MEET A FRIEND---!
11-2

---THIS IS MR. GENIE ---JUST IN FROM ARABIA!
THY PLEASURE IS INDEEDLY MOST EXTREME HONOR, NOBLE SIR!
UH--GAWRSH! YUH KINDER GOT ME THERE, BUT SAME TO YOU, BROTHER!

?
UH-HAW-HAW-HAW! UH-HAW!
WELL? WHAT'S SO FUNNY?

NO FEET!
WALT DISNEY

GAWRSH--- HOPE Y' AIN'T SORE CAUSE I LAFFED! YUH SEE, I NEVER KNOWED BEFORE THAT A-RABS DIDN'T HAVE FEET!
11-3

UH-HAW! MUST BE PURTY TOUGH WHEN YUH GIT CORNS!
SIR?
WHADDYA MEAN?

NO PLACE TO PUT THUH CORN-PLASTERS!
WELL, 'SCUSE ME ---I GOTTER BE GOIN'!

BOY--- THAT GUY GETS DOPIER EVERY DAY!
AS I HAVE SUGGESTED BEFORE --- SUCH UNPLEASANT PERSONS COULD BE READILY BOILED IN OIL!
WALT DISNEY

WHY SHOULD I BE FOOLIN' AROUND WITH SMALL POTATOES, THE WAY I'VE BEEN? WITH ALL THIS POWER, I'M GOIN' TO DO SOMETHIN' BIG--- SOMETHIN' FOR EVERYBODY!
AH! WELL SPOKEN, MASTER!
11-4

FIRST, I'LL GO GET MY CAR---HEY, WHAT AM I TALKIN' ABOUT? LET IT APPEAR---RIGHT HERE!

?
!
SNAP!

HEY, YOU! WHY DON'TCHA SIGNAL!?
WALT DISNEY

FED-UP WITH THE EASE OF PETTY MIRACLES, WHICH NO ONE ELSE BELIEVES, ANYWAY, MICKEY IS OUT TO USE THE LAMP FOR SOMETHING BIG AND BENEFICIAL!

ALL ENTHUSED OVER HIS PLAN TO HOUSE THE POOR IN A MODEL VILLAGE, MICKEY, LATE AT NIGHT, PREPARES TO TRANSFORM THE CITY DUMP!

TO MAKE WAY FOR HIS MODEL VILLAGE, MICKEY ORDERS ALL THE RUBBISH OFF THE CITY DUMP. A LONE MINION OF THE LAW HAS BEEN A FRIGHTENED WITNESS TO THE SCENE!

MIDNIGHT! AND THE GREATEST MIRACLE MICKEY HAS EVER TRIED IS UNDER WAY--- A MODEL VILLAGE, RENT FREE, TO HOUSE THE SLUM-DWELLERS!

ARRESTED FOR "CONSTRUCTING" HIS MODEL VILLAGE WITHOUT A BUILDING PERMIT, MICKEY, NEVERTHELESS, GOES AHEAD WITH HIS PLANS NEXT MORNING.

MICKEY IS AMAZED TO FIND THAT NONE OF THE TENEMENT FAMILIES HAS MOVED INTO HIS RENT-FREE VILLAGE! HE SCURRIES AROUND, LISTENING TO THEIR COMMENTS.

MICKEY'S FREE VILLAGE FOR THE POOR SEEMS TO HAVE BACKFIRED INTO A HORNET'S NEST! THE INVESTIGATING COMMITTEE REFUSES TO BELIEVE AT ALL IN HIS GOOD INTENTIONS!

WELL, MR. MAYOR, WHAT DO Y' WANT ME TO DO WITH MY MODEL VILLAGE?
AHEM--- IN VIEW OF THE FACT THAT YOU HAVE LEFT THE CITY WITH NO DUMP--- A MOST SERIOUS OFFENSE---
11-23

---AND HAVE VIOLATED PRACTICALLY ALL OUR ORDINANCES, WE--- AHEM, SHOULD DEAL HARSHLY!

BUT WE ARE GOING TO BE LENIENT! MERELY RESTORE OUR DUMP AS YOU FOUND IT AND NOTHING MORE WILL BE SAID!

HOWEVER---THIS MUST BE DONE WITHIN 24 HOURS, OR WE TAKE POSSESSION OF THE BUILDINGS!
OKAY-- YOU ASKED FOR IT!
WALT DISNEY

A PITY TO HAVE VANISHED THAT NOBLE VILLAGE! ONE OF MY BEST MIRACLES GONE BACK TO RUBBISH!
BETTER IT'S RUBBISH THAN GETTIN' IN THE CLUTCHES OF A BUNCH OF GRAFTERS!
CITY DUMP
11-24

ART THIS THY HOME, O, MASTER?
YEH, AND FOR ALL I ACCOMPLISHED, I MIGHT BETTER HAVE STAYED HERE!

A FAT LOTTA GOOD A MAGIC LAMP IS! PEOPLE ARE EITHER SCARED SILLY OR DON'T BELIEVE IT AT ALL!
INDEEDLY, THY WORLD HAST MANY HALF-WITS! NOW, IF THOU WISHEST TO REALLY HELP PEOPLE---

---TAKE THE LAMP TO MY LAND, WHERE FOLK BELIEVETH IN IT!
HUH? YOUR LAND- --TELL ME ABOUT IT!

Y' MEAN, IF I HAD THE LAMP IN YOUR COUNTRY I COULD HELP THE PEOPLE THERE?
INDEEDLY SO! THEY ARE NOT IGNORANT AND SUPERSTITIOUS LIKE MORTALS- --THEY BELIEVE IN MAGIC!
11-25

BUT, ALAS, MY PEOPLE HATH MANY TROUBLES! WHY, WHEN I WAS THERE YESTERDAY---!

YESTERDAY?
PARDON-- I WAS GOING BY GENIE STANDARD TIME! I FORGOT THOU USEST THE OLD PRIMITIVE RECKONING!

BY THY METHOD IT WAS ABOUT THREE THOUSAND YEARS! FORGIVE MINE ERROR!
OH! OH, SURE-- YEH, I--I SEE!

WHAT SAY, MASTER-- WOULDST COME WITH ME? 'TIS AN EASY TRIP BY FAST CARPET!
GOSH! I'VE A NOTION TO--- Y' MIGHT HAVE SOMEP'N THERE!
WALT DISNEY

THE GENIE TRIES TO INDUCE MICKEY TO GO TO "GENIELAND" WITH HIM TO WORK MIRACLES FOR THE BENEFIT OF THE INHABITANTS!

THE BIG ADVENTURE IS ON! TRAVELING BY MAGIC CARPET, MICKEY IS ON HIS WAY TO THE GENIE'S NATIVE LAND!

MICKEY MAKES AN ABRUPT ARRIVAL IN "GENIELAND," WHEN THE MAGIC CARPET SNAGS ON A STEEPLE!

PLEASE DON'T MIND GRANDPA! HE DOESN'T REALIZE YOU'VE COME HERE JUST TO HELP US POOR GENIES!
BUT HE MEANS NO HARM!
HUMPH! ALWAYS TALKIN' LIKE I WAS A CHILD!
G'WAN! CHILDREN GOT MORE SENSE!
Copr 1939, Walt Disney Productions World Rights Reserved
12-4

THERE! YOU HEAR THAT?
THAT'S THE YOUNGER GENERATION FOR YOU--NO RESPECT WHATEVER!

THINK THEY KNOW IT ALL, THEY DO! LAND KNOWS WHAT THEY LEARN IN SCHOOL NOWADAYS --- NOTHIN' BUT ABC MAGIC, CARD TRICKS AND SUCH PIFFLE!

WHY, WHEN I WAS THAT HIGH---
YEAH, WE KNOW, "---I WAS PULLING RABBITS OUT OF TURBANS AND SAWING WOMEN IN HALF!"
GRAMPA'S AN OLD FOGY--- GRAMPA'S AN OLD FOGY!
WALT DISNEY

CALL ME AN OLD FOGY, WILL YOU? I'LL TAN YOUR HIDES---!
HA-HA-HA! GRAMPA CAN'T TAKE IT ANY MORE---HE'S AN OLD SOREHEAD!
12-5

YOU LITTLE BRATS--- I'LL---!

HA-HA-HA! DOES GRAMPA ALWAYS FALL FOR THAT ONE!
WHOMP!

YOU WHIPPERSNAPPERS AIN'T SO SMART-- JUST WAIT--!
GRAMPA'S AN OLD FOGY- -GRAMPA'S AN OLD FOGY!
WALT DISNEY

DURN PESKY KIDS THINK THEY KNOW MAGIC! NOW, IF YOU WANT TO SEE A GOOD ONE, WATCH THIS!
12-6

DIDN'T KNOW THERE WAS A TOY BALLOON OVER YER HEAD, DID YOU?
NO! WHY, SURE ENOUGH- -THERE IS!

SPLOP!
YOU MEAN, THERE WAS! HEE-HEE-HEE!

VERY FUNNY!
OH, HEE-HEE-HEE! AIN'T THAT A PEACH, THOUGH?
HEE- HEE---
I'LL DIE LAUGHIN'!
WALT DISNEY

GUESS YOU THOUGHT THAT WAS PRETTY SLICK MAGIC, EH? BUT I GOT MORE --- HERE HOLD THIS ROPE!
12-7

?

!

WOW!
HO-HO! HEE-HEE-HEE! THAT WAS NO SNAKE --- IT WASN'T EVEN A ROPE! HEE-HEE --- DID **THAT** ONE FOOL YOU!

NOW, GRANDPA, STOP THIS! YOU MUSTN'T PLAY YOUR PRANKS ON OUR **GUEST**!
WHO **CAN** I PLAY 'EM ON? EVERY-BODY ELSE IN TOWN **KNOWS** 'EM! ALWAYS SPOILIN' M' FUN!
WALT DISNEY

I TOLD YOU, GRANDPA, I WON'T HAVE OUR GUEST ANNOYED BY YOUR TRICKS! YOU'VE **GOT** TO BEHAVE!
THERE Y' GO --- TREATIN' ME LIKE A CHILD AGAIN! I **NEVER** GET TO HAVE ANY FUN!
12-8
Copr. 1939, Walt Disney Productions
World Rights Reserved

ALL RIGHT! I'LL GO DOWN IN THE **CELLAR**, WHERE I CAN'T **BOTHER** ANYBODY! AND MAYBE I'LL **STAY** THERE, TOO!

OH-OH! HE'S GOING DOWN TO SULK AGAIN! CHILDREN --- FOLLOW GRANDPA AND WATCH HIM!

YOU SEE-- WHEN HE GETS MAD THIS WAY, HE QUITE OFTEN TRIES TO BURN THE HOUSE DOWN!
WALT DISNEY

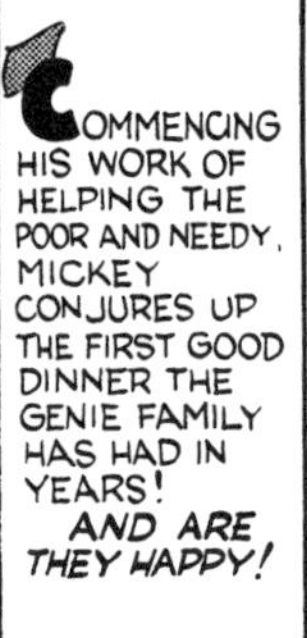
COMMENCING HIS WORK OF HELPING THE POOR AND NEEDY, MICKEY CONJURES UP THE FIRST GOOD DINNER THE GENIE FAMILY HAS HAD IN YEARS!
AND ARE THEY HAPPY!

12-9

NOW, THEN --- I'LL HAVE M' AFTER-DINNER SMOKE AND GET SICK!
GOSH-- WHY SMOKE, IF TOBACCO MAKES Y' SICK?
Copr. 1939, Walt Disney Productions
World Rights Reserved

OH, WE'VE HAD NO TABACKY IN YEARS --- THAT'S WHY I GET SICK!
BUT, I DON'T SEE HOW---?

IT'S THIS DURN **STRING** I'VE BEEN USIN' FOR A SUBSTITUTE!
!
Distributed by King Features Syndicate, Inc.

MICKEY'S FIRST ACT IN GENIELAND IS TO PRODUCE A BIG BANQUET FOR THE FAITHFUL SLAVE OF THE LAMP AND HIS FAMILY! BUT AFTER THE FEAST IS OVER---!

MICKEY WANDERS THROUGH THE STREETS OF GENIELAND TO LEARN JUST HOW POVERTY-STRICKEN THE COUNTRY REALLY IS. HE HEARS THE STORY OF A RAGGED AND STARVING BEGGAR!

12-12

GOSH--THESE PEOPLE ARE SURE POOR! THAT LITTLE OLD GUY HASN'T EVEN A CART TO CARRY HIS FIRE-WOOD!
12-14

WAIT A MINUTE, MISTER! HOW'D Y' LIKE TO HAVE A HORSE AND CART TO HAUL THAT LOAD FOR YOU?
HUMPH! I S'POSE YOU'RE THAT "MIRACLE MASTER" THEY'RE TALKIN' ABOUT!

WELL, I'LL THANK Y' TO MIND YER OWN BUSINESS! I'VE GOT FIVE STARVIN' KIDS, A WIFE AND A MOTHER-IN-LAW---

---NOW, Y' EXPECT ME TO FEED A HORSE, TOO!
WALT DISNEY

HERE'S A CASE WHERE I OUGHTA BE OF SOME HELP! THAT POOR WOMAN LOOKS ALL IN!
Copr. 1939, Walt Disney Productions
World Rights Reserved

PARDON ME, MADAM! THAT WASH LOOKS TOO BIG FOR YOU--- JUST LET ME TAKE CARE OF IT!
YOU? OH, I SEE-- YOU'RE THE "MIRACLE MASTER!"
12-15

I'LL FIX Y' UP IN A JIFFY! AHEM--LET ALL HER CLOTHES BE WASHED AND HUNG ON THE LINE!

!
WALT DISNEY

PLEASE, SIR, IS IT TRUE THAT YOU WORK MIRACLES TO HELP POOR FOLK LIKE ME?
THAT'S RIGHT! JUST TELL ME WHAT YOU NEED MOST AND YOU CAN HAVE IT!
12-16

WHAT I NEED MOST IS SOME NEW CLOTHES! COULD YOU---?
EASIEST THING IN THE WORLD! ANY PARTICULAR KIND?

WELL, ER--COULD I HAVE 'EM WITH TWO PAIRS OF TROUSERS? I HATE TO ASK TOO MUCH, BUT, ER---

---IT'S BEEN SO AWKWARD, HAVING MY BROTHER WEARING THE SAME PAIR!
WALT DISNEY

GOSH! I'VE SEEN SOME DILAPIDATED HOUSES AROUND HERE. BUT THIS WRECK IS THE WORST EVER!
12-18

WHAT HAPPENED--- DID THE WALLS OF YOUR HOUSE COLLAPSE?
NOPE! WE TOOK 'EM DOWN ON PURPOSE!

UH-- DOESN'T IT MAKE THE PLACE KINDA COLD?
NOPE! THAT'S WHY WE DID IT!

---WE NEEDED THE WOOD FOR THE FIRE!

I'VE HEARD THEY CALL YOU THE "MIRACLE MASTER" AND THAT YOU CAN DO ANYTHING! WOULD YOU MIND--- COULD I HAVE A NEW DRESS?
CERTAINLY, MA'AM! JUST ASK FOR ANYTHING YOU LIKE!
12-19

OH, THANK YOU, SIR!
THERE Y' ARE! A NEAT LITTLE STYLE, DON'T Y' THINK?
PLING!

OH, THIS IS JUST LOVELY!
F'R PETE'S SAKE! YOU'RE CUTTIN' IT FULL O' HOLES!

WELL, YOU SEE IT'S THE NEIGHBORS--- I DON'T WANT THEM TO THINK I'M SHOWING OFF!

PARDON ME, MADAM! WHAT SEEMS TO BE THE TROUBLE?
I'M LEAVING HOME ON ACCOUNT OF THAT GOOD-FOR-NOTHING LOAFER!
12-20

HERE I AM STARVING AND HE HASN'T BROUGHT HOME ANY FOOD FOR A WEEK!
ARE Y' SURE, MA'AM---?

---HE SEEMS TO HAVE DONE ALL RIGHT TODAY! LOOK!
!

SO! BEEN KEEPING IT ALL TO YOURSELF, HAVE YOU? I'LL TEACH YOU TO STARVE ME, YOU WRETCH!

F'GOSH SAKES--- SNOWING! IS THERE ANYTHING THAT CAN'T HAPPEN IN THIS CRAZY COUNTRY?
12-21

THIS IS TERRIBLE, WITH ALL THE POOR AND HOMELESS PEOPLE THERE ARE!
MOST UNUSUAL-- -QUITE UNPREPARED- --ONLY OCCURS ONCE IN A LIFETIME!

NEED WARM SHOES, TOO--- MOST UNCOMFORTABLE!
GOSH! WE'LL REMEDY THAT RIGHT NOW!

---LET HIM HAVE THE RIGHT KINDA SHOES FOR THIS WEATHER!

!
?
WALT DISNEY

ENOUGH HARDSHIPS IN THIS COUNTRY WITHOUT HAVIN' SNOW! I'M GONNA MAKE IT DISAPPEAR!
12-22

VANISH! AH--- THAT'S BETTER!
HE STOLE OUR SNOW MAN!
BAW-W! WE WERE HAVIN' FUN!

YOU AND YOUR VANISHING TRICKS! LOOK WHERE IT LEFT MY DONKEY!
WALT DISNEY

OF ALL THE NERVE! OUR NICE WARM SNOW HOUSE SNATCHED AWAY WITHOUT WARNING!
RIGHT IN THE MIDDLE OF MY BATH, TOO!
GOOD NIGHT- --CAN'T I PLEASE ANY-BODY?

WELL, I'VE LOOKED AROUND AND THE FOLKS SURE ARE IN A BAD WAY! I DON'T KNOW HOW I CAN HELP 'EM ALL!
WHY NOT SET UP A SUMPTIOUS PALACE, WHERE ALL MAY COME AND RECEIVE THEIR BENEFITS?
Copr. 1939, Walt Disney Productions World Rights Reserved
12-23

HAVE 'EM COME TO ME WITH THEIR TROUBLES--- YEH, THAT'S A GOOD IDEA! BUT WHY A PALACE?
YOU DON'T KNOW MY PEOPLE! THEY HAVE NO RESPECT FOR ANYTHING COMMONPLACE!

AS A MASTER OF MIRACLES, THEY EXPECT THE POMP AND CEREMONY BEFITTING SUCH A NOBLE PERSONAGE! THEY WOULD BE OTHERWISE DISAPPOINTED!

I S'POSE YOU OUGHTA KNOW! OKAY--I'LL PUT ON THE DOG FOR 'EM!
AH! NOW, EVERYONE WILL BE MADE HAPPY!
Distributed by King Features Syndicate, Inc.

In a setting considered necessary to command respect of Genieland's peculiar people, Mickey holds open court to relieve their many woes!

OH, SIR---CAN YOU HELP ME? MY HOUSE IS IN A TERRIBLE CONDITION---THE FURNITURE'S ALL TO PIECES---
GOSH--THAT'S PRETTY BAD!
12-28

---THE ROOF LEAKS--AND WHEN IT RAINS, OUR SOUP TASTES AWFUL---! WE DON'T REALLY MIND SLEEPING ON THE FLOOR---

---BUT WE HAVEN'T MUCH FLOOR LEFT, AND---!
CALM YOURSELF, MA'AM---I'M TAKIN' CARE OF EVERYTHING! WHEN Y' GET HOME YOU'LL FIND YOU'VE GOT THE BEST HOUSE IN TOWN!

OH, GOODY! NOW, I'LL SHOW THAT SNIPPY NEIGHBOR OF MINE WHO'S WHO!
WALT DISNEY

YES, LADIES---?
LOOK HERE--YOU GAVE HER A FINER HOUSE THAN I'VE GOT!
AND, WHY NOT?
12-29

IT'S ALL RIGHT, MADAM---I'VE JUST MADE YOUR PLACE EVEN BETTER! NOW, ARE Y' HAPPY?
OH, YES, INDEED!
WELL, I'M NOT!

OKAY, I'LL MAKE YOURS BETTER, TOO! NOW, YOU'VE EACH GOT A HOUSE FINER THAN THE OTHER! HOW'S THAT?
OH, LOVELY!
OH, GOODY!

ISN'T HE WONDERFUL?
WALT DISNEY

MICKEY IS MAKING GREAT PROGRESS IN CURING THE TROUBLES OF GENIELAND WITH HIS TRUSTY LAMP! HUNDREDS OF PEOPLE HAVE BROUGHT THEIR WOES TO HIM---AND STILL THEY COME!

GOOD MORNING, MA'AM! CAN I HELP YOU?
OH, SIR, I DON'T KNOW WHAT TO DO! OUR COW CAN'T GIVE ANY MILK AND WE NEED MILK FOR THE BABY!
12-30

THAT'S EASY--I'LL JUST HAVE YOUR COW GIVE ALL THE MILK Y' WANT!
I'M AFRAID YOU CAN'T DO THAT, MASTER!

TUT, TUT, LADY--DON'T Y' KNOW THIS LAMP CAN DO ANYTHING?
MAYBE SO---BUT THE TROUBLE IS---

---WE HAD TO EAT THE COW LAST WEEK!
!
?
WALT DISNEY

THE FAME OF THE "MIRACLE MASTER" HAS SPREAD LIKE WILDFIRE! DR. MICKEY'S "FIX EVERYTHING" CLINIC IS BUZZING LIKE A BEE-HIVE!

WHO'S NEXT?
I AM, SIR! BUT I'M NOT HERE TO ASK ANYTHING FOR MYSELF!
1-1

I CAME TO PLEAD FOR A MOST WRETCHED FAMILY SIR! THEY ARE IN THE VERY DREGS OF POVERTY!
GOSH---!

THEY ARE ABOUT TO BE EVICTED FROM THE LITTLE HOME THEY'VE HAD FOR YEARS---OH, IT'S AWFUL!
WELL, I'LL SURE SEE THAT THEY GET SOME MONEY! UH--ARE YOU A RELATIVE OR--?

NO---I'M THEIR LANDLORD!

WHAT'S YOUR TROUBLE, MISTER?
IT'S MY CAMEL, SIR---HE'S STARVING TO DEATH!
1-2

WELL, I CAN EASILY FIX THAT!
I HOPE YOU CAN, MASTER! HE'S PRETTY OLD, BUT HE'S ALL I'VE GOT LEFT!

WHAT DOES HE WANT---HAY OR OATS?
NEITHER---

---TEETH!

GOOD MORNING! UH--ARE YOU IN TROUBLE---?
OH, YES, SIR---TERRIBLE TROUBLE! I CAN'T STAY AWAKE TO DO MY WORK!
1-3

AND IF I KEEP FALLIN' ASLEEP ON THIS JOB--AWAAAA-HO-HUMMM--I'LL BE FIRED!

WELL--AHEM---DON'T Y' SLEEP NIGHTS?
NO! THAT'S MY WIFE'S FAULT---

---SHE EATS CRACKERS---IN BED...
Z-Z-Z-Z-Z-Z-Z-!
WALT DISNEY

JUST AS THE "LORD HIGH CALIPH-MAYOR" OF GENIELAND IS CONGRATULATING MICKEY ON MAKING EVERYONE HAPPY, COMPLAINTS START COMING IN!

AFTER MICKEY HAS RUBBED THE LAMP AND GRANTED EVERY WISH OF THE CITIZENS OF GENIELAND, HE IS DISCONCERTED TO FIND THAT THEY ARE STILL COMPLAINING!

IN SPITE OF THE BEST OF INTENTIONS, MICKEY IS BESIEGED BY INCREASING CROWDS OF IRATE CITIZENS, ALL DISSATISFIED WITH WHAT HE HAS DONE FOR THEM!

FED UP WITH THE THANKLESS TASK OF TRYING TO HELP PEOPLE, MICKEY FLEES FROM AN ANGRY MOB OF UNGRATEFUL CITIZENS!

AN EDUCATION FOR THURSDAY

JANUARY 15, 1940
–
APRIL 20, 1940

YESTERDAY'S THURSDAY, TODAY

The road to Hades is often paved with good intentions. But never was a road bumpier than "An Education for Thursday"—one of Floyd Gottfredson's most famous Mickey adventures, yet easily among his most infamous as well.

"Thursday" is often lauded as one of Gottfredson's *funniest* tales, and no wonder; its ridiculous climax depicts an elephant demolishing downtown Mouseton, comically ravaging everything and everyone in sight. Unfortunately, "Thursday" also has a tragic flaw: the title character is an extremely dated African aborigine stereotype.

"Thursday" is one of Gottfredson's rare follow-up tales: a sequel to "Mickey Mouse Meets Robinson Crusoe," itself a highly flawed story. In "Crusoe," Gottfredson struggled to keep the adventure storyline central as pesky gag characters dominated: villainous, lazy jungle "savages" and a highly unlikeable Crusoe. In "Thursday," the eponymous savage *is* the storyline, with no distractions whatsoever.

Significantly, the savages transformed from one story to the next. In "Crusoe," they reflected Gottfredson's earlier 1930s depictions of Africans: as displaced deep-Southerners. It was already an insensitive trope in 1939—and Gottfredson was no racist. He seems to have recognized that the characters pushed the boundaries of "funny" a bit too far.

Indeed, reading "Crusoe" and "Thursday" in order, you will perceive that the latter might have been meant as an apology for the former. In "Thursday," Friday's tribe are no longer Southern bumpkins, merely primitives. The Black characters aren't villainous or lazy this time; Thursday is "just" a nonstop, naïve source of gags. Unfortunately, this merely substitutes one awkward trope for another. The attempted apology reads much like a typical "Mickey gets an unruly pet" tale, except now the "pet" is a near-feral person.

Obviously, one can try to enjoy "An Education for Thursday" in spite of its faults—the same way that one enjoys a kitschy 1940s jungle movie, with similar comic-relief tribesmen. Today, of course, the humor comes not from the *intended* laughs, but from the laughably embarrassing 1940s social mores. It is too easy to forget how we once, naïvely, viewed other cultures; it's important to watch and remember, so it can't happen again.

Gottfredson evidently had his memory problems, too. Another difference between "Thursday" and "Crusoe" is a major continuity error; in "Crusoe," Mickey's adventure on Abalone Island was a movie studio set-piece. According to "Thursday," it happened in Mickey's real life!

You'd think that Gottfredson or Merrill De Maris might have remembered this rather crucial detail, but alas. If it's a mess, it must be Thursday... or Friday, depending on your point of view.

— Jonathan Gray

DID I DREAM I HAD ALADDIN'S LAMP--OR---? GOSH, IT SEEMED SO REAL---!
1-15

---OH-OH--- SOMEBODY AT THE DOOR!
RRRR-INNGG!

MR. MOUSE?
YES--!
ONE CASE OF WEST AFRICAN BANANAS--- SIGN HERE, PLEASE!

HUH? WEST AFRICAN BANANAS? BUT, UH--I DON'T KNOW ANYBODY IN AFRICA!
NEITHER DO I ---BUT WHY GET PERSONAL? SIGN HERE, PLEASE!

IT--IT'S MEANT FOR ME, ALL RIGHT! BUT, WHAT TH'---?
WALT DISNEY

BANANAS FROM WEST AFRICA! WHO THE HECK COULD'VE SENT 'EM--- AND WHY?
1-16

WELL, I MIGHT AS WELL OPEN IT UP AND---

YOWTCH!

GLUG--- GA-BOOCH!
WALT DISNEY

WHO ARE YOU? HOW COME YOU'RE SENT TO ME LIKE THIS?
GLUG--- GA-BOOCH!
1-17

Y' LOOK JUST LIKE "FRIDAY" THAT I USED TO KNOW---BUT HE COULD AT LEAST TALK!
GLUG--- GA-BOOCH!

GOSH! IS THAT ALL Y' CAN SAY?
BOOCH--- GA-BLUG!

FROM ISLAND. SOME PLACE BY AFRICA. 12TH MOON, 9TH DAY 1939
DEAR MICKEY MOUSE--- THIS NOT ME--- THIS MY ALMOST-TWIN BROTHER, NAME "THURSDAY". I SENDUM TO YOU FOR EDUMCATION 'CAUSE HE NEEDUM BACKGROUND POLISHED. YOU KEEP REST OF BANNANAS FOR PAY. GOODY-GOOD-BYE, I SEE YOU NEVER.
FRIDAY.
WALT DISNEY

MICKEY HAS QUITE A JOB ON HIS HANDS TRYING TO TRAIN AN IGNORANT SAVAGE WHO DOESN'T EVEN SPEAK ENGLISH!

FACED WITH THE BIG JOB OF TRAINING THURSDAY IN THE WHITE MAN'S WAYS, MICKEY FINDS HE HAS TO START FROM SCRATCH!

THIS IS BATH, SEE? YOU WASHUM-- UNDERSTAND?
UM- GLOOB!
SOAP
1-22
Copr 1940, Walt Disney Productions World Rights Reserved

GOSH, MY OWN NEPHEWS MAKE MORE FUSS THAN HE DOES!

A LONG TIME LATER.
GOOD NIGHT, HE'S BEEN IN THAT TUB FOR AGES! I'D BETTER GO SEE IF HE'S DROWNED---!
The BLEATING BUGLE

WELL, F'R---! HE DIDN' TAKE A BATH-- HE DRANK IT!
SOAP
WALT DISNEY
Distributed by King Features Syndicate, Inc.

---AND NOW, MY FRIENDS, I WILL ENTERTAIN YOU WITH A FEW IMITATIONS OF WILD ANIMALS I HAVE KNOWN---!
1-23

---FIRST, A LION---
ARR-ROAR-R-R-!

--R-ROARR--

--RROAR-R-
-UH-
GLUG--
GUG--
OW!
WALT DISNEY

PFOOO-OO-OOH-!
NO USE THURSDAY--- Y' CAN'T BLOW THAT FLAME OUT!
1-24

?

HERE, LET ME SHOW Y'! THIS CAN'T BE DONE BY YOUR PRIMITIVE METHODS, BUT---!

HEY---!!
POP

I MIGHT'VE KNOWN---YOU'D FIND SOME WAY TO DO IT!
GLOOB!

NOW, WHERE'D THAT THURSDAY GO TO? MINNIE'S ON HER WAY OVER AND I WANT TO GIVE HER A SURPRISE!
1-25

EEEEEEEEEK!

---EEK! HELP! MICKEY---HELP!!

POW! THUD!

"BUDDEM-GLY!"
WALT DISNEY

WHERE DID THIS BEAST COME FROM? CALL THE POLICE! DON'T STAND THERE AND LET ME BE MURDERED! DO SOMETHING!
BUT, MINNIE, HE'S NOT DANGEROUS--- HE'S JUST SORTA--- PRIMITIVE! OF COURSE, HE SHOULDN'T 'A BOPPED Y' ON THE HEAD,
BUT HE DOESN'T KNOW ANY BETTER!
1-26

HIS BROTHER SENT HIM FROM AFRICA---TO BE EDUCATED! I'M TEACHIN' HIM OUR WAYS AND---!
MICKEY MOUSE, HAVE YOU LOST YOUR MIND? ARE YOU HARBORING THIS BLOODTHIRSTY SAVAGE IN YOUR HOME?

OH, HE'S ALL RIGHT! LOOK, THURSDAY--- YOU BE NICE TO THIS LADY --SHE BIG FRIEND! YOU KNOW--LIKE-UM MUCH, SEE?

BOOGIE-WOOGIE!
EEK! OUCH-- LET GO OF ME!
SEE, MINNIE--- HOW FRIENDLY HE IS!
WALT DISNEY

THURSDAY'S IDEA OF A FRIENDLY GREETING DOESN'T APPEAL TO MINNIE--- IN FACT, SHE DOESN'T CARE FOR IT AT ALL!

KEEP AWAY FROM ME, YOU JUNGLE APE!
SMACK!
!
1-27

UMBOPA SQUIRMP---!
UNH-UNH! MAN NO HIT LADY--NO-NO--- NOT DO!

NOPI-NOPI? BOP-- UM KANOODLE--!
YEH, I SEE ---BUT, MAN NO HIT LADY! LADY HIT MAN---OKAY!

OKI-OKI!
WELL--- MY GOODNESS- ---!
WALT DISNEY

I STILL SAY IT'S IMPOSSIBLE! YOU CAN'T KEEP A SAVAGE IN YOUR HOME---IT'S JUST TOO FANTASTIC!
BUT HE'S BEIN' EDUCATED, MINNIE! LOOK HOW HE ENJOYS THAT SIMPLE PAINTING!
1-29

FIDDLESTICKS! YOU KNOW VERY WELL IT ONLY REMINDS HIM HE'D LOVE A FISH DINNER!
MAYBE SO-- BUT IF THAT'S HIS PRIMITIVE WAY OF ENJOYING THE PICTURE, AT LEAST IT'S HONEST!

TO HIS SIMPLE MIND THAT'S A GREAT PIECE OF WORK AND HE DOESN'T NEED TO PUT ON THE ARTY FRONT THAT OUR CIVILIZED--!
MICKEY--- LOOK!

!
WALT DISNEY

ALL RIGHT--IF YOU WANT TO KEEP A WILD MAN IN YOUR HOUSE, GO AHEAD! DON'T BLAME ME IF HE EATS THE FLOWERS OFF YOUR RUGS!
AW, HE'S NOT SO BAD, MINNIE!
1-30

THERE'S SOME PEOPLE MINNIE JUST DOESN'T TAKE TO!

!

HEY! STOP!!
UM-GLOOB!
WALT DISNEY

GOSH--BEFORE THURSDAY CAME THERE USED TO BE FOOD IN HERE! NOW THERE'S NOT EVEN AN ONION! WHAT A GUY!
1-31

TRYIN' TO TEACH CIVILIZED WAYS AND MANNERS TO A SAVAGE IS SOME JOB---AND SAY-- I HAVEN'T SEEN HIM FOR TWO OR THREE HOURS!

I'D BETTER HUNT HIM UP BEFORE---?!!
YIPE YIPE---!!

UM-SLOUP--!
OWOOO--- YOW-W-W--!!
WALT DISNEY

THE IDEA! TRYIN' TO EAT PLUTO! WILL Y' EVER LEARN THE THINGS Y' SHOULDN'T DO?
NO PMAFF? NOPI-NOPI?
2-1

'LO, MICKEY! WHO'S YER FRIEND--- OR IS HE A RELATIVE?
HIS NAME'S THURSDAY! HE'S FROM AFRICA--- HASN'T LEARNED ANY ENGLISH YET!

BOOPA-DOOPA-- UM-TOTA!
WELL, F'R---!!?
NICE-MANNERED LI'L GUY, AIN'T HE?
WALT DISNEY

F' GOSH SAKES! HE NEVER ACTED LIKE THAT BEFORE!
I'VE TUK NOTICE, MICKEY, THET FURRINERS IS VERY PERLITE!
2-2

WHUR'S HE A-HURRYIN' OFF TO, MICKEY?
DARNED IF I KNOW! SOME IDEA SEEMS TO'VE STRUCK HIM!

I MIGHT'VE KNOWN HE WAS ONLY AFTER SOMEP'N TO EAT, BUT---

---GOOD GOSH---!

---HE'S GIVIN' IT AWAY! WHAT IS THIS?
BOOPA-DOOPA-- UM-TOTA!
THANKS--- DON'T MIND IF I DO!
WALT DISNEY

WELL, THIS BEATS ME! THURSDAY'D MURDER HIS AUNT FOR A PLATE O' BEANS -- BUT HE GIVES HIS FOOD TO YOU! WHAT'VE Y' GOT, GOOFY?
HUH? OH! JEST BOLONEY!
2-3

WELL, I GOTTA BE GOIN'! SO LONG, MR. THURSDAY!
WAIT A MINUTE! CAN Y' EXPLAIN WHAT THIS GREAT CHARM IS Y' SEEM TO HOLD?

GAWRSH -- AIN'T I NICE TO ALL YER FRIENDS? IT'S JEST MUH NATCHERAL GIFT O' TACT AN' PERLITENESS!

WELL, S'LONG MICKEY, I CAN'T WASTE THE WHOLE DAY STANDIN' HERE GABBIN' WITH YOU!
WALT DISNEY

NOW, WE'RE GOIN' OUT TO SHOW Y' AROUND, THURSDAY, AND YOU BE SURE AND BEHAVE! NO MONKEY BUSINESS, SEE?
UM-GLOOB!
2-5

GOOD MORNING, MICKEY! TEE-HEE --- YOUR FRIEND LOOKS CUTE MADE UP LIKE A LITTLE CANNIBAL! I DON'T EVEN RECOGNIZE HIM!
BUT HE'S THE REAL THING, CLARABELLE! HE'S JUST IN FROM AFRICA AND I'M TRYIN' TO CIVILIZE HIM!
!

NOW, MICKEY, DON'T SPOOF ME WITH ---
EEEK!!
NO, Y' DON'T! YOU LEAVE THAT HAT ALONE!

WHOA, CLARABELLE- --OOPS-- PASSED OUT!
PMAFF!
WALT DISNEY

OH, IT'S YOU, MICKEY! I THOUGHT--- THERE WAS A WILD MAN--- A SAVAGE--!
YEH, THAT'S THURSDAY! Y' GOT SCARED AND PASSED OUT WHEN Y' SAW HIM!
2-6

HE DOESN'T MEAN ANY HARM, BUT- --HE IS PRETTY PRIMITIVE AND --- WELL, I'LL BUY Y' A NEW HAT, CLARABELLE!

MISSY-- UM-GOOKOO, HUH?
WALT DISNEY

SCARIN' POOR CLARABELLE LIKE THAT! CAN'T I EVER TEACH Y' BETTER? CIVILIZED FOLKS DON'T EAT BIRDS OFF LADIES' HATS--- THEY JUST DON'T!
UH-UH?
2-7

NO! NO EATUM ALL TIME! WHITE MAN NO DO! NOPI-NOPI!
UM-UM! WHI' MAN NO DO--- T'URSDAY NO DO! NOPI-NOPI!

WELL, WHADDYA KNOW? THE LITTLE RASCAL'S LEARNIN' TO TALK! AND I SEEM TO HAVE PUT OVER MY LECTURE, TOO!

GLOOB! UM-SLOUP!
OOOH! WHAT A GUY!
WALT DISNEY

AFTER PAYING FOR ALL THE DAMAGES, MICKEY DECIDES THAT FOR THE BEST INTERESTS OF ALL CONCERNED, THURSDAY'S PLACE IS IN THE HOME!

IN SPITE OF PLUTO BEING SAFELY LOCKED IN THE CELLAR, ONCE MORE THE EVIDENCE OF A CHICKEN DINNER IS FOUND IN HIS HOUSE!

NIGHT FALLS AGAIN! AND ONCE MORE MICKEY TAKES UP WATCH FOR THE MYSTERIOUS PROWLER!

THIS NIGHT PROWLIN' HAS GOT TO STOP! AND THE ONLY SURE WAY IS TO LOCK Y' IN!
CLICK!
2-19

I HATE TO BE SO TOUGH WITH THE LITTLE GUY, BUT HE JUST WON'T LEARN!
CLICK!

A FEW HOURS LATER.

WELL, THIS IS ONE NIGHT I CAN HIT THE HAY WITHOUT WORRYIN' WHAT THURSDAY'S UP TO!

BUT--WHAT IS THIS?
WALT DISNEY

HOTEL RITZ-DUFF,
RITZ-
2-20

SMACK!

SURE IS NICE TO KNOW THURSDAY'S LOCKED UP IN HIS ROOM! TONIGHT I CAN SLEEP IN PEACE-- --MMM--Z- Z-Z-Z---
WALT DISNEY

OH, I SAY, MY MAN--YOU CAWN'T GO IN! THIS IS THE RITZ-DUFF HOTEL---WE DON'T CATER TO CIRCUS FREAKS!
2-21

UMBOPA SQUIRMP!
YOW-W!

AND, THINKING THE LITTLE SAVAGE SAFELY LOCKED UP, MICKEY SLUMBERS BLISSFULLY ON!
Z-Z-Z-Z Z-MMM- -Z-ZZ-- -Z--

ATTRACTED BY THE NOVELTY OF A REVOLVING DOOR, THURSDAY TRIES TO GET INTO THE HOTEL RITZ-DUFF! HE HAS A LITTLE TROUBLE WITH THE DOORMAN--- AND ALSO WITH THE DOOR!

REFUSING TO ACCEPT DEFEAT FROM A REVOLVING DOOR, THURSDAY WINS BY A DIRECT ASSAULT!

THURSDAY DISCOVERS THAT WILD GAME ABOUNDS IN THE PALATIAL LOBBY OF THE RITZ-DUFF HOTEL!

THURSDAY'S PRIMITIVE IMPULSE TO SPEAR A LEOPARD IN THE RITZ-DUFF LOBBY RESULTS DISASTROUSLY. THE LEOPARD HAPPENS TO BE A COAT WITH A LADY STILL IN IT!

LITTLE DOES MICKEY KNOW THAT HIS PRIMITIVE GUEST IS RUNNING LOOSE IN THE SWANKY HOTEL RITZ-DUFF AND CREATING A FURORE!

A 'PHONE CALL FROM THE HOTEL MANAGER FAILS TO SHAKE MICKEY'S BELIEF THAT THURSDAY IS SAFELY UNDER LOCK AND KEY!

SO BACK TO SLEEP HE GOES!
Z-ZZ-ZZ-Z--
2-29

MEANWHILE, THURSDAY IS BUSY DODGING VARIOUS IRATE EMPLOYEES OF THE HOTEL!

--AND MY DEAH--HER **GOWN**!
UP!
YES, I KNOW--**UTTERLY** PASSE!
---AND ABSOLUTELY **NO** NAIL POLISH--!

!!?!

UM-PNAFF??

MICKEY SLEEPS ON, SUBLIMELY UNCONSCIOUS OF THURSDAY'S NOCTURNAL ESCAPADE!
KNR-R-W-W--KSPLLT--MUMBLE-MILK 'N HONEY--MMM-Z-Z---!
3-1

BUT---AT THE RITZ-DUFF HOTEL ---
STOP--IN THE NAME OF THE HOUSE DETECTIVE!

GRANDE HALLE DE BANQUETTE

OHH!!
EEK!
MY WORD!

STOP--YOU BLASTED HEATHEN---!
Copr. 1940, Walt Disney Productions World Rights Reserved
3-2

CRASH!

THE RITZ-DUFF **AGAIN?** BUT, I TELL Y', YOU'RE **CRAZY**! HE'S LOCKED IN HIS ROOM! ALL RIGHT, I **WILL**---!

THERE! SLEEPIN' LIKE A LAMB, JUST AS I THOUGHT! THOSE PEOPLE MUST'VE BEEN **SEEIN'** THINGS!
Z-ZZ---ZZZ--
WALT DISNEY

MORNING! MICKEY FINDS THURSDAY STILL LOCKED IN HIS ROOM AND IS INDIGNANT THAT THE LITTLE GUY WAS ACCUSED OF THE RIOT IN THE RITZ-DUFF HOTEL!

SHUCKS! HOUDINI COULDN'T HAVE GOTTEN OUT OF THAT ROOM LAST NIGHT!
3-4

"---PANDEMONIUM REIGNED, WHEN A GRASS-SKIRTED SAVAGE, ARMED WITH A SPEAR, UPSET THE SERENE DIGNITY OF THE CITY'S SWANKIEST HOSTELRY!"

"---THE VANDAL MADE GOOD HIS ESCAPE AND, ACCORDING TO WITNESSES, FLED AT SUPER-SPEED TOWARD THE HOME OF MICKEY MOUSE---!"

WELL, FOR PETE'S SAKE! IT SOUNDS LIKE THURSDAY---BUT IT COULDN'T BE!
GOSH!

IN SPITE OF THE NEWSPAPER STORY OF THURSDAY'S HOTEL ESCAPADE, MICKEY IS STILL UNCONVINCED! THE FOLLOWING NIGHT HE AGAIN LOCKS THE LITTLE AFRICAN IN!

YOU COULDN'T HAVE GOTTEN OUT---AND Y' WON'T TONIGHT, EITHER!
NOPI-NOPI?
3-5

BUT LITTLE DOES MICKEY KNOW---!!

AUK!
EL CABBAGO CIGARO

!
EL CABBAGO CIGARO

---IT'S IMPOSSIBLE, I TELL Y'! SOMEBODY MUST BE CUCKOO! ALL RIGHT--HOLD THE 'PHONE AND I'LL GO TO HIS ROOM RIGHT NOW AND PROVE IT!
WALT DISNEY

WHAT NERVE! TRYIN' TO TELL ME THURSDAY'S OUT RAISIN' CAIN, WHEN I'VE GOT HIM LOCKED IN HIS ROOM!
3-6

I S'POSE HE COULD GET OUT THE WINDOW--WITH THIS ON IT!

AFTER ALL, THE WHOLE IDEA WAS TO MAKE SURE HE COULDN'T GET INTO TROUBLE---

---ANY TIME HE GETS OUT OF-
--HUH?
GOOD GOSH---
HE IS OUT!
WALT DISNEY

AFTER INCARCERATING THURSDAY TO KEEP HIM OUT OF TROUBLE, MICKEY IS ASTOUNDED TO FIND HIM MISSING, ALTHOUGH BOTH DOOR AND WINDOW ARE LOCKED!

NOW, OFFICER --D-DON'T WORRY! I'LL PAY FOR THAT TIRE THAT THURSDAY DAMAGED!
HMMPH--- I'LL SAY YUH WILL! BUT JUST THE SAME, I GOT A WARRANT HERE FOR---
P.D.
3-11

LOOK, OFFICER --- I'LL ADMIT HE'S GOT INTO PLENTY OF TROUBLE --AND ALL THAT--- BUT I'VE MADE GOOD FOR EVERYTHING --SO---

---SO, Y' SEE, AS LONG AS ALL THE DAMAGE HAS BEEN COVERED, YOU'VE GOT NO RIGHT TO ARREST HIM FOR---
YEAH, YEAH! OKAY, SONNY BOY. BUT---

---THIS WARRANT'S FOR YOU --- FOR MAINTAININ' A PUBLIC NUISANCE!
WALT DISNEY

---MUMBLE-MBLE---MAINTAINING-PUBLIC-NUISANCE, WHO-WILFULLY---MUMBLE---MALICIOUS-MISCHIEF---BLAH-BLAH---FELONIOUS-ASSAULT--BREAKING-AND-ENTERING---BLAH-BLAH---
3-12

---ARE-HEREBY-ORDERED-FORTHWITH-TO-ABATE-THE-SAID-NUISANCE-WITHIN-24-HOURS!
AND S'POSIN' I CAN'T GET RID OF THE "SAID NUISANCE," --WHAT THEN?

IN THAT CASE, YOUNG MAN, THE COURT WILL BE COMPELLED TO TAKE FULL CHARGE OF THE MATTER!

THANKS-- THAT'S ALL I WANTED TO KNOW! WE'LL MOST LIKELY SEE Y' TOMORROW!
EH!!? NOW, LOOK HERE---!
WALT DISNEY

NO DOUBT ABOUT IT, I'VE GOT TO GET RID OF THURSDAY--- BUT WHAT THE HECK CAN I DO WITH HIM?
3-13

I COULD SEND HIM BACK WHERE HE CAME FROM--- BUT WHERE DID HE COME FROM? ALL I KNOW IS JUST AFRICA!

IF HE WASN'T SO DARN WILD---OH, HELLO, GOOFY!
H'YA, MICKEY! MORNIN', MR. THURSDAY!

THERE IT GOES AGAIN! GOSH DARN--I'D LIKE TO KNOW YOUR SECRET, GOOFY! HE TREATS Y' LIKE A--- LIKE A KING!
UM-TOTA! OOOOH---UM-TOTA!
WALT DISNEY

BOOPA-DOOPA --UM-TOTA!
THANKS! DON'T CARE IF I DO!
BOY! IF HE'D ONLY BEHAVE LIKE THAT FOR ANYBODY ELSE!
3-14

NICE LI'L GUY! WHAT I COME OVER FER, MICKEY, WUZ TO **SEE** IF YOU'D GO TO THUH CIRCUS WITH ME!
HECK! I CAN'T GO **ANYWHERE** 'TIL I FIND A WAY TO GET RID O' THAT DOGGONE PEST!

AND WHAT TO DO WITH HIM IS--- **CIRCUS??** YOU SAID **CIRCUS**! WHY DIDN'T I THINK O' THAT BEFORE?

GAWRSH! WHUT TH'!!?
Distributed by King Features Syndicate, Inc.
WALT DISNEY

SIDE SHOW ENTRANCE
POLA ROLEY
I SHOULD'A THOUGHT OF IT BEFORE ---THIS OUTFIT WILL BE TICKLED PINK TO TAKE THURSDAY OFF MY HANDS!
WORLD'S FATTEST
HUMAN
BARLEY AND BAILEM'S
SIDE SHOW TICKETS
3-15

NOW, TO FIND THE BOSS AND--
JAM'N JIVE
WILDEST MAN ALIVE!
CAPTURED AT TERRIFIC COST IN DARKEST AFRICA
DANGER KEEP DISTANCE
Copr. 1940, Walt Disney Productions World Rights Reserved

AFRICA
DANGER
PMAFF! BOOGIE-WOOGIE-WOOGIE!
!

HALP!! A CANNIBAL!

CAN Y' USE A REALLY **WILD** WILD MAN IN YOUR SHOW? HIS NAME'S THURSDAY AND HE'S DIRECT FROM AFRICA!
HE SURE LOOKS THE PART ALL RIGHT! BUT CAN HE ACT?
3-16
Copr. 1940, Walt Disney Productions World Rights Reserved

HE DOESN'T **NEED** TO ACT--- I TELL Y', HE'S THE REAL THING!
OH, SURE--- THEY **ALWAYS** ARE! WELL, WHADDYA WANT FOR HIM, SON?

NOTHING! HE'S ABSOLUTELY FREE! ONLY FROM NOW ON YOU'RE RESPONSIBLE--NOT ME!
HUH!!?
Distributed by King Features Syndicate, Inc.

HAPPY DAYS ARE HERE AGAIN---!
WALT DISNEY

COULD MICKEY BE CROWING A LITTLE TOO SOON? **YOU** KNOW THURSDAY!

ELATED OVER HAVING DISPOSED OF THURSDAY WITH A CIRCUS SIDESHOW, MICKEY IS ENJOYING LIFE ONCE MORE!

BOY, WHAT A DAY! NOT A CARE IN THE WORLD!
3-18

OH, NO? THAT'S WHAT YOU THINK!

SMART GUY, HUH? TELLIN' ME YUH HAD A WILD MAN FOR MY SHOW, THEN HANDIN' ME THIS!
Y' MEAN-- HE'S NOT---?

DON'T GET FUNNY! THAT ZULU'S THE REAL THING ---AND YOU KNEW IT, YUH CROOK!
WALT DISNEY

THINKING THAT HE HAD DISPOSED OF HIS "PROBLEM CHILD" WITH A CIRCUS, MICKEY'S DREAM IS RUDELY SHATTERED WHEN THE SIDESHOW MANAGER RETURNS THURSDAY FOR BEING TOO WILD!

GOSH -- IF HE'S TOO MUCH FOR A CIRCUS TO HANDLE, WHAT THE HECK AM I GOIN' TO DO WITH THE GUY?
3-19

OH-OH! WHILE I'M SITTIN' HERE STEWIN' ABOUT HIM, HE'S SNEAKED OFF! I BETTER FIND HIM QUICK!

HE WENT THIS WAY-- I CAN SEE THAT!

OH, F'R PETE'S SAKE! WHAT NEXT?
CITY AQUARIUM
WALT DISNEY

---STEALIN' FISH OUTA THE AQUARIUM--- THAT'S THE LAST STRAW!
POLIC COUR
UM-GLOOCH- --?
3-20

WHAT!? HAVEN'T YOU DISPOSED OF THIS NUISANCE, AS THE COURT ORDERED? DON'T YOU RECALL THE COURT'S FINAL WARNING?
I DO! IF I DIDN'T GET RID OF HIM IN 24 HOURS, YOU WOULD TAKE CHARGE! WELL--- I DIDN'T GET RID OF HIM!

AH, NOW--AHEM- --THE COURT IS ALWAYS FAIR! WE ARE WILLING TO BE LENIENT AND --AH, EXTEND THE TIME LIMIT!

NO, SIR--- I WOULDN'T THINK OF ASKING THE FAVOR ---THE LAW'S THE LAW! GOOD DAY, SIR!
WALT DISNEY

REALIZING THAT IT IS HOPELESS TO TRY AND MAKE A "SILK PURSE" OUT OF THURSDAY, MICKEY ALLOWS HIM TO BE TAKEN BY THE POLICE.
3-21

POOR LITTLE GUY, I HATE TO LET HIM DOWN, BUT WHAT COULD I DO? AND, GOSH KNOWS I NEED A LITTLE REST!

FIRST TIME I'VE BEEN ABLE TO RELAX SINCE THURSDAY CAME! BOY, WHAT A NUISANCE HE TURNED OUT TO BE!

TING-KLING-KA-LING!
AT LEAST, I CAN ANSWER THE DOORBELL AND KNOW IT ISN'T SOMEBODY WITH A BILL FOR DAMAGES!

HE'S YOUR PROPERTY AGAIN, SON! THE LAW FINDS WE GOT NO LEGAL GROUNDS TO HOLD HIM!
OWW-W!!
WALT DISNEY

AGAIN "THE CAT COMES BACK"! MICKEY'S PEACE ENDS ABRUPTLY WHEN THE POLICE CLAIM THEY HAVE NO LEGAL RIGHT TO HOLD THURSDAY!

YUH SEE, SINCE HE'S AN ALIEN, WE CAN'T HOLD HIM EXCEPT FOR DEPORTATION! AND NOBUDDY KNOWS WHERE TO DEPORT HIM--- SO THERE Y' ARE!
YEH- --SO HERE I AM!
3-22

AND, MIND YUH-- NO MONKEY BUSINESS! SEE THAT YUH KEEP THAT BIRD OUTA TROUBLE, THAT'S ALL!
YEH-- THAT'S ALL! IT'S JUST SO SIMPLE AND EASY!

BOOM-BIDDY-- BUM-BIDDY--- BUM-BUM- BOOM!
HUH!!?

NOW, WHERE THE HECK DID HE GET THAT? AND WHAT'S THE IDEA--??
BOOM- BIDDY-- BUM-BIDDY--- BUM-BUM- BOOM!
WALT DISNEY

DARNED IF I KNOW WHERE HE GOT THAT--- BUT IT SEEMS TO KEEP HIM AMUSED, SO I S'POSE I SHOULDN'T KICK!
BOOM- BIDDY-- BUM- BIDDY--- BUM- BUM- BOOM!
3-23

BUT---AFTER THREE HOURS WITHOUT PAUSE---!
ENOUGH IS ENOUGH! GOSH, CAN'T Y' DO ANYTHING IN A CIVILIZED WAY?
UM- PMAFF?

YOU'D THINK DRUMMIN' WAS THE MOST IMPORTANT THING IN LIFE, THE WAY HE--- HUH!!?
BOOM- BIDDY- BUM- BIDDY-- BUM- BUM- BOOM

F' GOSH SAKES--- WHAT IS THIS!!?
BOOM-BIDDY-- BUM-BIDDY--- BUM-BUM-BOOM!
WALT DISNEY

THURSDAY HAS DEVELOPED A NEW MANIA ---A SUDDEN YEN FOR DRUMMING! HIS CEASELESS. MONOTONOUS POUNDING IS GETTING MICKEY DOWN!

ONE MORE REASON I'VE GOTTA GET RID OF HIM---THE WHOLE NEIGHBORHOOD WILL BE RAISIN' CAIN!
BOOM-BIDDY--BUM-BIDDY--BUM-BUM--BOOM
3-25

SAY! HE LIKES TO DRUM SO MUCH--HOT DOG---AN INSPIRATION!

CLUB CONGO
NOW
CAL CABWAYS CONGOLIERS

OOOOH--BOOGIE-WOOGIE!
AND HOW! BOY--- I'VE FOUND A PLACE FOR Y' AT LAST!
REHEARSAL DO NOT DISTURB!
WALT DISNEY

FINDING THAT THE ONE THING THURSDAY CAN DO HARMLESSLY IS TO BEAT A DRUM, MICKEY GETS THE BRIGHT IDEA OF TRYING TO PUT HIM IN A BAND!

REHEARSAL DO NOT DISTURB
IF THEY'LL ONLY TAKE Y', MY TROUBLES WILL BE OVER!
3-26

HEY! WAIT---!

OWW-W!
GIMMIK!
BO K!

OOOOOH!!

SA-AY---DAT BOY'S HOT STUFF! WE KIN USE HIM!
BOOM-BIDDY-BUM-BUM-
WALT DISNEY

YEH, MAN---LOOKA DAT BOY DRUM! IF YOU HIS AGENT, WE GWINE MEK A DEAL RIGHT NOW!
BOOM-BIDDY-BUM-BIDDY--BUM-BUM-BOOM!
OKAY---HE'S ALL YOURS!
REHEARSAL DO NOT
3-27

YASSUH---HOTTEST NOVELTY AH EVAH SEEN! DOGGONE IF AH COULDN'T BILL 'IM AS A GENUWINE AFRICAN AN' GIT AWAY WID IT!

BOY-OH-BOY---WHAT A RELIEF! GUESS I'LL GET MINNIE AND GO OUT AND CELEBRATE!

---YEH, MINNIE, COULD Y'---?
JUST A MINUTE, THERE'S SOMEBODY AT THE DOOR!
TING-KLING-KA-LING!

LOOK YERE, AH DON' WANT NO MO' O' DIS BABY! WHAT GOOD TO A BAND AM A DRUMMER, WHICH YO' CAIN'T MAKE 'IM STOP?
WALT DISNEY

IT'S TOO DEEP FOR ME! ALL OF A SUDDEN HE'S GOT NO INTEREST IN LIFE EXCEPT BANGIN' ON A DRUM!
BOOM -BIDDY-- BUM- BIDDY--- BUM- BUM- BOOM!
3-28

WELL, BY GOSH, I'M GOIN' TO FIND SOME PLACE THAT'LL TAKE THAT PEST OFF MY HANDS!

AT THE COUNTY ORPHANS' HOME.
--- SO, YOU'VE HEARD ABOUT THURSDAY AND YOU'RE AFRAID- --IS THAT IT?
ER--NOT AT ALL! IT'S THE, ER--LEGALITY OF IT---WE MUST HAVE PROOF THAT HE IS AN ORPHAN!

THEN, AT THE STATE REFORM SCHOOL.
---BUT, I TELL Y' HE BELONGS HERE! NOBODY COULD NEED REFORMIN' MORE THAN HE DOES!
I QUITE AGREE, SIR! BUT THIS INSTITUTION ONLY TAKES IN THOSE WHO CAN BE REFORMED!
Distributed by King Features Syndicate, Inc

GOSH, THE WHOLE WORLD SEEMS TO KNOW WHAT HE IS--- NOBODY'LL TAKE HIM!
---BIDDY- BUM-BUM- BOOM!
WALT DISNEY

IN A DESPERATE EFFORT TO GET RID OF HIS "PROBLEM CHILD," MICKEY HAS TRIED EVERY INSTITUTION IN TOWN. HE CAN'T EVEN CRASH THE STATE REFORMATORY!

I CAN'T GET RID OF HIM- --AND I CAN'T KEEP HIM! WHAT THE HECK--?
BOOM- BIDDY--BUM- BIDDY---!
3-29

BIDDY- BUM-BUM- BOOM!
THAT INFERNAL DRUMMING ---IT'S DRIVIN' ME COO-KOO!

BOOM-BIDDY-- BUM-BIDDY--
IT'S DRIVIN' THE WHOLE NEIGHBORHOOD NUTTY--OUCH! WE'VE STOOD ENOUGH--!

---BIDDY- --BUM-BUM- BOOM!
---FOR DAYS NOW!
DON'T I KNOW IT!
Y' GOTTA DO SOMETHING!
DO WHAT?
SOMETHING--ANYTHING!
YOU DO IT!
DO WHAT?
ANYTHING!
AW, SHUT UP!

BOOM- BIDDY--BUM- BIDDY---BUM-BUM- BOOM!
MORNING, NOON AND NIGHT--- HE NEVER STOPS! AND WHY? WHAT'S IT MEAN TO HIM?
3-30

---BUM-BUM- BOOM!!

Distributed by King Features Syndicate, Inc.

HUH!? WHAT'S WRONG? WHAT WAS THAT LOUD SILENCE I JUST HEARD?

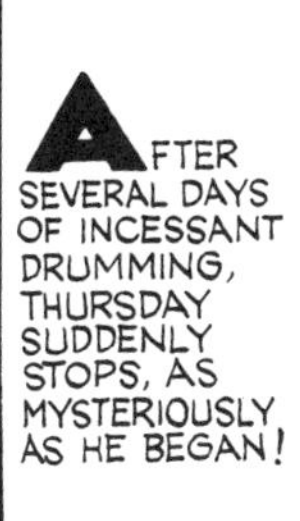
AFTER SEVERAL DAYS OF INCESSANT DRUMMING, THURSDAY SUDDENLY STOPS, AS MYSTERIOUSLY AS HE BEGAN!

YESTERDAY Y' COULDN'T'VE BLASTED HIM LOOSE FROM THAT DRUM! NOW ALL HE DOES IS STARE INTO THE DISTANCE!
4-1
Copr. 1940, Walt Disney Productions World Rights Reserved

WELL, WHATEVER MADE HIM QUIT, IT WAS JUST IN TIME SO THE NEIGHBORS DIDN'T CALL OUT THE MILITIA!

LOOK HERE, CONFOUND YOU--- THIS INFERNAL QUIET IS GETTING ON OUR NERVES! WHERE'S THAT DRUM---?
B-BUT I THOUGHT--- YOU COMPLAINED ---!?

OF COURSE! BUT THIS AWFUL SILENCE IS DEAFENING---WE CAN'T SLEEP! IF HE'S GOIN' TO STOP DRUMMING HE'S GOTTA TAPER OFF GRADUALLY!
WALT DISNEY
Distributed by King Features Syndicate, Inc.

DOGGONE---THIS SUDDEN QUIET MAKES ME NERVOUS! I'D LIKE TO KNOW WHAT HE'S GOT ON HIS MIND!
4-2

AT LEAST, WHEN HE WAS BANGIN' ON THIS THING HE KEPT OUT O' MISCHIEF!

LOOK, THURSDAY! DON'T Y' WANTA BEAT THE DRUM AWHILE? YOU KNOW--- BOOM-BOOM-BOOM?
Distributed by King Features Syndicate, Inc.

UG-GLOOMPH!
WELL, I'LL BE---!?? WHEN HE'S THROUGH, HE'S THROUGH!
WALT DISNEY

MICKEY IS COMPLETELY PUZZLED WHEN THURSDAY SO SUDDENLY LOSES ALL INTEREST IN DRUMMING!

FOR WEEKS NOW, ALL HE'S DONE IS GAZE OUT, LIKE HE WAS EXPECTIN' SOMEONE!
4-3

UM-GLOOB! ELLUMPAN! ELLUMPAN!!
?
!!

ONE AFRICAN ELEPHANT--- SIGN HERE, PLEASE!
WELL-- UH-- WHAT--- ???
M'JUMJO!
Distributed by King Features Syndicate, Inc.

I MUST SAY, YOU HAVE THE DARNDEST THINGS DELIVERED HERE! GOOD DAY!

AN ELEPHANT-- FROM AFRICA--!!? HOW TH' HECK---?
M'JUMJO! BOOGIE-WOOGIE!

DEAR BROTHER THURSDAY-- I HEAR YOUR DRUM CALL, AND SO
SENDUM YOUR PET. EXCUSE DELAY, BUT MESSAGE FULL OF STATIC.
GIVE MANY REGARD TO MR. MOUSE.
FRIDAY.
4-4

SO THAT'S WHAT YOUR DRUMMIN' WAS ALL ABOUT! BUT TO AFRICA ---WHY, THAT'S IMPOSSIBLE! IT'S---!
UGGLE-OOCH---BOOM -BOOM--GA-BLUG-- BOOM ---FOODELI-RAKI-SAKI--BOOM- --DITTEM-DOTTEM-WOTTEM-CHOO! GLOOB! ELLUMPAN!

WELL, THANKS! THAT MAKES IT PERFECTLY CLEAR!
WALT DISNEY

THE ANSWER TO THURSDAY'S DRUM MESSAGES ARRIVES IN THE FORM OF A PET ELEPHANT FROM HOME! MICKEY INSISTS IT'S IMPOSSIBLE- --BUT HERE'S THE ELEPHANT!

DRUMS HEARD CLEAR TO AFRICA! ABSURD! ---HEY!! NO, Y' DON'T--!
4-5

NO, THURSDAY! COME BACK-- STOP! STOP THAT THING, I TELL Y'---!!
Distributed by King Features Syndicate, Inc.

HEY, CUT IT OUT! LIE DOWN! GO HOME- --OUCH!

HI-YO, M'JUMJO! OOWAH!
!
!
!
TRASH

HEY, THURSDAY, STOP-- DOGGONE Y'! COME BACK!
TRASH
Copr 1940, Walt Disney Productions World Rights Reserved
4-6

GOOD NIGHT! THIS IS THE WORST YET!

---I TELL Y', SERGEANT, IT'S SERIOUS---HE'S GOT AN ELEPHANT THIS TIME! THAT'S WHAT I SAID--- YES--ELEPHANT! YOU'D BETTER SEND YOUR RIOT SQUAD-- QUICK!

NO TIME TO LOSE! IT MIGHT AS WELL BE A CARLOAD O' DYNAMITE!

OMIGOSH! IT'S STARTED!
STOP
WALT DISNEY
Distributed by King Features Syndicate, Inc.

WITH THURSDAY JOY-RIDING ON AN ELEPHANT, MICKEY FEARS THAT ANYTHING CAN HAPPEN ---AND IT DOES!

WHICH WAY---?
YE MEAN, TH' RUNAWAY CIRCUS TRAIN? THAT WAY!
STOP
GO
4-8

GOSH KNOWS, HE MADE ENOUGH TROUBLE FOR ME WITHOUT AN ELEPHANT! I HATE TO THINK WHAT'S GOIN' ON NOW!
Copr. 1940, Walt Disney Productions
World Rights Reserved

SAY-- DID YOU SEE A LITTLE AFRICAN GO BY ON AN ELEPHANT ---?

OH---WAS THAT AN ELEPHANT? I THOUGHT IT WAS AN EARTHQUAKE!
Distributed by King Features Syndicate, Inc.

THURSDAY AND AN ELEPHANT --- WHAT A COMBINATION! I'LL BE RUINED!
4-9

NO NEED TO ASK IF THEY CAME THIS WAY---!

ALLA TIME, MY FRUIT, SHEEZA WRECK! WHAT AM I -- SOMEBODY IN FUNNY PAPERS?!

OWW-- TOO LATE AGAIN--!
ANTIQUE CHINA and GLASSWARE
YEH-- YA SHOULD 'A BEEN HERE, MISTER! HONEST---A REAL ELEPHANT WENT BY!
WALT DISNEY

FOLLOWING THE TRAIL OF THURSDAY ON HIS ROLLICKING ELEPHANT JAUNT, MICKEY DISCOVERS HAVOC IN LARGE GOBS!

OH-OH! WAS IT-- THE ELEPHANT?
IT WAS! HE JUST STOPPED TO SCRATCH HIS BACK!
4-10

GRADUALLY THE WHOLE TOWN IS RISING UP!
WHEEE-E-E-UUU-U-U---!
P.D.

WOOO-WEEE-E-E-E-E--EE.
MAYOR
F.D.

BOY--I'D SURE HATE TO BE TH' GUY THEY'RE GONNA HOLD RESPONSIBLE FOR ALL THIS! CHANCES ARE, HE'LL GET LIFE!
YEH-- ULP ---HE PROB'LY WILL!
WALT DISNEY

FROM ALL PARTS OF TOWN COME TALES OF DISASTER! ONE AFRICAN ELEPHANT PLUS ONE PRIMITIVE SAVAGE EQUALS ONE EARTHQUAKE!

THURSDAY'S ELEPHANT ESCAPADE IS THE LAST STRAW! AN AROUSED CITIZENRY WILL STAND NO MORE---AND MICKEY FINDS HIMSELF ON TRIAL AS KEEPER OF "PUBLIC MENACE NO. ONE"!

MYSTERY! ON THE DAY THAT THE COURT SENTENCE FALLS DUE, THURSDAY DISAPPEARS, LEAVING A NOTE WHICH NO ONE CAN DECIPHER! DAYS PASS--- AND PEACE STILL REIGNS!

JUST CHECKING UP AGAIN FOR THE POLICE! STILL NOTHIN' HEARD FROM THAT CONGO CRIME WAVE?
NOT A THING! HE DROPPED OUTA SIGHT WEEKS AGO AND THAT'S ALL I KNOW ABOUT IT!
4-18

WORST OF IT IS, HE MIGHT TURN UP ANY TIME! THIS SUSPENSE IS AWFUL!

MORNIN', MICKEY! ONLY ONE LETTER FOR YOU TODAY!
G-GOSH--- IT'S FROM---!
MAIL

DEAR MICKEY MOUZE:
THURZDAY HOME TODAY.
THANKZ FOR EDUMCATION
AND BACKGROUND
POLIZHMENT. HE NO
LIKE YOUR COUNTRY.
ZAY NOBODY HAVE FUN--
ALL TIME WANTUM FIGHT.
THURZDAY GENTLE--
LIKEZ PEACE.
COME ZEE UZ
ZOMETIMEZ.
FRIDAY.
IT'S-IT'S TRUE! HE'S GONE! MY WORRIES ARE OVER!
WALT DISNEY

BOY--IT'S GREAT TO LIVE AGAIN! JUST THINK-- THAT PESKY LITTLE SAVAGE IS GONE FOR GOOD!
YEAH? TOO BAD! HE ALLUS SEEMED LIKE A NICE LI'L GUY TO ME!
4-19

HE WAS MORE THAN NICE TO YOU, GOOFY! THAT'S A MYSTERY I NEVER COULD FIGURE OUT!
MUSEUM OF NATURAL HISTORY
'TAIN'T NO MYSTERY! THEM SIMPLE-MINDED FOLK ARE JEST NATCH'RULLY IMPRESSED BY SOOPERIOR INTELLECK!

AN' SPEAKIN' OF INTELLECK, HOW COME YUH BRUNG ME INTO THIS HERE MUSEEM?
JUST ABSENT-MINDED, I GUESS! I WAS THINKIN' OF THURSDAY AND SORTA WANDERED INTO AFRICA!
AFRICA
Distributed by King Features Syndicate, Inc.

HUH? WOTZA MATTER---?
WELL, F'R--- DO YOU SEE WHAT I SEE?

WANDERING INTO THE NATURAL HISTORY MUSEUM WITH GOOFY, MICKEY SUDDENLY FINDS THE ANSWER TO AN OLD MYSTERY!

BOY-OH-BOY! AT LAST I KNOW WHY THURSDAY THOUGHT YOU WERE SUCH HOT STUFF-- LOOK--!
I'VE TOLE YUH, MICKEY, MR. THURSDAY WUZ A JEDGE OF CHARACTER! I COULD SEE HE WUZ PLENTY SMART---!

YEAH? WELL, LOOK AT THAT!
HUH? LOOKS FAMILIAR, SOMEHOW--!
SACRED TOTEM OF WEST AFRICAN TRIBE
4-20

DON'T Y' SEE? HE THOUGHT YOU WERE A LIVING TOTEM POLE!
WELL---THUH GOL-DURN DIM-WITTED MONKEY! I ALLUS SAID HE DIDN'T HAVE NO SENSE!

I NEVER DID HAVE NO USE FER HIM, THUH CONSARNED LI'L IDJUT--!
OH, HA-HA-HA! BOOPA-DOOPA--UM-TOTA!

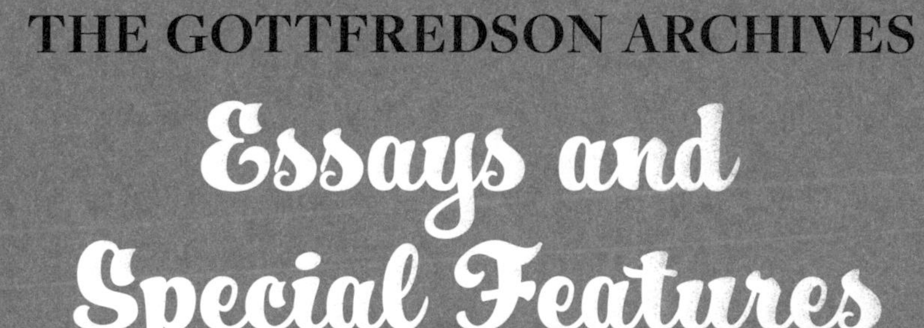
THE GOTTFREDSON ARCHIVES
Essays and
Special Features

Gottfredson's World: MIGHTY WHALE HUNTER 

Every country that loves Mickey Mouse has had its own edition—or editions—of Floyd Gottfredson's epics. And each country's Disney comics publisher has tried to make its own version unique, usually by asking homegrown talent to create their own covers or vignettes based on the stories.

In this series we're proud to anthologize these images, both foreign and domestic, old and new—and give you a sense of how far Gottfredson's classic adventures have traveled over the years. In the case of "Mighty Whale Hunter," of course, it's a trek best taken by *ship*... [DG]

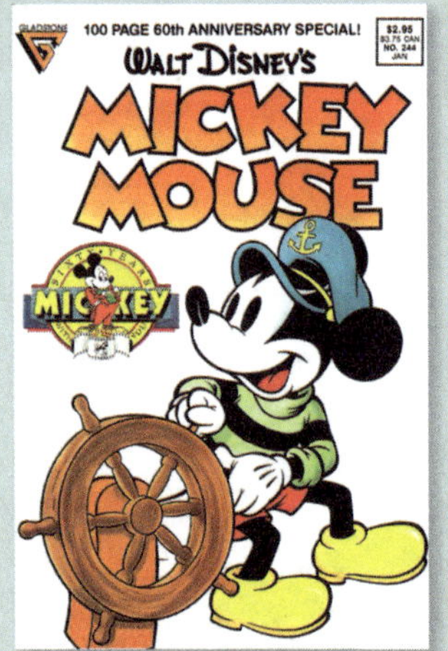

FROM LEFT CLOCKWISE:

Mickey Mouse 244 (1988), art by Daan Jippes. While the cover was drawn with "Mighty Whale Hunter" in mind, the story is not actually in the issue! Image courtesy Thomas Jensen.

Italian *Albi d'oro* 28 (1939). Art by Enrico Mauro Pinochi; images courtesy Leonardo Gori.

Italian *Topolino collezione ANAF* 32 (1983). Art by Romano Scarpa; image courtesy Leonardo Gori.

French *Journal de Mickey* 1834 (1987). Pencils by René Guillaume, inks by Patrice Croci; image courtesy David Gerstein.

Italian *Topolino d'oro* 21 (1973). Art by Marco Rota; image courtesy Leonardo Gori.

The Cast: JOE PIPER

Of the many villains that Gottfredson pits against Mickey, the artfully incompetent Joe Piper is among the most likeable. His protective, almost paternal attitude towards eager apprentice Mickey is genuinely endearing. We marvel with amusement at the cheek and bravado with which Piper shows Mickey the ropes of the plumbing business—even while seeming in dire need of a beginner's course himself!

When we learn that Piper is really a robber, not a plumber, the aura of sloppiness and incompetence still lingers around him. Despite his gang's ingenious scheme to rob the bank with a folding bathtub, we never perceive Piper as a criminal genius; only as a laid-back, likeable oddball who is slightly intimidating at worst—and probably not the sharpest knife in the drawer.

The final revelation—that Piper and his pals are actors—seems to suggest not only that Piper's role as a plumber was fictitious; perhaps his robber role, too, is an act rather than his true nature. Revealing a narcissistic streak that vaguely anticipates *Batman*'s Joker, Piper and his gang seem to derive more pleasure from their clever performance in disguise than from any potential outcome of their theft!

It is entertaining to note how the newly introduced Detective Casey bears a striking visual similarity to Piper; almost as if Gottfredson had intended to depict the inept *lumpenproletariat*—Piper—and a righteous guardian of the law, Casey, in a kind of Brechtian mirror. Furthering the comparison, while Casey is smart and alert in "The Plumber's Helper," he would later develop a Piper-like laid-back confidence and a defiant pride in his less-than-professional skill!

While Piper remains a memorable figure, he never reappeared in later American comics. But Gottfredson's late 1930s stories earned a special place in the memories of Italian readers. During World War II, American comics were banned in Fascist Italy, and prewar Mickey Mouse albums became collectors' items—nostalgically treasured and cherished even as cities fell in ruins. Years later, fueled by that nostalgia, great postwar Italian Disney authors like Luciano Bottaro, Guido Martina and Romano Scarpa revived key prewar Gottfredson characters for their own new stories: Dr. Vulter, Dr. Einmug, the Phantom Blot—and of course our Joe Piper. *Topolino* ("Mickey Mouse") was a comic book for all ages in the 1960s; so Italian authors could write not only for new kid readers, but for readers of their own generation, who were sure to remember the thrill of Gottfredson's original masterpieces.

Joe Piper has thus reappeared several times in Italian stories by various authors—perhaps a couple every decade—enough to keep him alive, but never quite enough to make him an established character in readers' minds. We like to think that Piper, with his slightly enigmatic true identity, enjoys staying just a little bit mysterious!

— Francesco Stajano and Leonardo Gori

ABOVE: Wak! Donald recalls Mickey's adventure with Joe Piper in "Donald Duck and the Pipe of Peace" (1961), written and drawn by Luciano Bottaro.

EVERY GREAT ARTIST needs some down time. The need hit Floyd Gottfredson in late 1938, when illness forced a cutback in his output. For the *Mickey Mouse* Sunday strip, Gottfredson trained a permanent replacement, Spanish-born Manuel Gonzales. Then Gottfredson delegated a month of dailies to a promising new penciler: Ross Louis Wetzel.

Born March 11, 1917, Wetzel was an artist from the start—drawing up a storm at Chicago's Etta Flagg Young Elementary School, then becoming a print cartoonist for Austin High School's *Austin Times.* Father Fred Wetzel at first resisted Ross' artsy aspirations: "My son should not starve in a garret!'"[1] But others encouraged the boy, including artist and future wife Janice May Johnson. In 1935, Ross followed Janice to the American Academy of Art. Then, in 1938—work with Disney? Why not?

"I sent for a tryout brochure," Wetzel recalled. "They asked prospective employees to solve certain drawing problems. Draw Goofy climbing a barbed wire fence..." Soon Wetzel had another problem to solve: making it to California in time to start his tryout period with Disney!

Wetzel and Gottfredson quickly crossed paths. "I had always admired his work," Wetzel remembered. "It seemed that Floyd had gotten behind schedule and needed help." Soon Wetzel had penciled four weeks of strips: almost all of the "Unhappy Campers" story arc. "I never realized how hard a comic strip artist worked until this experience!" Wetzel's *Mickey* style—round and stagey, redolent of animation—gave his serial a special flair.

"Unhappy Campers" established Wetzel as a permanent hire, enabling him to join the Animation Department as an in-betweener. Soon he was assisting master animators: Ollie Johnston on *Pinocchio* (1940), Eric Larsen on *Bambi* (1942).

Then, it seemed, came a better job offer. King Features Syndicate headhunted Wetzel to take over the *Felix the Cat* comic strip from creator Otto Messmer. Wetzel excitedly left Disney for the position. Alas, unbeknownst to Wetzel, King had removed Messmer against his will. When the *Felix* IP owners found out, they demanded Messmer's reinstatement.[2] Poor Wetzel was left jobless.

But like a cat—like Felix!—Ross landed on his feet. He and Janice had married in 1941; now they set up an art firm and got busy with commission work. Then, with World War II intensifying, Ross joined the US Army Air Forces' First Motion Picture Unit. Numerous animated flight training films featured that stagey Wetzel style.

His trademark look spread further in peacetime, when Ross opened The Cartoonists, a Chicago animation house specializing in commercials. Decades of exciting ad art followed. Then abstract art. Then a Chicago serigraph business, Ross Wetzel Studios, which evolved into a major frame shop. Wetzel's late 1970s retirement saw him turn from serigraphs to large watercolors, which he continued to create until his passing in 2013. Today, Ross Wetzel Studios is managed by Wetzel's daughter Susan Lindstrom, best known as the founder of the Paper Source stationery-store chain.

Ross Wetzel only spent a short while with Gottfredson's Mouse, but "Unhappy Campers" marked a turning point in his life. "Nobody in Chicago had my [Disney] background," he later explained, "so we were in the perfect position to... get into TV." Isn't it just like Mickey to help a buddy along? [DG]

ABOVE: Ross and Janice Wetzel in 2000. Photo © and courtesy Susan Lindstrom.

RIGHT: Early trial drawings of Mickey by Ross Wetzel, 1938. Image courtesy Susan Lindstrom.

1 All quotes and most biographical information: Susan Lindstrom, "Ross," e-book, http://www.photobookpress.com/assets/client_books/SusanLindstrom_Ross_42213.pdf (accessed May 13, 2013).

2 John Canemaker, *Felix: The Twisted Tale of the World's Most Famous Cat* (New York: Pantheon, 1993), p. 149.

Gottfredson's World: THE PLUMBER'S HELPER

The calmly enigmatic—some would say idiotically enigmatic—Joe Piper "took off" in Italy like nowhere else. In fact, his magnum opus has been published so many times there that you'd expect Mr. Piper to be Italian himself! Hmm... extra servings of manicotti, meatballs and lasagna *would* explain our chubby plumber's unpipelike girth. [DG]

ABOVE LEFT THREE: Italian *Albi d'oro* 29-31 (1939). Art by Enrico Pinochi; images courtesy Leonardo Gori.

ABOVE RIGHT: Dutch *Mickey Maandblad* 1985-02. Art by Michel Nadorp; image courtesy Roy Kooijman.

BOTTOM LEFT: Italian *Topolino collezione ANAF* 33 (1983). Art by Luciano Bottaro; image courtesy Leonardo Gori.

BOTTOM RIGHT: Italian *Albi d'oro* 43 (1947, 2nd series). Art by Michele Rubino; image courtesy Leonardo Gori.

Gottfredson's World: TRAVELS OF 1939

Mickey was going places in early 1939—or *was* he? Gottfredson's wild "Robinson Crusoe" island was really just a movie studio "location" shoot, while a camping drive in "Unhappy Campers" only succeeded in bringing Mickey back home! As these classic covers show, however, getting there is half the fun. [DG]

ABOVE LEFT: Italian *Albi d'oro* 32 (1939). Art by Enrico Pinochi; image courtesy Leonardo Gori.

ABOVE MIDDLE: Italian *Topolino collezione ANAF* 34 (1984). Art by Romano Scarpa; image courtesy The Walt Disney Company.

ABOVE RIGHT: *Mickey Mouse* 243 (1988), illustrating "Unhappy Campers." Art by Daan Jippes; image courtesy Thomas Jensen.

Much has been written of the inspirational relationship between the Mickey Mouse theatrical cartoons and the syndicated *Mickey* comic strip produced by Floyd Gottfredson. But surely, there is no animated antecedent to one of Gottfredson's greatest creations, the Phantom Blot.

...Or *is* there?

On title alone, the 1933 short *The Mad Doctor* would seem an unlikely source for an international criminal mastermind—even one with a penchant for frequenting dark and stormy nights, skulking, and scaring. However, consider that the titular "mad doc" comes to us in the form of a mysterious figure cloaked head-to-toe in black; who, not so coincidentally, slithers through dark and stormy nights, skulking and scaring!

When the actual Blot eventually made his bow, fortune eluded him in the form of cheap cameras and secret formulas. But our mysterious phantom would find a path—however winding—to eventual felonious fame.

In 1941, Gottfredson's comic strip continuity was reformatted to feed America's growing appetite for comic *books*; appearing in Dell's *Four Color* (series I) 16. It was here, in the book's title, that our villain—heretofore known only as "the Blot"—was rechristened the *Phantom* Blot.[1]

In 1949 the original Blot story was redrawn, by artists Dick Moores and Bill Wright, in monthly installments for *Walt Disney's Comics and Stories* 101-106. Gottfredson's art would return, with certain panels redrawn by Paul Murry, for 1955's *Mickey Mouse Club Parade* giant comic.

To this point, the Phantom Blot had still appeared in only *one* story, albeit presented in four distinctly different versions. But half a world away, things had begun to pop...

In Italy, renowned Disney comic artist Romano Scarpa and writer Guido Martina would revive Gottfredson's Blot in a lengthy thriller later known as "The Blot's Double Mystery" (1955).

1964 would see a divergent path for the black-cloaked blackguard, beginning with an unexpected North American revival in the Paul Murry-drawn "Return of The Phantom Blot." This serial, in *WDC&S* 284-287, was followed immediately by an ongoing *Phantom Blot* comic book title, published between 1964 and 1966.

Not all Blots were created equal. The Scarpa Blot, like later European incarnations, remained a deadly, often world-threatening mastermind. The Blot of 1960s American comics was somewhat less deadly and more blustery; though, by the publishing standards of the period, still a major force for evil.

Comic books would be the Blot's sole domain until December 30, 1987, and the jaw-dropping surprise of an *animated* appearance on Disney's *DuckTales*. This cartoon Blot exuded more 1960s bluster, less 1939 mystery; but that would be rectified by a more Gottfredson-esque—if still blustery!—version in TV's later *House of Mouse*.

Today there is no stopping the Blot as a multimedia presence; from plastic figurines to the *Disney Epic Mickey* video game series. But the circuitous route taken—from 1933 animated imagery and 1939 newspaper strips to 21st century celebrity—has been full of twists and turns worthy of a twisted criminal mind.

— Joe Torcivia

LEFT: Paul Murry's bourgeois detective Mouse is outmatched in this cover detail from *Walt Disney's Comics and Stories* 284 (1964).

RIGHT: An unmasked Blot can still hypnotize Mickey in "The Blot's Double Mystery" (1955; version from *Mickey and Donald* 9, 1987). Story by Guido Martina, art by Romano Scarpa.

1 In the strips for May 24 and 25, 1939, Chief O'Hara refers to the Blot as a "phantom," but the actual compound name begins with *Four Color* 16.

The prim 1950s were a tough time for funnybooks. Self-proclaimed moral guardians claimed that comics caused delinquency—and publishers, including Disney licensee Dell, reacted by trying to publish tamer, less scary stuff.

For *Mickey Mouse Club Parade* 1 (1955), Mickey artist Paul Murry redrew many pages of Gottfredson's "Mickey Mouse Outwits the Phantom Blot," the idea being to make the Blot's deathtraps a little less deadly! This segment replaced the strips for June 1-3, 1939 (page 164):

After Mickey's first escape, the original Gottfredson story takes over for awhile. Then this segment replaces the strips for July 4-13 (page 173). If the Blot could use a cat as an accomplice, perhaps he could also use a fish (!)...

HE **FORGOT** A GUY CAN FLOAT ON HIS BACK EVEN IF HE IS ALL TIED UP!

I CAN EASILY FLOAT HERE ALL NIGHT! SOMEONE IS BOUND TO SPOT ME IN THE MORNING! HEH, HEH! THAT PHANTOM IS SURE CARELESS---

THUD!
YIPE! I'M PINNED TO THE PIER!

HE SURE--- **YEEK!** HE SURE KNEW WHAT HE WAS DOING! I FORGOT THESE WATERS ARE FILLED WITH **SWORDFISH!**

YEOW! I ZIGGED THE RIGHT WAY THAT TIME---BUT WILL I THE **NEXT**?

BUT, **BOY!** IF I CAN JUST RUB THIS ROPE OVER HIS SHARP SWORD BEFORE HE PULLS HIMSELF LOOSE---

MADE IT!

OH, GEE! WHERE'D HE GO? NO TELLING WHAT DIRECTION HE'LL CHARGE FROM NOW!

MAYBE IF I LOOK UNDER, I CAN SPOT HIM--- OMIGOSH!

NOW THEN! IF I CAN PULL MYSELF UP THIS ROPE, I'LL BE SAFE---

OW!

THANKS! I DON'T THINK I COULD'VE MADE IT WITHOUT YOUR HELP!

THAT SETTLES ANOTHER ONE OF THE "BLOT'S" FANCY SCHEMES TO DO AWAY WITH ME!

BUT IN SPITE OF HIM, I'M STILL HALE AND HEARTY!

I BETTER DUCK IN HERE AND PICK UP MY DISGUISE! I'M STILL ON THE CASE!

"BLOT" HAS **SCARED** ME--- BUT SURE AS SHOOTIN' HE HASN'T SCARED ME **OFF**!

HEY! JUST A MINUTE! WHAT WERE Y' DOIN' ON THAT PIER?
WHY---UH---

NO TRESPASSING ON PIER
CONDEMNED
CAN'T Y' READ SIGNS?
YES, BUT---

Y' COULDA LOST YER **LIFE** OUT THERE! ONE STEP ON THOSE OLD ROTTEN PLANKS AND "**SPLOOSH**" YOU'D BE FEEDIN' THE FISHES!
MY---**I WAS** FOOLISH!

I CAN'T LET HIM KNOW WHO I AM AND GIVE AWAY THIS DISGUISE!
WELL! I WON'T GO OUT THERE AGAIN, OFFICER!
YOU'RE DURN TOOTIN' Y' WON'T!

'CAUSE I'M RUNNIN' Y' IN FER NOT OBEYIN' THAT "NO TRESPASSIN'" SIGN!

SHORTLY---
THE OFFICER'S GONE! YOU'RE FREE TO GO NOW, MICKEY!
THANKS, MR. O'HARA! AND I'M STILL IN THIS CASE WITH BOTH FEET!

I'M DARN GLAD YE ARE---THINGS ARE LOOKIN' MIGHTY BLACK! THE "BLOT'S" RUNNIN' WILD---EVEN GRABBIN' CAMERAS FROM PEOPLE ON THE STREETS IN BROAD DAYLIGHT!

By this time Dell was grabbing *pages* out of the *story* in broad daylight! In this trade-in for the strips of August 12-18 (page 184), a positively thick Phantom Blot enlists the silliest animal assistant of all. Shouldn't this critter be *Oswald's* enemy?

Bwoom! Beyond this, Paul Murry redrew three additional "Blot" pages—but these pages were just direct Gottfredson tracings, in some cases because original art had gone missing. Maybe (gasp!) the Blot *stole* it? Rumors were flying around Mouseton in 1955...

Gottfredson's World: MICKEY MOUSE OUTWITS THE PHANTOM BLOT

Given its milestone status, the Blot's debut has most often been reprinted in Mickey "best-of" anthologies—which means, oddly enough, that it has rarely gotten a *cover* all to itself. Luckily, those that do exist are strikingly iconic... just like Gottfredson's black-cloaked blackguard! [DG]

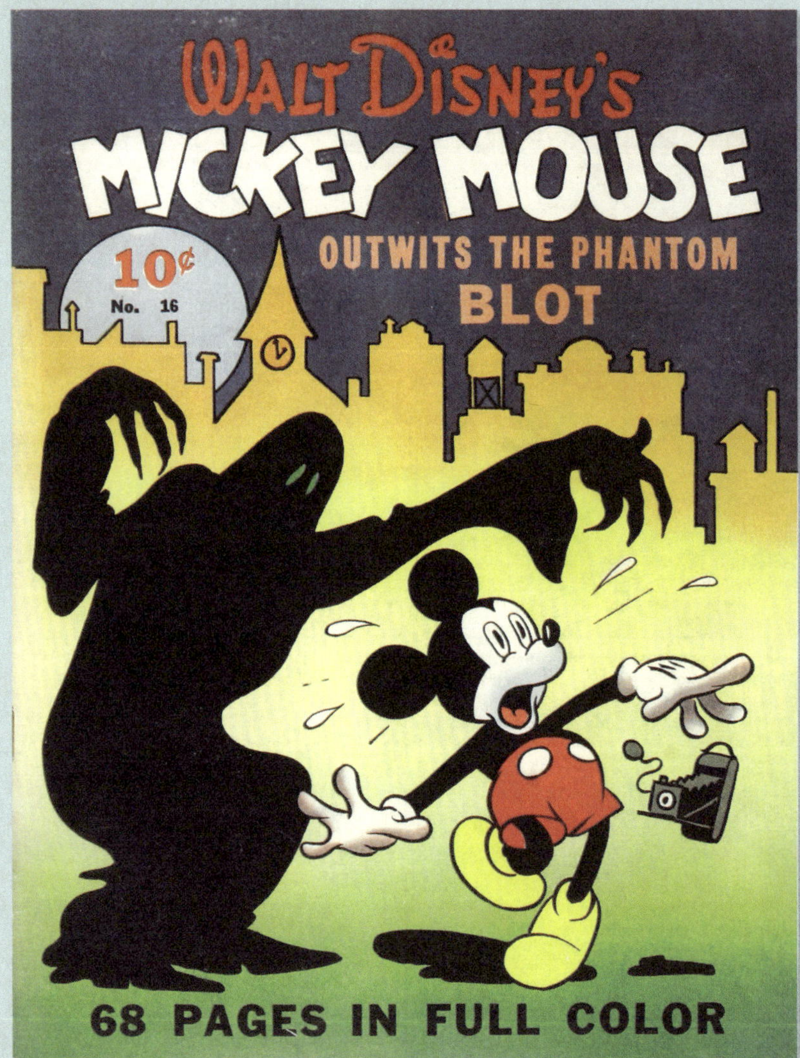

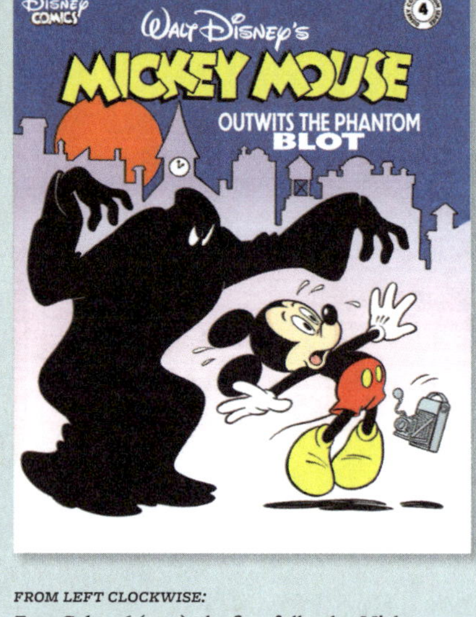

FROM LEFT CLOCKWISE:

Four Color 16 (1941), the first full-color Mickey Mouse comic book in the United States. Artist unknown; image courtesy Heritage Auctions.

French *Le Journal de Mickey* 2390 (1998). Art by Angel Rodriguez; image courtesy Francois Willot.

Disney Comics Album 4 (1990). Pencils by Todd Kurosawa, inks by Larry Mayer; image courtesy Thomas Jensen.

Dutch *Donald Duck presenteert* special (2013). Art by Jan-Roman Pikula; image courtesy Ferdi Felderhof.

MICKEY MOUSE OUTWITS THE PHANTOM BLOT. Painting by Floyd Gottfredson, July 1978. Image courtesy Malcolm Willits.

276 MICKEY MOUSE OUTWITS THE PHANTOM BLOT. Painting by Floyd Gottfredson, June 1981. Image courtesy Malcolm Willits.

The Cast: O'HARA AND CASEY

As we've seen in past volumes of this series, Mickey Mouse began life as a curious, determined ragamuffin—and remained curious and determined even as he "matured" into a de facto grownup. This made him the ideal star for crackerjack detective yarns; in particular, the type in which an authority figure needed to be impressed or outwitted.

Gottfredson had already paired Mickey with authority figures like Captain Churchmouse and Captain Doberman; but sailors and pilots were geared toward action-adventure tales, not detective stories. Pulp sleuths were the flavor of the day, so why not create ongoing mystery-based mentors for Mickey? Enter Chief Seamus O'Hara and his right-hand man, Detective Casey.[1]

O'Hara was established from the start as one of the few genuine good guys in the oft-corrupt Mouseton power structure. His thick Irish accent was there for humor—but O'Hara was also a wise, gently cynical friend whom the reader intuitively wanted Mickey to help. In a world where Mickey's closest peers were an eccentric (Goofy) and an egotist (Horace), the Chief took Mickey's aspirations seriously like few others could. As the Chief developed, one could even argue that he functioned as a surrogate father figure—making it all the more gripping, now and then, when circumstances put O'Hara and Mickey at odds.

The most frequent wedge between the two was Casey, who functioned as a rival for Mickey. Then as now, Casey isn't keen on an amateur sleuth like Mickey getting into official police work. But unlike Mickey's other rivals, Casey is never malicious. Nor is he entirely inept, at least under Gottfredson's pen; he just chases clues too impulsively. At worst he is a blowhard—and even a blowhard can find a new angle on a case! Now if only Mickey and the Chief didn't have to tiptoe around Casey's easily-shattered *ego*...

Chief O'Hara stands as one of the most recognizable symbols of Mickey's Golden Age. But he also became identified—from the 1950s to the 1980s—with many formulaic, non-Gottfredson mystery potboilers. Rather than hiring Mickey as a special agent when a creative approach was needed, Silver Age O'Hara hired Silver Age Mickey because Mickey was a reliable Mr. Perfect... and because O'Hara himself was now too inept even to catch jaywalking grannies. Casey, meanwhile, was almost never seen.

Thankfully, the modern-day O'Hara—as written by the likes of Romano Scarpa, Byron Erickson and Andrea Castellan—has regained his Gottfredson-era intelligence and wit. And if O'Hara is back to being a big cheese, Casey is once again the stinky flavor that gives the cheese its delicious taste.

— Jonathan Gray

LEFT: The Paul Murry-drawn "Return of the Phantom Blot" (*Walt Disney's Comics and Stories* 284-287, 1964) was among the finest American Mickey tales of its era—but reflected the inept O'Hara of other, weaker stories.

ABOVE: Italian master Romano Scarpa carried on Casey in "Mickey Mouse in the Delta Dimension" (1959; version from *Mickey Mouse Adventures* 11, 2006). Color by Scott Rockwell.

1 The Chief's first name of Seamus was established by modern Mickey scribe Byron Erickson. As for Casey, no one knows whether that's his first or *last* name—which makes sense, given his frequent state of confusion.

Ever rub a magic lamp and wish for a pile of classic comics? Er—no? Well, we did. And the results were this nice little collection of vintage "Miracle Master" covers, including a striking sample by classic Disney publicity artist Hank Porter. (Next time, maybe we'll wish for world peace.) [DG]

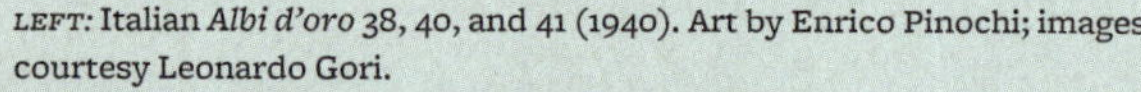

LEFT: Italian *Albi d'oro* 38, 40, and 41 (1940). Art by Enrico Pinochi; images courtesy Leonardo Gori.

RIGHT THREE: *Better Little Book* 1429 (1942). Art by Hank Porter; image courtesy Larry Lowery.

BOTTOM: Italian *Topolino collezione ANAF* 36 (1983). Art by Romano Scarpa; image courtesy Leonardo Gori.

MICKEY MOUSE AND THE MAGIC LAMP (based on "The Miracle Master"). Painting by Floyd Gottfredson, May 1979. Image courtesy Malcolm Willits.

THE HEIRS OF GOTTFREDSON:

OSAMU TEZUKA

» *BY* RYAN HOLMBERG

THE FINAL WORKSPACE of Osamu Tezuka (1928-1989), manga and anime grandmaster, is located in Tezuka Productions' animation studio in Niiza, northwest of Tokyo. On a wall in that office—preserved more or less as-is since the artist's death in 1989—there hang framed sketches of Donald Duck and Woody Woodpecker, personally dedicated by Carl Barks and Walter Lantz to Japan's most famous cartoonist. There are works by other giants besides, including an animation drawing from Winsor McCay's *Gertie the Dinosaur* (1914). But there is no obvious trace of the individual who most shaped Tezuka's style: Floyd Gottfredson.

Often championed as "the god of manga" by fans, Tezuka has had a profound effect on comics and animation—and not only in Japan. As Japanese pop culture spreads across the globe, Tezuka's work has gained a diverse international following. An older generation in North America knows him as creator of the animated series *Astro Boy* (1963-66) and *Kimba the White Lion* (1965-66). In India, Tezuka's eight-volume biographical *Buddha* (1972-83) is a perennial favorite. There is no escaping Tezuka for historians, whether they are studying the explosive growth of postwar manga or the roots of *shōjo* girls' comics and cute *kawaii* characters.

LEFT: Osamu Tezuka in the early-to-mid-1950s. Photo © and courtesy Tezuka Productions; used with permission.

RIGHT: Cover to Tezuka's *Manga College* (1950). All Tezuka comics images © Tezuka Productions; used with permission.

And in the beginning, there was Disney. Tezuka declared his debt to the studio's animation and comics on numerous occasions. However, it appears that he may not have been fully aware of *whose* Disney artistry, exactly, he adored and emulated. On the occasion of Mickey Mouse's 60th anniversary, Tezuka described

ABOVE: From "Mickey Mouse Outwits the Phantom Blot" as seen in *Four Color* 16 (1941). Compare with the *New Treasure Island* sequence on pages 282-283. All Disney images © Disney; used with permission.

a famous pirated Mickey manga, Bontarō Shaka's *Mickey's Show* (*Mikki no katsuyaku*, 1934), as "having steered me toward becoming a cartoonist... It was so close to the real thing," he added, "that it would be worth showing the Disney studio itself."[1] The young Tezuka copied *Mickey's Show* obsessively. Yet he seems to have never realized that Shaka's manga was based on imported editions of Floyd Gottfredson's work.

Tezuka recalled receiving a large batch of Disney and Disney-style comics in the spring of 1946 from an American GI.[2] On another occasion he admitted to owning many copies of Dell's *Walt Disney's Comics and Stories*.[3] For his first full-on Disney-styled manga, *The Streamline Case* (*Ryūsenkei jiken*, 1948), he borrowed cars and characters from Gottfredson's "Island in the Sky" (1936-37), which had been reprinted in *WDC&S* in 1940. For *Manga College* (*Manga daigaku*, 1950)—a tutorial in comics form—Tezuka featured the skinnier Mickey of early 1940s Gottfredson as a cover model for aspiring cartoonists to follow.

Tezuka's Gottfredson influences are often integrated with copying from other Disney talents like Carl Buettner, Al Taliaferro, Don Gunn, and Paul Murry. As their names were not made public until the 1960s, Tezuka could not have been aware of the identities of these different draftsmen. Into the 1970s, Tezuka, like most other fans, spoke of Disney comics and animation as Walt Disney's personal creations.

Nonetheless, Gottfredson's influence on Tezuka is exceptionally strong, inscribed deeply upon even the artist's legendary beginnings. Tezuka's breakout work, *New Treasure Island* (*Shintakarajima*), drawn in the summer and fall of 1946 and published in January 1947, might not be the most popular manga on record. But when it comes to narratives of how Japan became a comics empire, the stature of *New Treasure Island* is unmatched.

This is not for its story, which is unexceptional. A young boy named Pete—cast in the mold of the precocious youth detectives made popular by mystery writer Ranpo (*Continued on Page 284*)

BELOW: From *Four Color* 16 (1941). Compare with the *New Treasure Island* sequence on page 283.

282. Pages 2-5 of Tezuka's *New Treasure Island* (1947), inspired by Gottfredson's "Phantom Blot." English translation by Ryan Holmberg, lettering by David Gerstein.

BWOOOT!

BWOOO...

SHOOT! IT'S GONE!

ABOVE: Cover to Tezuka's *The Mysterious Underground Men* (1948).

Edogawa—has found a treasure map amongst the belongings of his late father. Pete and his uncle sail by steamship toward the treasure island. Pirates and cannibals complicate their quest. Eventually, with the help of a Tarzan-like character named Baron, the good guys free themselves from evil's clutches and obtain the sought-for chest of riches—sailing home with a select party of African animals and big plans to open an exotic petting zoo for kids back home.

New Treasure Island had an enormous impact on postwar manga, with Tezuka's contemporaries frequently recycling its scenes and staging. Most famous today are the story's first five pages, showing young Pete racing in his roadster to the wharf and leaping into a speedboat to catch his uncle's departing steamer. The sequence was apotheosized as ground zero of postwar manga by Motoo Abiko (*Ninja Hattori-Kun*), who recalled his 1940s encounter with it: "When I opened to the main text, the shock was so great that I almost blacked out... Two pages with nothing but driving. What was so exciting about it? I felt this biological pleasure as if it was myself in that car speeding toward the wharf... It was like watching a movie!"[4] Other writers have similarly described the scene as being done in a key frame or storyboard style.

Historians once claimed that, with this sequence, Tezuka invented "cinematic techniques" for manga. But as it turns out, *New Treasure Island* was informed strongly by the influx of American "ten-cent" comics during the Occupation. A glance at World War II airplane nose art will tell you that American GIs held funny animal comics dear to their hearts. The accidental byproduct of GI taste: authors of Japanese kids' comics began appropriating heavily from Dell. A copy of "Mickey Mouse Outwits the Phantom Blot" (Dell *Four Color* 16 [series 1], 1941) evidently found its way into Tezuka's hands in 1946, for most of the opening sequence of *New Treasure Island* has been appropriated directly from Gottfredson's depiction of Mickey chasing the Blot, first in his car, then on surfboard, before leaping to catch the tire of a plane as Pete does a rope dangling from his uncle's ship.

Tellingly, later sequences in *New Treasure Island*—as well as the manga's cover—were visibly inspired by another Disney comic: Jack Hannah's and Carl Barks' famous "Donald Duck Finds Pirate Gold" (*Four Color* 9, 1942). The oversized action and lack of verbiage of the *Blot*-derived passage might also have been inspired by similar wordless action sequences in "Pirate Gold." Other episodes in *New Treasure Island* indicate the influence of the animated Mickey films *The Castaway* (1931) and *Trader Mickey* (1932), the latter adapted by Gottfredson into the continuity "Mickey Mouse Sails for Treasure Island" (also 1932).

It is important to realize that *New Treasure Island*—though remembered as Tezuka's creation—was actually a collaborative work. The other creator was Shichima Sakai (1905-69), an important figure in the postwar Osaka manga scene. On the cover of *New Treasure Island*, Sakai is credited for the book's story (*gensaku*) and "composition" (*kōsei*), and Tezuka for its "drawing" (*sakuga*). In the 30s and early 40s, Sakai had worked as head animator for both Nikkatsu and a government-sponsored studio. Many of his productions reflect intimate familiarity with the early Mickey Mouse films. It is well known that Tezuka, as a child in the 30s, not only frequented movie theaters showing Disney and Fleischer films, but also watched them at home on a Pathé Baby projector. It is possible that Mickey references in Tezuka's early work stem from reviewing these 9.5mm toy films after the war. But considering that Sakai had studied some of the same movies professionally as an animator in the late 1930s, one cannot so easily attribute the innovations of *New Treasure Island* to Tezuka alone.[5] Still, it is only in Tezuka's subsequent comics that one sees further "Phantom Blot" influences. From Gottfredson, Tezuka learned a number of things: dynamic character movement, techniques of squash and stretch, expressions of temperamental emotion, and comical facial caricature.

One image from "The Phantom Blot" with which Tezuka seems to have been particularly taken with was that of Mickey running low to the ground through his secret underground passage. The pose was transferred to the top panel of page four of *New Treasure Island*, showing Pete dashing along the wharf. It was reused later in Tezuka's *The Mysterious Underground Men* (*Chiteikoku no kaijin*, 1948)—a book whose cover title is rendered in that tottering font typical of Mickey movie posters—and then again in the short story "Little Q Detective" ("Q chan torimono chō," 1948).

A subsequent scene in *New Treasure Island* shows Pete jumping down into his boat in a manner very close to how Mickey leaps from his sidecar in "The Phantom Blot." It too was reused in *The*

Mysterious Underground Men, in one case tellingly right next to the running pose.

In the early 1950s, Tezuka seems to have still had "The Phantom Blot" at his side. In "New World Luloo" (*Shin sekai lulū*, 1950-52), a science fiction story, there are at least two panels—a cigar-puffing editor who looks like Gottfredson's bulldog detective Casey, and an angry boy artist who stomps out of his office like Mickey charging down the street—which suggest, if not "The Phantom Blot" specifically, then at least Gottfredson's influence more generally.

ABOVE: Pose to pose: Gottfredson alongside Tezuka's "New World Luloo" (serialized in *Comics and Stories for Boys and Girls*, 1950-52). English translation by Ryan Holmberg, lettering by David Gerstein.

The early 1950s mark the high point of Tezuka's "Disney era." In 1952, through Disney's agents in Japan, he even drew authorized manga versions of *Bambi* and *Pinocchio*. A diligent student, Tezuka had mastered the studio's vocabularies of caricature and movement, as well as its atmosphere of enchanting fantasy. From there he moved on to develop a distinct style of his own that would shape, in small and large ways, much of Japanese cartooning for the next couple of decades.

As Tezuka's star rose, the original impact of Disney comics was gradually obscured. Not only was it hidden behind more general talk of "Disney style" in Tezuka's work, which most people assumed to have derived from the films. For decades *New Treasure Island*, the strongest evidence of Gottfredson's contribution, was unavailable to most readers. Commanding huge sums on the manga market, the existing copies had been sequestered by collectors. Tezuka refused to allow republication, claiming that the original art had been adulterated by Sakai. A remake was published in 1984, but it was visibly modernized with breakdowns and character stylization that clearly did not belong to 1946.

Thankfully, an archival edition of *New Treasure Island* was finally issued in 2009, thus opening the way for a more accurate historiography of the development of comics form in Japan. That Tezuka owed a lot to Gottfredson—and a lot to the Blot—was made clear for anyone to see. ●

1 Tezuka Osamu, "Atomu wa mikkii no oikko mitai na mono," *Kinema junpō* (Late November 1988), pp. 194-95.

2 Tezuka, "Boku o michibiitekureta Moozaruto," *Watashi no Moozaruto* (Tokyo: Kidoku shobō, 1976), pp. 261-63.

3 Tezuka Osamu and Ono Kōsei, "Ame komi o kataru" (1979), rpt. in *Tezuka Osamu taidanshū*, vol. 3 (Tokyo: Kōdansha, 1997), pp. 98-9.

4 Fujiko Fujio, *Futari de shōnen manga bakari kaitekita* [Abiko Motoo, 1975-76] (Tokyo: Nihon tosho sentaa, 2010), pp. 20-22.

5 Nakano Haruyuki, *'Shintakarajima' no hikari to kage: nazo no mangaka Sakai Shichima den* (Tokyo: Shōgakukan Creative, 2011).

It's been a long time since the Western world naïvely perceived Africans as primitives—so understandably, Gottfredson's highly dated Friday and Thursday tales have been out of the spotlight for quite awhile. These two vintage covers, presented here as documents of their time, show us how the story was anthologized back in the day. [DG]

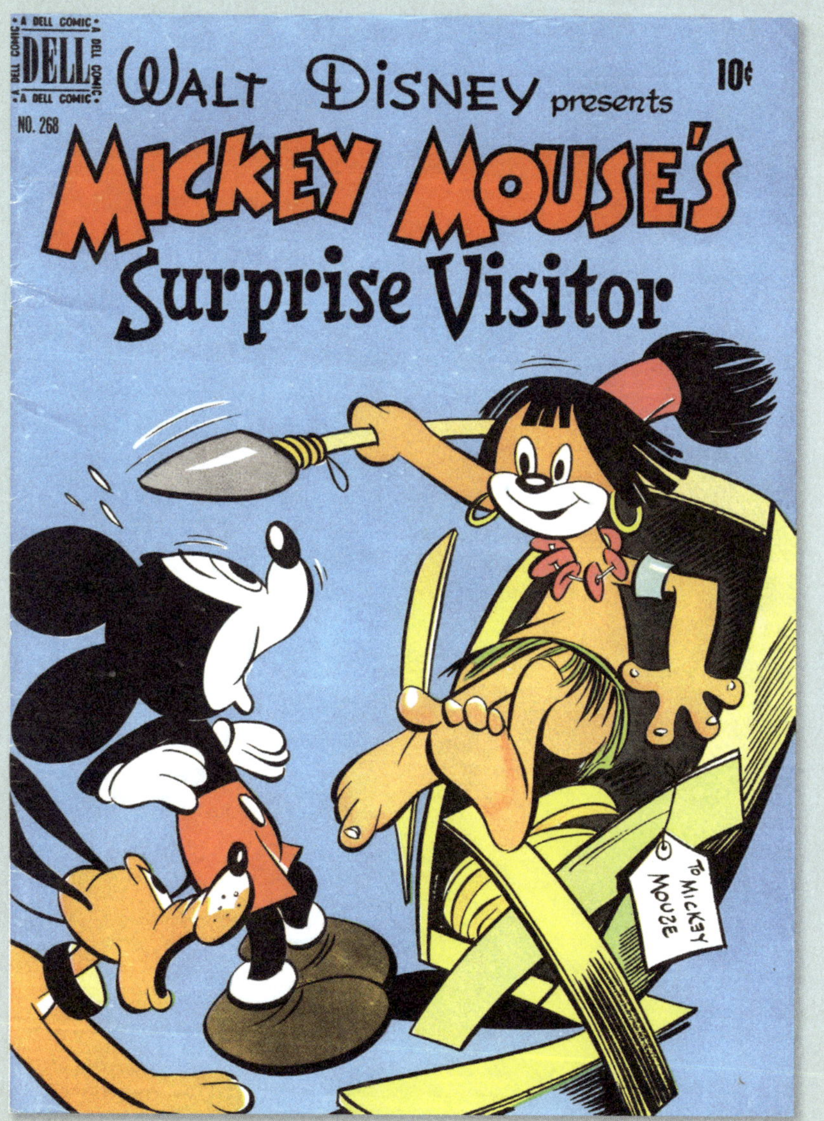

LEFT: *Four Color* 268 (1950). Art by Dan Gormley; image courtesy Thomas Jensen.

RIGHT: *Italian Topolino collezione* ANAF 37 (1984). Art by Romano Scarpa; image courtesy The Walt Disney Company.

Left: Years before the forest fauna of "Mickey Mouse Meets Robinson Crusoe," Floyd Gottfredson animated this jungle beast for the Silly Symphony cartoon *Cannibal Capers* (1930). It was one of very few scenes that Gottfredson—more typically an assistant—took charge of himself.

"[Animator Norm Ferguson] did about four extremes of a lion running out of the jungle... he said, 'Take this and animate it.'... One funny thing happened... [future Mickey Mouse *strip writer] Roy Williams came to work, I think about a month after I did. I was working on animating that lion and he came up and looked over my shoulder... he exclaimed, 'This is amazing. I just had no idea that animation was done this way. You're marvelous; you're remarkable.' And I said 'Look, I'm not an animator. I'm just an in-betweener.' But do you know that to this day when I run into Roy out on the lot, he'll come up and slap me on the shoulder and ask how the lion is doing."*

— Floyd Gottfredson to David R. Smith, 1975

ABOVE: 1939 King Features Christmas card drawing by Floyd Gottfredson (Mickey and orphans) and Al Taliaferro (Donald and nephews). Image courtesy Carl Guderian.

ABOUT THE EDITORS

DAVID GERSTEIN is an animation and comics researcher, writer, and editor working extensively with the Walt Disney Company and its licensees. Gerstein's published work includes *Mickey and the Gang: Classic Stories in Verse*; *Walt Disney Treasures – Disney Comics: 75 Years of Innovation*; and *The Katzenjammer Kids: 100 Years in Norway*. He has also worked with Disney to preserve the *Mickey Mouse* newspaper strips seen in this volume.

GARY GROTH co-founded Fantagraphics Books and *The Comics Journal* in 1976. And he is still at it.

THOMAS ANDRAE is an internationally recognized authority on social theory and Cultural Studies and an instructor at California State University East Bay. He is co-founder and senior editor of *Discourse: Journal for Theoretical Studies in Media and Culture*. He is the author of *Carl Barks and the Disney Comic Book: Unmasking the Myth of Modernity*; and *Creators of the Superheroes*; and co-author of Bob Kane's autobiography, *Batman & Me*; *Siegel and Shuster's Funnyman: The First Jewish Superhero* (with Mel Gordon); and *Walt Kelly: The Life and Art of the Creator of Pogo* (with Carsten Laqua).

CRAIG McCRACKEN has been working in television animation for over twenty years. He is the Creator and Executive Producer of the Emmy- and Annie Award-winning series *The Powerpuff Girls* and *Foster's Home for Imaginary Friends*. He also served as Art Director and Storyboard Artist on Cartoon Network's *Dexter's Laboratory*. Currently, he is working as the Creator and Executive Producer for Disney Channel's new comedy adventure series, *Wander Over Yonder*. He lives in Los Angeles with his wife, fellow animator Lauren Faust.

BYRON ERICKSON has spent the last 28 years of his life editing and writing Disney comic books, first for Gladstone and then for Egmont in Denmark. Some wags claim he's best known as Don Rosa's Disney editor, but he prefers to be remembered for the over two dozen Mickey Mouse stories he's written, most of which were drawn by Cèsar Ferioli.

LEONARDO GORI is a comics scholar and collector specializing in Italian Disney authors and syndicated 1930s newspaper strips. With Frank Stajano and others, he has written many books on Italian "fumetti" and American comics in Italy. He has also written thrillers, which have been translated into Spanish, Portuguese, and Korean.

FRANCESCO "Frank" STAJANO was imprinted on Disney comics at preschool age and never grew out of it: the walls of his house are covered in bookshelves and many of them hold comics. He has often written about Disney comics, particularly with Leonardo Gori. In real life he is an associate professor at the University of Cambridge in England.

THAD KOMOROWSKI began his professional association with Disney comics as a teenager, writing character dialogue for American editions of European *Uncle Scrooge* stories. Today a historian and archivist, Komorowski maintains the blog *whataboutthad.com*, devoted to the art of animation, comics, and live-action film. He is the author of *Sick Little Monkeys: The Unauthorized Ren & Stimpy Story*.

JONATHAN GRAY was born in 1979 in Birmingham, Alabama. Best known as an artist and writer for his online comics "Chip and Walter" and "Time Trouble," he has done work since 2003 for Archie Comics (*Sonic the Hedgehog*) and various Disney licensees (*Mickey Mouse*, *DuckTales*). He credits his mother for introducing him to comics… to keep him from playing crazy stupid amounts of video games. Currently he is a fulltime production artist for Archie Comics.

JOE TORCIVIA is a comics historian renowned for decades of Disney, Warner Bros, Hanna-Barbera, and DC Comics scholarship. He has also worked as a dialogue writer for American editions of European Disney comics. He maintains the blog "The Issue At Hand" (*tiahblog.blogspot.com*), featuring a light-hearted look at pop culture.

RYAN HOLMBERG is a historian and translator of Japanese comics. He is a frequent contributor to *The Comics Journal*, *Artforum*, and *Art in America*. His most recent book project is the English translation of Osamu Tezuka's *The Mysterious Underground Men* for PictureBox, Inc. He is currently working on a study of the impact of American cartooning on Japanese manga.